Praise for *Management Lessons from Mayo Clinic*

"A landmark. Through deep study, respectful listening, and eloquent reporting, the authors connect 'service success' to the very core of healthcare's mission and to the very soul of the healthcare workforce."

—DONALD M. BERWICK, MD, MPP, former Administrator,
Centers for Medicare and Medicaid Services,
and President Emeritus and Senior Fellow,
Institute for Healthcare Improvement

"This book is an essential read for those managing labor-intensive, highly interactive service businesses, and offers thought-provoking guidance to anyone seeking to build a customer-focused culture."

—GEORGE DAY, PHD, Geoffrey T. Boisi Professor Emeritus,
Wharton School, University of Pennsylvania

"An extraordinary book that provides wonderful lessons on how to build and sustain service excellence in any business organization. It also offers superb insights on how unshakable core values can drive a successful culture."

—STEPHEN W. BROWN, PHD, Edward M. Carson Chair
and Professor of Marketing Emeritus,
W. P. Carey School of Business, Arizona State University

"Great insight into how a successful service organization operates . . . offers valuable information for businesses striving for service excellence."

—COLIN V. REED, Chairman and CEO,
Ryman Hospitality Properties, Inc.

"Mayo Clinic is an amazing management story. . . . This book gives more than an inside look into one of the world's most famed and revered brands, it provides a detailed and inspiring blueprint for what it takes for any service brand to truly achieve greatness."

—KEVIN LANE KELLER, E.B. Osborn Professor of Marketing,
Tuck School of Business, Dartmouth College

"A must-read for organizations looking to restore service to its rightful place."

—DAN J. SANDERS, *New York Times* bestselling author of *Built to Serve*

"Berry and Seltman speak eloquently to what an organization can achieve when it has clearly defined its core mission and focuses every aspect of the enterprise on that mission."

—J. MICHAEL MCGINNIS, MD, Leonard D. Schaeffer
Executive Officer, Senior Scholar, and Executive Director,
NAM Leadership Consortium

"Powerful and valuable insight into how to create a culture and environment that provide the best quality and experience."

—GARY SHORB, former CEO, Methodist Healthcare,
and Executive Director, The Urban Child Institute

"Whether part of healthcare or an executive in a corporation, the lessons to be learned from Mayo are both inspirational and timeless. This wonderful book is a must-read for anyone in pursuit of excellence."

—CHARLES S. LAUER, former VP, Publisher,
and Editorial Director, *Modern Healthcare* magazine

"Berry and Seltman have now defined a new gold standard for service with their extraordinary assessments of the prestigious Mayo Clinic's service culture and management."

—JAMES D. ROGERS, former President and CEO,
Kampgrounds of America, Inc.

"*Management Lessons from Mayo Clinic* can help all service managers build better businesses and better brands that endure and thrive no matter how complex and difficult the environment."

—IAN MORRISON, PHD, author of *Healthcare in the New Millennium*

"*Management Lessons from Mayo Clinic* should be required reading for every healthcare leader."

—QUINT STUDER, Founder and CEO, Studer Group

"Full of strategies and tactics managers can use every day to lead with creativity, compassion, and communication."

—KIP TINDELL, former Chairman and CEO, The Container Store

"A remarkable story of a dynamic business model driven by customer-first advocacy and passionate teamwork."

—JOE V. TORTORICE JR., Founder and CEO, Jason's Deli

MANAGEMENT LESSONS FROM
MAYO CLINIC

INSIDE ONE OF THE WORLD'S MOST ADMIRED SERVICE ORGANIZATIONS

Leonard L. Berry
Kent D. Seltman

New York   Chicago   San Francisco   Athens
London   Madrid   Mexico City   Milan   New Delhi
Singapore   Sydney   Toronto

1 2 3 4 5 6 7 8 9   LCR   22 21 20 19 18 17

ISBN   978-1-260-01183-8
MHID   1- 260-01183-6

e-ISBN 978-0-07-159074-7
e-MHID   0-07-159074-9

This publication is designed to provide accurate and authoritative information in regard to the subject matter covered. It is sold with the understanding that the publisher is not engaged in rendering legal, accounting, or other professional service. If legal advice or other expert assistance is required, the services of a competent professional person should be sought.
          —*From a declaration of principles jointly adopted by a committee of the American Bar Association and a committee of publishers.*

McGraw-Hill Education books are available at special quantity discounts to use as premiums and sales promotions or for use in corporate training programs. To contact a representative, please visit the Contact Us pages at www.mhprofessional.com.

CONTENTS

ACKNOWLEDGMENTS

Researching and writing this book thrust us into the roles of both student and teacher. Before we could teach, we first had to learn. We now have studied a remarkably successful service organization and, in this book, teach its lessons. We have had an enlightening and rewarding journey.

We began this project believing that we already understood Mayo Clinic and what makes it tick. And we did know many things. However, as we write these words to thank those who have helped us, it is clear to us how much more we learned. The disciplined exploration and personal reflection required to write a good book is a wonderful way to learn. The process forces you to dig deep, to see what you haven't seen before, to consider new patterns and connections. It is one thing to have ideas that resonate in your mind; transforming those ideas into words on a printed page forces clearer, deeper thinking. When your words are going to be on a printed page for a long time, you want to get them right.

We have done our best to get the words right in portraying the real Mayo Clinic, in accurately telling its service story, and in teaching its lessons. We are grateful to many people who have helped us on our journey to a completed manuscript. Carleton Rider, who retired at the end of 2007 from Mayo Clinic following a distinguished administrative leadership career that included being the first chief administrative officer of Mayo Clinic Jacksonville, encouraged us to write this book. Although historical accounts of Mayo Clinic have been published in book form, no book has ever been published on Mayo Clinic's service culture, strategy, management, and systems. Rider felt that such a book could make a genuine contribution, not only to external audiences of corporate, not-for-profit, and healthcare organization managers but also to the internal audience of

Mayo Clinic itself. With thousands of new staff members joining Mayo Clinic each year, such a book could be useful in capturing and reinforcing the uniqueness of Mayo Clinic. And in telling the service story of Mayo Clinic, this book could also help many patients, who number over 500,000 each year, understand the background of their excellent patient experiences.

Carleton Rider was one of seven individuals whom we asked to carefully read and critique a draft of our manuscript. Mayo Clinic's complexity, stemming from its age, size, governance structure, and type and breadth of services, among other factors, increases the opportunity for inadvertent errors as well as misinterpretation of historical events. Thus we recruited a group of prepublication reviewers with broad and diverse Mayo Clinic experience to help us tell the story as accurately and completely as possible. The review process proved invaluable, and we wish to thank the other members of the review team in addition to Carleton Rider: John La Forgia, Dr. Robert Waller, Dr. Michael O'Sullivan, Robert Smoldt, Matthew Dacy, and Dr. James Donnelly, Jr.

John La Forgia, chair of the division of public affairs at Mayo Clinic, not only offered excellent insights on our manuscript but also championed this project and secured the internal support for the independence that this study required.

Dr. Waller retired as Mayo Clinic's CEO in 1999. A Clinic physician for 30 years, he played key leadership roles in Mayo's geographic expansion. Dr. Waller was always available to us and always gracious when we called with "just a few more questions."

Dr. O'Sullivan started as a resident in pathology at Mayo Clinic in 1964, joined the clinical pathology staff in 1969, and retired as CEO of Mayo Clinic Scottsdale in 2002. Dr. O'Sullivan had an amazing career at Mayo, providing leadership during the early years for some of the Clinic's most successful ventures.

Robert Smoldt retired from Mayo Clinic in 2008 following a nearly 36-year career in administrative and management positions, including chief administrative officer. Smoldt knows the inner workings of the Clinic's management systems. He was our go-to person for a wide range of issues requiring clarification or amplification.

Smoldt has devoted considerable thought to improving healthcare public policy and has much insight to offer in any discussion of the future of healthcare.

Matthew Dacy is director of Mayo Clinic Heritage Hall in the department of development. A skilled writer and editor, Dacy also is an astute student of Mayo Clinic's history. We benefited greatly from his detailed, constructive suggestions.

Dr. James Donnelly, Jr., who recently retired as the Thomas C. Simons professor of business at the Gatton College of Business and Economics, University of Kentucky, was our seventh external reviewer. We reached out to him not only because of his background as a prolific book author but also because of his experiences as a Mayo Clinic patient. Professor Donnelly's careful reading of the manuscript through the lens of both patient and author was extremely helpful.

This book was written with the blessing and cooperation—but not under the control—of Mayo Clinic. We thank Mayo Clinic's leaders, all of whom supported this project and participated in one or more candid, in-depth interviews. We are grateful not only for their time and insights but also for the trust they extended to us. Among the Clinic leaders who helped us are: Dr. Denis Cortese, Dr. George Bartley, Dr. Victor Trastek, Dr. Glenn Forbes, Dr. Hugh Smith, Shirley Weis, Doreen Frusti, Craig Smoldt, Dr. Dawn Milliner, Dr. Stephen Swenson, James G. Anderson, Robert Brigham, and Jeffrey Korsmo.

In Chapter 1, we describe how we conducted the research that underlies this book in two distinct phases. Both phases involved personal interviews with numerous current and former Mayo Clinic staff members. We thank each of our interviewees, a number of whom readers meet in the pages that follow. We also thank the many employees across the three Mayo campuses for their efforts in locating the specific details and data our book required as well as those who facilitated our work in countless ways: Nicole Babcock, Adam Brase, Virginia Bruce, Dorothy Burch, Amy Davis, Lindsay Dingle, Jean Engler, Susan Fargo-Prosser, Daniel Goldman, James Houck, Patrick McCarty, Heidi Miller, Jim Nassens, Robert Nellis,

Donly Okrzynski, Marie Perhay, Gail Prechel, Clifford Romme, Ann Schauer, Alan Schilmoeller, Kimberley Schmidt, Tripp Welch, Laurie Wilshusen, and Renee Zeimer.

We also thank Glenda Bessler and Shirley Deffenbaugh, longtime members of Leonard Berry's "book team." Glenda Bessler has served as Berry's splendid administrative assistant for more than 20 years and always embraces a new book project with good cheer even though it means considerably more work for an already hard-working professional. This book is the sixth one Glenda has helped bring to fruition. Shirley Deffenbaugh, who lives in Seattle, is a gifted copy editor who absolutely will not tolerate needlessly long sentences. This is the fourth book on which Shirley has provided assistance.

We appreciate the opportunity to work with McGraw-Hill and our editor, Mary Glenn, and her associates. Mayo Clinic is a global brand and so is McGraw-Hill. We thought it made sense to bring these two brands together to see if we could create some magic with this book.

Kent Seltman thanks his wife, Kristine, and daughters, Lee and Ann, for loving affection and support even as his passion for this book delayed production in his family-focused furniture shop. Happily, the family members all know firsthand that good comes from hard work on big projects—Kristine as a creative and committed mother, Lee as a civil rights attorney in the U.S. Department of Justice, and Ann as a colon and rectal surgeon whose 30th and final year of education was completed at Mayo Clinic. He also thanks Lee who critiqued the manuscript on behalf of general readers who have not been to business school or who do not work in healthcare. He also wishes to acknowledge Dr. Patricia Simmons, Franklin Iossi, and Robert Smoldt who explained the Mayo culture as it existed early in his career and guided and mentored him in "the Mayo Way."

Leonard Berry thanks his wife, Nancy, and sons, Matthew and Jonathan, for their love and for their pride in this book's publication. He, in turn, feels great pride in their pursuits, Nancy as an active community leader and member of several local and regional boards of directors, including the College Station Medical Center; Matthew as head of fantasy sports for the ESPN network where he is known as "the talented Mr. Roto;" and Jonathan as a creator of new television shows and other entertainment services. Leonard Berry also thanks Dr. Donald Berwick and Maureen Bisognano, the leaders of the Institute of Healthcare Improvement (IHI), for their passion and commitment to improving healthcare safety, effectiveness, and efficiency. Their work and the jewel of an organization they head are an inspiration.

To the people of Mayo Clinic, we did our best to tell your story accurately, interestingly, and usefully. To our readers, thank you. We believe you will receive a good return on your investment.

Leonard L. Berry
College Station, Texas

Kent D. Seltman
Rochester, Minnesota

CHAPTER 1

THE 100-YEAR BRAND

*O*n a Sunday afternoon in late June, I was picking up a rental car at the Minneapolis airport. An electronic sign over the car blinked my name, so it was easy to find. Under the windshield wiper lay a handwritten message, filling both sides of a legal-sized page. Curious, I started reading.

The note was from a woman who had seen my name displayed on the sign and took a chance that I was the same Dr. Cortese who treated her father years ago at Mayo Clinic in Rochester, Minnesota. He had early-stage lung cancer, and I was on a team developing experimental treatments using laser and light-activated, cancer-killing drugs. Her father had received three treatments, and she wanted to thank me for caring for him. That was 15 years ago. The daughter was at the airport that day because she had flown in from California to attend his funeral. He had died suddenly the night before from a heart problem.

I was touched, not only because she took the time in her grief to write the note, but also because it reminded me of what I find so compelling and rewarding about medicine—caring for patients.

The best physicians and healthcare providers are part engineers and part artists. The engineer sees the problem and applies technology to fix it. Thanks to the engineers, patients benefit from CT scans, minimally invasive surgeries, and computer-guided, pinpoint treatments. The engineering approach has helped patients immensely and has saved many lives. It's measurable, visible, and almost always reimbursable.

The artist knows when the patient needs a warm smile, reassuring words, or a gentle hug. It's the artists who make every patient feel welcome, comfortable, secure, hopeful. The artist sees the anxiety and reassures the

new mother that her baby's fever is nothing to worry about. The artist lis-
tens to the middle-aged patient unloading his frustration over failed
attempts to quit smoking. The artist knows when there's nothing more the
engineer can do and helps the patient and family cope at the end of life.
What the artist does is why I became a physician.

This is an excerpt from an essay written by Mayo Clinic president
and chief executive officer Dr. Denis Cortese in 2002 when he headed
Mayo's Jacksonville, Florida, practice.[1] He shared it with the staff in
an internal newsletter. We begin with this story because it evokes a
powerful truth applicable to all managers regardless of what they
manage: organizational excellence is never only about the science. It
also is about the "artistry" that Dr. Cortese describes—the human
touch, teaching, collaboration, generous acts, personal courage, and
core values that guide decision making and inspire extra effort.

This is a book about the art of service that takes readers inside
an exceptional service organization, Mayo Clinic, and teaches its
lessons. The book is written for all managers who rely on the
performances of people to create differentiated value for customers.
It is about a legendary healthcare organization, but it is not a healthcare book. It is a book about sustainable service excellence and what
drives it. It is about the power of unshakable core values and the
leaders—Dr. William Worrall Mayo and his sons Drs. William and
Charles Mayo—who lived and taught them and created the cultural
and infrastructural investments to sustain them.

The medical practice opened for business more than 140 years ago
in the small, isolated Minnesota town of Rochester and came to be
called "Mayo Clinic" in the early 1900s. That Mayo Clinic still exists
after all this time is noteworthy; that it created one of the most influential and valuable service brands in the world—and has successfully
maintained, extended, and protected the brand for so long—is truly
remarkable. To this day, the Clinic uses little advertising to promote
clinical care. It had no marketing staff until 1986, and from then until
1992 the marketing department consisted of one person.

With so much focus in management circles on the "new"—
new concepts, new theories, new models, new technologies—it is

refreshing, revealing, and inspiring to learn from a world-renowned institution that established its foundation for success in the early 1900s and continues to depend on that foundation in its twenty-first century success. Mayo Clinic illustrates that an organization's basic concept of the business can be so right that it can endure for the ages. The Clinic showcases the promise of the "modern-traditional" enterprise that aligns strategy with values, innovation with tradition, talent with teamwork, and science with art.

Mayo by the Numbers

Five days each week, a small city moves in and out of Mayo Clinic. Day-shift employees begin to show up at about 5:00 a.m., and over the next 24 hours more than 42,000 employees, students, and volunteers will work or study on the three Mayo Clinic campuses in Minnesota, Arizona, and Florida. Surgical patients begin arriving at the hospitals as early as 5:30 a.m. for the 300 surgeries performed on a typical weekday. The numbers increase by 6:45 a.m. when patients begin reporting to the laboratory to have their blood drawn. By midafternoon, up to 13,500 patients—each typically accompanied by one or more family members or friends—will have received medical services at Mayo Clinic. By the end of the day, as many as 65,000 people—patients, their family members and friends, as well as employees, students, and volunteers—will have converged on one of the Mayo Clinic campuses to participate in the real-life drama, and in many cases true life or death drama, of twenty-first century healthcare delivery.

During this 24-hour period, patients will undergo more than 4,600 procedures or diagnostic studies—such as an X-ray, a CT scan, or an MRI—in radiology, and one of about 230 Mayo Clinic radiologists will read the images and complete the report, usually in less than 90 minutes. The 2,500 Mayo Clinic physicians will conduct more than 9,000 examinations or consultations. About 375 patients will be treated in one of the three emergency departments in Mayo Clinic's hospitals, and nearly 1,300 patients will spend the night as hospital inpatients.

Mayo Clinic is the first integrated, not-for-profit medical group practice in the world and one of the largest. As a multispecialty medical group, it brings together doctors from virtually every medical specialty—joined by common systems and values—who work together to care for patients. For more than a century, Mayo Clinic has been a major medical institution. In 1912, more than 15,000 individual patients were registered at Mayo Clinic. Twelve years later, when the Mayo brothers were at the height of their careers, Mayo doctors were seeing about 60,000 patients and performing more than 23,600 surgeries per year. (See Table 1-1.) The practice had access to more than 1,500 hospital beds and 27 operating rooms. By 1983, the practice, with 276,800 individual patients, was about four and a half times larger than it was in 1924.

Table 1-1
Then and Now

	1924*	1983†	2007‡
Patients			
Individual patient registrations§	60,063	276,800	520,000
Hospital admissions		63,600	135,000
Surgeries	23,628	30,800	76,300
Hospital beds	1,507	1,848	2,400
People of Mayo Clinic			
Mayo physicians and medical scientists		889	2,706
Administrative and allied health staff		5,350	35,971
Residents, fellows, students		1,504	3,229
Total		7,743	41,906**
Operating Performance (in millions)			
Total revenue		$411.6	$7,322.4
Total expenses		$353.1	$6,699.6
Excess of revenues over expenses		$58.5	$622.8

*Sketch of the History of the Mayo Clinic and the Mayo Foundation (W. B. Saunders: Philadelphia, 1926), pp. 30–31.
†Mayo Clinic annual report, 1983.
‡Mayo Clinic annual report, 2007.
§Each patient counted once every 12 months, regardless of the number of physician visits or hospitalizations.
**While over 54,000 persons were employed in Mayo Clinic organizations at the end of 2007, only 41,906 worked on the three campuses that are the subject of this book.

In 1983, Mayo Clinic operated much as it had from the outset in Rochester, Minnesota, but in that year strategic decisions set the organization on an accelerated growth trajectory that continues today. The Rochester hospitals—Saint Marys Hospital and Methodist Hospital—became part of Mayo Clinic in 1986 and the Clinic expanded to Jacksonville, Florida, in 1986 and Scottsdale, Arizona, in 1987. The impact of these changes is detailed in Table 1-1. From 1983 through 2007, the patient volumes nearly doubled, and the number of physicians and research scientists increased by more than 200 percent. Revenue in 2007 totaled $7.3 billion (more than 17 times the revenue in 1983), while the excess of revenue over expense increased to $622.8 million (more than 10 times the amount in 1983).

Although known throughout its history largely for the medical services it provides to patients, Mayo Clinic thinks of itself as "a three-shield organization." The central and larger shield in the Mayo Clinic logo (see Exhibit 1-1) represents patient care. But integrally linked to patient care are the complementary shields of medical research and medical education. The tripartite mission was defined by the Mayo brothers—Drs. William and Charles Mayo—who believed that they were better doctors because they had studied and observed other doctors on a "vacation" each year. (Dr. Charles Mayo and his bride Edith even spent their honeymoon touring hospitals and surgical clinics on the East Coast and in Chicago.) The brothers also engaged with their colleagues around the world through their research publications. The brothers established the original endowment to support medical research and education at Mayo Clinic. Medical education and medical research programs are true complements to Mayo Clinic's primary focus on clinical medicine.

Exhibit 1-1

Mayo Clinic is distinctive in that it is a major academic medical center with a medical school that is not university-based.[2] Today, the College of Medicine at Mayo Clinic comprises five fully accredited schools with residents and students numbering about 3,200 annually. The educational program is part of Mayo Clinic's medical and charitable mission. In 2007, more than $166 million of Mayo Clinic funds and benefactor gifts combined to help support the $215 million cost of Mayo's education programs. Established in 1972, the Mayo Medical School is a small, highly competitive medical school with about 200 students in its M.D. and M.D./Ph.D. programs. Dating back to 1917, Mayo Graduate School now enrolls about 250 master's and Ph.D. students in biomedical sciences programs. The Mayo School of Graduate Medical Education for resident and fellowship physicians stems from a program developed in 1915 in collaboration with the University of Minnesota. Though no longer affiliated with the university, the Graduate Medical Education program today trains more than 2,200 resident physicians and clinical fellows in 280 different programs at Mayo Clinic. Mayo Clinic has provided academic training to allied health professionals for over a century. Today, the Mayo School of Health Sciences has about 600 students in 34 different programs in the health-related professions. By design, the school places about half of its graduates in Mayo Clinic employment. Every year, the Mayo School of Continuing Medical Education offers approximately 170 different short courses for about 15,500 non-Mayo physicians.

Mayo Clinic physicians and scientists, beginning with the Mayo brothers themselves, have used medical research in support of improved diagnostic tools and techniques as well as improved treatments for patients. Mayo Clinic researchers Drs. Edward Kendall and Phillip Hench were awarded the 1950 Nobel Prize in medicine for the discovery of cortisone. In 2007, the annual research budget for Mayo Clinic was about $495 million with $179 million of that coming from Mayo Clinic funds and benefactor gifts. The research ranges from basic science research in laboratories to clinical research directly involving patients, population research (epidemiology), and translational research that takes findings from laboratories and applies them to patient care initially in "clinical trials." About 80 percent of Mayo Clinic physicians are actively involved in research on the more than 7,000 approved projects underway at any time.

A Medical Mecca

During their lifetimes, much of the international recognition brought to the Mayo brothers and the Clinic that bore their name was based on their contributions to the science of medicine and to innovative surgical techniques. Over the seven decades since their deaths in 1939, the evolution of medical science has superseded the brothers' scientific and technical contributions. Stunning at the time, these contributions are historical footnotes today. The Mayo brothers' most significant legacy is a living enterprise that is a dynamic monument to their organizational genius. The basic management structure and systems and clinical care model they created during their careers still endure today. They endure not because of stubborn worship of the past, but because they produce stellar clinical results, organizational efficiency, and interpersonal service that often exceed patients' expectations and thus earn their loyalty.

In 1961, an independent consumer research firm called Social Research studied the image of Mayo Clinic held by first-time patients when they arrived for care. Among the principal perceptions of these patients were that Mayo was "the place to go if you are really sick" and was "a court of last resort—the 'Supreme Court' of Medical Opinion." The report authors wrote:

> People are convinced that Mayo will come up with the diagnosis and the solution. They expect both clarification and resolution of conflicting medical opinions, diagnoses, and/or treatments. The belief that Mayo can give you a definitive answer is a very prominent facet of its image.[3]

In 1962, Social Research followed up with a study of nonpatient attitudes toward Mayo Clinic. The researchers found that the Clinic was considered an important national institution and had qualities of a cherished myth. It stood as a symbol of what is best in American medicine, which was intimidating for some people because other clinics, however good they might be, were unlikely to alter or reverse a Mayo diagnosis. As the researchers wrote: ". . . one senses in the non-patients we talked with . . . relief that it had never been, and is not yet, necessary for them to turn to Mayo."[4]

Recent research that we present later suggests that Mayo Clinic remains a medical "mecca," a term used by the Social Research investigators in their 1961 report.[5] The activities of the Clinic today are carried out with different tools, but the humane values, clinical and administrative models, and philosophical underpinnings from the Mayo brothers' time have changed little as the organization has adapted to new eras of medical science, public policy, healthcare finance, and patient expectations. The brothers' astute insights into the soul of medicine still prevail in the management of this organization.

The Spirit of the Clinic

Late in his life, Dr. William Mayo identified three conditions that he considered essential to the future success of Mayo Clinic:

1. Continuing pursuit of the ideal of service and not profit.
2. Continuing primary and sincere concern for the care and welfare of each individual patient.
3. Continuing interest by every member of the staff in the professional progress of every other member.

In 1975, Dr. Emmerson Ward, then chair of the board of governors, offered a fourth condition:

4. A willingness to change in response to the changing needs of society.

In 1984, Robert Roesler, who retired from Mayo in 1983 following 37 years in administration, added two more conditions that he felt were implicit in the Mayo brothers' actions but had been left unstated:

5. Continuing effort toward excellence in everything that is done.
6. Continuing conduct of all affairs with absolute integrity.[6]

Roesler considered these six conditions to be part of "the spirit of the Clinic" that Dr. William Mayo discussed in a 1919 address to the Mayo Alumni Association in which he sought to explain the Clinic's success:

> *In view of the large number of sick who come here to be cared for, it would be natural to attribute the cause of their coming to work well done, but since good work is being done everywhere, there must be another and deeper reason. Perhaps this other reason may best be summed up in one phrase, "the spirit of the Clinic," which incorporates the desire to aid those who are suffering, the desire to advance in medical education by research, by diligent observation, and by the application of knowledge gained from others and, most important of all, the desire to pass on to others the scientific candle this spirit has lighted.*[7]

Contemporary research is confirming a social profit and financial profit connection in companies that depend on people to serve customers.[8] Companies create social profit when their activities produce net benefits to society beyond the marketing of goods and services and the creation of employment opportunities, essential elements in producing financial profits. Social profit involves investing financial and nonfinancial resources (such as knowledge) toward a better quality of life. Social profit is a form of profit sharing, except the profits are not restricted to financial profits, and the sharing extends beyond the organization.[9]

Social profit depends on a spirit of generosity. Researchers are learning that generosity is an input to service organization success, not just an outcome, because it wins the hearts of stakeholders—including those who perform the service for customers—and strengthens their commitment. Whereas selfishness saps human energy from service, generosity has an opposite, positive effect.[10] The Mayo brothers' uncommon generosity and dedication to generating social profit through their medical practice underlie the service success story that unfolds in this book. Perhaps more than any other factor, exceptional generosity was the spark that defined the spirit of the Clinic. The purpose of the enterprise goes far beyond making money.

Chapter 5 tells the story of the Mayo brothers giving their thriving medical practice and most of their personal wealth to a not-for-profit charitable organization called Mayo Properties Association in 1919. Dr. Will discussed his and Charlie's philosophy with a newspaper writer in 1931:

> *By 1894 my brother and I had paid for our homes. Our clinic was on its feet. Patients kept coming. Our theories seemed to be working out. The mortality rate among our cases was satisfyingly low. Money began to pile up. To us it seemed to be more money than any two men had any right to have.*
>
> *We talked it over a lot, that year of 1894. Then we came to a decision. That year we put aside half of our income. We couldn't touch a cent of that half for ourselves. I know it may sound mawkish, it may sound like egotism and arrogance, when it was none of those things— but that money seemed, somehow, like holy money to us.*
>
> *From 1894 onward we have never used more than half of our incomes on ourselves and our families. . . . My brother and I have both put ourselves on salaries now. The salaries are far less than half our incomes. We live within them.*
>
> *That holy money, as we call it, had to go back into the service of the humanity that had paid it to us.*
>
> *We try to take up the medical surgical education of selected and promising men where the state leaves off. My interest and my brother's interest is to train men for the service of humanity. What can I do with one pair of hands? But, if I can train 50 or 500 pairs of hands, I have helped hand on the torch. And we have the hands to train—nearly 300 of them now with the Mayo Foundation, and a waiting list of some 1,400. They are the ones who will carry on.[11]*

THE 100-YEAR BRAND   *11*

Learning from Healthcare

Can a book about a healthcare organization—even a world-class institution such as Mayo Clinic—actually offer important, practical lessons for managers outside of healthcare? Healthcare is after all dissimilar from most other services in significant ways. First, healthcare customers are usually sick or injured and under considerable stress. Second, inpatients not only enter the service facility but they live in it. Few service industries have their customers sleep over; hospitals do. Third, healthcare is a "need" service rather than a "want" service. The presence or possibility of illness thrusts people—often reluctantly—into the role of healthcare consumers. Consumers want to go out to eat, take a vacation, talk on the telephone, and attend a football game. They do not want to get a physical exam, have a mammogram, or undergo a surgical procedure. Fourth, healthcare services are inherently personal. Other services do not require people to bare themselves—emotionally and sometimes physically—to the degree required by healthcare. Fifth, healthcare customers often require a more holistic and customized service than other service customers require. Healthcare services need to be tailored not only to a patient's specific medical condition but also to the patient's age, mental status, personality, preferences, education, family situation, and financial constraints. Serious illness intensifies the need for "whole-person" service. Sixth, healthcare customers are at risk of being harmed beyond their existing medical problems. In seeking medical care, they may be subject to an incorrect diagnosis leading to an incorrect treatment plan or harmed by medication errors, hospital-acquired infections, or something else. A lot can go wrong in the delivery of healthcare services.[12]

The dissimilarities of healthcare from most other services actually make a well-run healthcare institution like Mayo Clinic especially valuable for managers in general to study. Imagine what can be learned from an organization that serves customers who (1) arrive with some combination of illness or injury, pain, uncertainty, and fear; (2) give up most of their freedoms if hospitalized; (3) need the service but dread it; and (4) typically relinquish their privacy (and modesty) to clinicians they may be meeting for the first time. Mayo Clinic and other well-run healthcare organizations serve just these kinds of special customers who are called patients and *still* earn high praise and fierce loyalty from them. Yes, indeed, a successful healthcare organization offers important lessons for most business organizations.

Of course, many services share some common dynamics with healthcare services:

- The core benefit from the service is intangible; it comes from a performance, and customers incur an expense rather than acquire tangible assets.
- The performance is labor- and skill-intensive, contributing to considerable variability from one service provider to the next.
- The customer is physically present to receive the service, requiring time and place synchronization with the provider of the service.
- The service is perishable. When the physical and human resources available to deliver the service are unused, the value that they might have created perishes.
- Customer demand for the service is unevenly distributed and is sometimes urgent.
- Customer needs and preferences are diverse, thus requiring the organization to have a portfolio of skills and other resources readily available.
- Reliability of the service—accuracy and dependability—is essential.
- Multiple service providers contribute to the customer's experience, necessitating coordination of their performances.
- The service chain is complex with numerous interdependent parts.[13]

While all the service characteristics enumerated fit healthcare, so too do they apply in full or in part to service industries ranging from power plants to airlines to restaurants. Managers and clinicians within healthcare can learn lessons from Mayo Clinic, and so can managers in other service sectors. Effectively operating organizations whose product is a performance is sufficiently challenging so that leaders always can learn from other service enterprises. This book shares insights and inspiration from one of the very best organizations in one of the most challenging of all service sectors.

The Research

Our overriding goal in writing this book is to clearly and accurately explain how a highly complex labor- and skill-intensive service organization has functioned so well for so long and to show how its lessons apply to others inside and outside of healthcare. To attain this goal, we first had to acquire an in-depth understanding of the organization. Superficial understanding would not suffice. To write a book worth reading, we needed to hear the perspectives of many people—patients as well as staff members—who know Mayo from actual experience. We also needed to know Mayo from our own experiences, listening to the "sounds" of the Clinic, observing how it conducts itself, and absorbing how it feels to serve and be served by Mayo Clinic. We needed to blend observational and historical research with more conventional personal interview and survey research.

We have done this research, capitalizing on a confluence of factors that provided an opportunity to look deeply inside a conservative, quiet, and proprietary institution to learn how and why it serves the way it serves. One factor was Len Berry's sabbatical research leave to study Mayo's service culture and systems during the 2001–2002 academic year. Another was Kent Seltman's impending retirement from Mayo Clinic; he had served as its director of marketing from 1992 to 2006 and had led or supervised many Clinic studies of patients, staff members, and the healthcare market. Our collaboration on this project gave us the benefit of *both* "outsider" and "insider" perspectives. A third factor was Mayo Clinic's cooperation through the participation of its leadership and staff in interviews and in allowing us to use proprietary research information in the book. Our book is strictly independent of the Clinic, which had no control over its content. Even so, this notoriously "private"

organization allowed us full access. A fourth factor was the availability of several "big picture" observers of Mayo—retired Mayo
CEOs and senior administrators from several different eras—who
gave us keen insights that we may not otherwise have obtained.
Readers meet these individuals and many more Mayo staff
members—past and present—in the pages ahead. Although the Clinic
had no control over the book's content, we did ask six of our big-
picture observers to read a draft of the book to ensure its accuracy.

We conducted the primary research for the book in two phases.
The sabbatical research was conducted prior to the decision to write
this book, but it provided a strong foundation for it. The research
problem investigated was to identify the ideal service experience
from the perspectives of patients, clinicians (doctors and nurses),
and nonclinical staff members (allied health staff and administrative
personnel). The research was conducted at Mayo's Minnesota and
Arizona campuses and included transcribed interviews with about
1,000 people from the groups listed here. The research also included
transcribed personal observations of hundreds of clinician-patient
interactions in exam and hospital rooms. Observing numerous
surgeries, staying in Mayo's Saint Marys Hospital as a patient, and
flying on the Mayo One emergency rescue helicopter service were
also part of the sabbatical research experience. The research focused
on 14 medical disciplines that were selected to provide broad representation of outpatient and inpatient services and differing levels
of acuity: cardiology, cardiac surgery, dermatology, emergency
medicine, endocrinology, executive exam program, family medicine,
gastroenterology, medical and radiation oncology, neurology, orthopedic surgery, transplant surgery, thoracic surgery, and urology. It
was a rare opportunity for an external researcher to study the Clinic's
service culture and systems from the inside and leave with a treasure
of knowledge about an exemplary medical institution that deserves
its high reputation (evident even to one untrained in medicine) but
also has opportunities to improve (which were shared with Mayo's
leadership and, where applicable, are shared in this book).

The second phase was the research done specifically for this book.
Kent Seltman conducted dozens of in-depth interviews with both

active and retired Clinic staff members, including present and former CEOs, clinical and administrative leaders, doctors, nurses, and others. The interviews typically lasted for about an hour. Many exploratory interviews designed to generate insights and thought patterns that could help us refine the structure and themes of this book were completed before we wrote the first word. Additionally, more targeted interviews focused on the subject matter of a particular chapter were conducted during the writing process. Some respondents were interviewed multiple times. All interviews were transcribed.

We also consulted Clinic research pertinent to our topic, and we used historical information provided by archival and library staff. We also relied on relevant published business literature to help present ideas and support our conclusions.

This is a book about a real organization and real people. We use the actual names of the people we quote except when referring to Clinic patients. Individuals who are quoted without an accompanying citation provided original material in either first or second research-phase interviews. We asked the individuals interviewed to verify the accuracy of the quoted material attributed to them before the book went to press. We also gave them the opportunity to clarify or elaborate on their comments.

Progressive in a Traditional Way

Labor-intensive service organizations commonly become less effective as they age. They become more bureaucratic and rule-driven, less flexible and nimble, less hungry. Service organizations depend on the personal commitment and energy of the performers of their services to become—and remain—excellent organizations. Too often, these performers lose their spark, their "volunteerism," their extra effort in serving. As a result, once-successful or highly promising enterprises falter.

Service organizations need to learn how to act young when they no longer are young, and Mayo Clinic offers a rich case study from which to learn about staying service strong. Progressive in a traditional way, the Clinic continues to live its values, execute its care model, adhere to its management system, and both create and embrace new medical knowledge despite the perils of time, growth, success, and prestige. Its long existence has benefited millions of patients and millions more will benefit in the future. We have written this book to benefit another big group: managers and service providers who want to improve the service of their organizations as well as to sustain and continue improvement as their organizations age. People inevitably decline when they age. Organizations need not decline; they can get better.

The book moves, broadly speaking, from the Clinic's core values to its core strategy to how it implements and sustains the values and strategy. Historical events and perspectives are intertwined with the present-day picture of Mayo Clinic. We liberally use stories and quotes to illustrate our points. We interpret themes from each chapter in the form of "lessons for managers." The chapters build on one another, and we encourage readers to read them in sequence; to skip a chapter is to miss a segment of Mayo's art of service.

In 1895, Dr. William Mayo addressed the graduating class of the medical department of the Minnesota State University on the importance of thoroughness in medicine:

> *Above all things let me urge upon you the absolute necessity of careful examinations for the purpose of diagnosis. My own experience has been that the public will forgive you an error in treatment more readily than one in diagnosis, and I fully believe that more than one-half of the failures in diagnosis are due to hasty or unmethodical examinations. Say to yourselves that you will not jump at a conclusion, but in each instance will make a thorough and painstaking physical examination, free from prejudice, and your success is assured.*[14]

In researching and writing this book, we have endeavored to carefully examine and interpret the underpinnings of Mayo Clinic's durable service excellence because its story teaches valuable management principles that are applicable in other organizations. Welcome to the book. Enjoy and benefit from the journey.

NOTES

1. Denis A. Cortese, "The Note on the Windshield," *Mayo Clinic Checkup*, July 2002, p. 2.
2. Thomas R. Viggiano, Wojciech Pawlina, Keith Lindor, Kerry D. Olsen, and Denis A. Cortese, "Putting the Needs of the Patient First: Mayo Clinic's Core Value, Institutional Culture, and Professionalism Covenant," *Academic Medicine*, November 2007, p. 1089.
3. "A Study of Attitudes toward Mayo Clinic," Report for Mayo Clinic, Social Research, Inc., December 1961, p. 55.
4. "A Study of Non-Patient Attitudes toward the Mayo Clinic," Research report for Mayo Clinic, Social Research, Inc., October 1962, p. 53.
5. "A Study of Attitudes toward Mayo Clinic," p. 56.
6. Robert C. Roesler, *Principles and People: Key Elements of Mayo* (Rochester, MN: Mayo Foundation, June 1984), p. 27.
7. As quoted in Roesler, p. 6.
8. See Rajenda S. Sisodia, David B. Wolfe, and Jagdish N. Sheth, *Firms of Endearment: How World-Class Companies Profit from Passion and Purpose* (Upper Saddle River, NJ: Wharton School Publishing, 2007) and Leonard L. Berry, *Discovering the Soul of Service: The Nine Drivers of Sustainable Business Success* (New York: Free Press, 1999).
9. Berry, 1999, pp. 35–38.
10. Leonard L. Berry, "The Best Companies are Generous Companies," *Business Horizons*, July–August 2007, pp. 263–269.
11. J. T. Logan, "The Mayo Clinic," *The Free Methodist*, February 13, 1931, p. 8.
12. Leonard L. Berry and Neeli Bendapudi, "Health Care: A Fertile Field for Service Research," *Journal of Service Research*, November 2007, pp. 111–122.
13. Leonard L. Berry, "Leadership Lessons from Mayo Clinic" *Organizational Dynamics*, Fall 2004, pp. 228–242.
14. William Mayo, (address, Minnesota State University) published in *Northwest Lancet*, 1895, vol. 15, pp. 221–225.

CHAPTER 2

PRESERVING A PATIENT-FIRST LEGACY

I could say "thank you" a thousand times, and still it would be inadequate to express the depth and breadth of my gratitude to the fine physicians, nurses, and support staff who attended my wife . . . during her recent surgical stay.

From my vantage point, three things in particular make Mayo Clinic unique and superior to all other health care facilities I have ever seen. First, the academic excellence and professionalism that is evident at every level. Second, the team approach to caring for each patient, with each doctor, nurse, and support staff contributing to the assessment, care, and recovery of each patient. And finally and of particular significance to us, the exemplary manner in which they give the highest priority to the patient-first [concept] in action and in attitude.

Before coming to Rochester, our journey had taken us to [another] surgeon who, at least on paper, appeared to be one of the most highly regarded experts in the field anywhere in the world. We eagerly awaited our visit with him, and [my wife] had prepared a list of questions to be sure she covered everything she wanted to learn from him. When he entered the room wearing a pin on the lapel of his lab coat that said "Patients First," we were both eager. But when [my wife] asked the first question, he responded that if he took the time to answer all of her questions, he would not have time to answer the questions of all the other patients who . . . had come from all over the world to see him.

By stark contrast, at Mayo "patients first" is not a mere lapel pin; it is a way of life.[1]

When this letter of thanks to the leadership of Mayo Clinic was written, neither the author, an attorney, nor his wife, the patient who is a nurse, realized that the letter was highlighting the primary value of Mayo Clinic: "The needs of the patient come first." The patient shared in a subsequent interview that the lapel pin on the surgeon's lab coat ironically clarified what she really needed in a healthcare provider. When the promise of the pin was not honored in her actual experience, the disappointment was compounded. Following the visit with the surgeon, the patient and her husband told some friends about the experience. One responded, "Well, you need to go to Mayo Clinic." The patient followed this advice, and she reports that she learned firsthand that "putting patients first is not just a slogan at Mayo Clinic."

Dr. Glenn S. Forbes, CEO of Mayo Clinic in Rochester, explains how this came to be: "If you've just communicated a value but you haven't driven it into the operations, into the policy, into the decision making, into the allocation of resources, and ultimately into the culture of the organization, then it's just words." He adds:

What makes Mayo Clinic distinct is that we have said, "The needs of the patient come first," from the beginning. Over generations, we have driven the needs of the patient into our thinking about how policies were developed. We've driven it into our thinking about how we structure ourselves and our governance and how we allocate resources. We've driven it into our thinking when we recruit people and form staffs. We've driven it so broadly and deeply into our management and operations that it becomes part of a culture. Thus, when we bring an issue forward, it's not a thin layer of, oh yes, that was the marketing mantra that somebody thought of last week. No, this is driven much more deeply into the fabric of the organization. That's what makes us different.

Mayo Clinic's 100-year-old brand is built on a foundation of core values that permeate the entire organization. The topic of this chapter—"the needs of the patient come first"—is chief among them. Other important values such as teamwork in patient care and organizational leadership and providing time-efficient care are discussed in chapters that follow. These values guide decisions and behaviors from Mayo Clinic's registration desk to its boardroom. They encompass the medical, ethical, and service decisions in patient care. They pervade both operational and strategic business matters, as well as human relations with patients and fellow employees. And they sustain the organization by creating a rock-solid basis from which to operate.

In this chapter, we explore how "the needs of the patient come first" value lives in the employees of Mayo Clinic today as it did in the lives of its founders. Sustaining patient centricity (and the related values that support it) is the most important responsibility of Mayo Clinic's management—yesterday, today, and tomorrow. We explain in detail how this core value is embedded in the Clinic's culture; how the organization supports, highlights, and sustains it; how it energizes and empowers employees and resonates with patients and their loved ones; and how it has evolved to keep pace with society.

A Living Value at Work

"The needs of the patient come first" core value has significantly contributed to the long-term success of Mayo Clinic. It is relevant and important to Mayo Clinic's key customers: patients and their families, referring physicians, and most payers—employers and the insurance companies who pay for much of healthcare in the United States. But the value is also relevant and important to the more than 42,000 employees of Mayo Clinic—the doctors, nurses, clinical technicians, and many support staff members. Caregivers feel rewarded by giving their best to those they serve. The values come to life anew each day through the human experiences orchestrated by staff members in their labor-intensive services delivered to patients and their families.

As with so much else at Mayo Clinic, the values emerged from collaborations. The first and most important was the collaboration among the Drs. Mayo—William Worrall Mayo and his sons William

James and Charles Horace—and the sisters of St. Francis of Assisi who built and operated Saint Marys Hospital. The collaboration with the Franciscan community began in 1883 following a devastating and lethal tornado in Rochester, Minnesota. To help manage the seriously injured, Dr. W. W. Mayo requested help from the Franciscan sisters who operated a school in town. After the immediate crisis was over, Mother Alfred proposed that the sisters build a hospital in Rochester. Dr. Mayo initially demurred because hospitals were viewed as places where patients went to die and because he believed that Rochester was too small to support a hospital. Mother Alfred persisted with her idea, and eventually Dr. Mayo agreed that he would use the sisters' hospital. Saint Marys Hospital opened in 1888.[2]

In the collaboration that developed, the Drs. Mayo found the sisters to be partners whose values overlapped their own. Both the doctors and the sisters were focused on the needs of individuals. Sister Mary Eliot Crowley, a member of the Franciscan community and administrator for Franciscan sponsorship at Saint Marys Hospital today, explains it this way: "Dr. Mayo's focus was on the person and a person's illness, and the Franciscan sisters focused on the person's spiritual as well as physical care needs." She adds that they were united as well in their concern for the "vulnerable and the poor."

The values driving the brand today were distilled by the Clinic's founders, William and Charles Mayo, in the first two decades of their careers. This distillation emerged from their reflections on their experience of providing care to thousands of patients. Their father, the Franciscan sisters, their physician colleagues, and the entire staff of the organization were all important contributors to the values that became the essence of Mayo Clinic.

Dr. William J. Mayo eloquently articulated these values in a commencement address to the Rush Medical College in 1910: "The best interest of the patient is the only interest to be considered, and in order that the sick may have the benefit of advancing knowledge, union of forces is necessary.... It has become necessary to develop medicine as a cooperative science."[3] This statement, which identifies two complementary values, has shaped Mayo Clinic for each succeeding generation. Mayo Clinic's contemporary pronouncement of its core value— "the needs of the patient come first"—is obviously derived from this statement. As Dr. Mayo's statement suggests, the needs of the patient can be met only by partnerships and teamwork among the employees providing and supporting patient care.

Business leaders outside the healthcare industry might suggest that building a corporate consensus around a humane value like "the needs of the patient come first" is more natural for a healthcare organization than for commercially driven competitors in other service market sectors such as retail, finance, or hospitality. But, as the letter opening this chapter reveals, sustained focus on the needs of the patient is not endemic in healthcare operations—it is not a slam dunk. The patient whose experiences are described in the letter told us that no one at the four prestigious healthcare institutions she visited before coming to Mayo Clinic really listened to her medical story. At Mayo Clinic, however, a nurse practitioner listened attentively to a 45-minute account of a long medical history. That nurse and the gastroenterologist who also met with the patient, again for a generous amount of time, created various hypotheses for the underlying problems from the detailed medical history they took time to hear. With these hypotheses in mind, the doctor ordered medical testing that focused on the root of the problem, which in turn led to a surgical solution. In terms of this patient's experience, the patient-centric approach at Mayo Clinic was unique.

The absence of patient-focused healthcare may be the root of the social and political angst about healthcare policy and practice in the United States. In February 2007, the *New York Times* reported that Dr. Richard F. Daines, the New York state health commissioner, perceived the "State's system as payout-centric, not patient-centric." According to the article, Daines stated that, "The state's efforts have to focus on what is best for patients, and we will bring the institutions into alignment with patients rather than the other way around."[4]

Certainly, thousands of individual professionals in healthcare do put the needs of patients above everything else. Mayo Clinic is not the only organization that strives to reach this standard. Moreover, Mayo Clinic providers do fall short with some patients, and this is a concern for the Clinic's leadership. Nonetheless, Mayo Clinic's brand research shows that more than 90 percent of its patients report that they say "good things" about Mayo Clinic to friends and family. The 100-year brand was created by word of mouth, first from thousands and now from millions of patients who have had a patient-first clinical experience at Mayo Clinic. They have talked about it because it is different from their experiences elsewhere. The preservation of this value is central to understanding how a strong brand has remained a strong brand over time. It has survived generations of physicians and allied health staff members, as well as 11 CEOs. Living the primary value is how it all begins.

A Patient-Centered Culture

Patients and visitors at Mayo Clinic frequently seek out physicians and administrative leaders in a quest to learn about the courses or training that Mayo uses to create the patient-focused service they experience. Some want the trainers to come to their companies and teach the course. However, there is no such "super" course required of all employees. Even if there were, it would not have the same effect in other organizations. Some conclude that patient-focused service grows out of the work ethic of the agrarian culture created by the Northern European farmers who settled in southeast Minnesota where the Clinic was founded. It is true that many of the Rochester employees do live on farms; even more are just one or two generations away from the soil. It is also true that Minnesotans have a reputation for being nice human beings—"Minnesota nice." But that does not account for the fact that Mayo Clinic's Jacksonville, Florida, and Scottsdale/Phoenix, Arizona, operations have patient satisfaction scores equal to those of Rochester. Patient-centered service exists in these locales as well.

"The needs of the patient come first" is woven into the fabric—the culture—of Mayo Clinic, and the Clinic might not exist today were this not the case. The secret is not a course, a training program, a strategic goal, or a report card score. As we discuss in later chapters, the service systems and procedures, the design of clinical and public space, salaried physicians, and team medicine all provide compelling manifestations of the key value, reflecting it but also reinforcing it. Strategic plans and all the significant operational strategies as well as the Clinic's operational tactics revolve around "the needs of the patient come first." This primary core value directs the organization by defining its "reason for being."

Although there is no single course that teaches the patient-first value, leaders and programs frequently address the topic. For instance, the value is emphasized in the new-employee orientation program. Robert F. Brigham, chief administrative officer in Jacksonville, reports, "New employees hear this in their first five minutes of orientation, because that is how I begin my talk." Rochester employees see the value emphasized in a "Mayo legacy" film that starts their orientation. The message is then reiterated in subsequent presentations. On the Rochester campus, the values are reinforced by additional orientation programming at three months, four months, and a year. But months and years after orientation, employees know the primary value while most of the other orientation details are dim memories or forgotten. Employees know "patient needs come first" because they live and experience it every day on the job. Most employees can recite the value-statement version—"the needs of the patient come first." They might call it the "mission statement" or the "key strategy," but the message is ingrained.

Increasingly, however, Mayo leadership is not content to trust the acculturation process completely, particularly in the assimilation of new physicians. A physician communications course has recently been developed, for example. The course varies slightly by campus, but each "stresses communication to improve that very personal relationship between the physician and the patient," emphasizes Dr. Daniel L. Hurley, one of the course leaders in Rochester. The Jacksonville practice requires all physicians—not just new hires—to attend its course. Even though the patient satisfaction scores are already high, Dr. William J. Maples, chair of the quality, safety, and service committee in Jacksonville, is not satisfied, "I know that we can do better." Among other behaviors, the course challenges physicians to listen to a patient's opening narrative without interrupting. Also the physicians are taught to ask, "Is there anything else?" to ensure that patients are not holding back important information or concerns. "We've seen our patient satisfaction scores improve—we think that the course is helping," Dr. Maples concludes. In 2006, the leadership in Jacksonville decided to put the entire workforce through a similar patient/employee communication program.

Still, in the end, even these educational initiatives would not succeed if the messages were foreign to the culture of Mayo Clinic. Jane Campion, an emeritus administrator, puts it this way: "If you are committed to the Mayo values, Mayo becomes part of your DNA." An analogy might clarify. Few chemistry professors can recall learning the periodic table of the elements, yet most know it perfectly. None of their undergraduate or graduate classes required them to memorize it, but when they understand the discipline of chemistry, they know the periodic table. Similarly, when one understands how to be a Mayo Clinic employee, the value has been internalized—the employee knows it. It is transmitted culturally, not didactically.

Preserving the Value

Mayo Clinic has codified its values, culture, and expectations in a document called the Mayo Clinic Model of Care (see Exhibit 2-1), which it gives to all employees. Although not formally adopted until 1998, the document essentially reflects how the Clinic has functioned throughout its history. For much of this history, the reach back to the founders was either first- or secondhand. Richard W. Cleeremans, an early leader in systems and procedures for Mayo Clinic, for instance, joined Mayo in 1950 and retired in 1992. He quips, "I didn't know Jesus Christ, but I knew the 12 apostles." Then he explains that he didn't know the Mayo brothers, but he worked with and for leaders who had been chosen by and trained under them. He also knew the children of both Drs. Will and Charlie

Exhibit 2-1
Mayo Clinic Model of Care

The Mayo Clinic Model of Care is defined by high quality, compassionate medical care delivered in a multispecialty, integrated academic institution. The primary focus, meeting the needs of the patient, is accomplished by embracing the following core elements (attributes) as the practice continues to evolve.

Patient Care

- Collegial, cooperative, staff teamwork with multispecialty integration. A team of specialists is available and appropriately used.
- An unhurried examination with time to listen to the patient.
- A physician takes personal responsibility for directing patient care over time in a partnership with the local physician.
- Highest quality patient care provided with compassion and trust.
- Respect for the patient, family, and the patient's local physician.
- Comprehensive evaluation with timely, efficient assessment and treatment.
- Availability of the most advanced, innovative diagnostic and therapeutic technology and techniques.

The Mayo Environment

- Highest quality staff, mentored in the culture of Mayo and valued for their contributions.
- Valued professional allied health staff with a strong work ethic, special expertise, and devotion to Mayo.
- A scholarly environment of research and education.
- Physician leadership.
- Integrated medical record with common support services for all outpatients and inpatients.
- Professional compensation that allows a focus on quality, not quantity.
- Unique professional dress, decorum, and facilities.

(as the Mayo brothers are commonly referred to inside the Clinic). To Cleeremans, the legacy was close at hand. By the late 1990s, however, few who had touched the first or second generations of Mayo

Clinic remained actively involved in the institution. Further, in the mid-1980s, a period of significant growth had begun. For instance, in 1985 before expanding to Jacksonville and Scottsdale, Mayo Clinic employed a total of 8,159 people including 832 staff physicians. In 1997, when the board of governors appointed and charged the Mayo Clinic model of care task force to codify the care model, the total number of employees—23,182—had nearly tripled, and the number of physicians had grown to 1,527. Dr. Kerry Olsen, who chaired the codification project, explains its genesis:

> With our rapid growth over the previous decade, we were concerned that new physicians who had not trained at Mayo would not understand the practice styles and values that had made Mayo successful. We were also concerned that short-term financial pressures could lead to practice changes that could hurt Mayo in the long term. Thus, we defined the essential elements of our model of care that must be preserved largely by mentoring so as to ensure continuation of the patient experience that makes Mayo Clinic unique and valued.

Dr. Dawn Milliner, who coordinates the clinical practice advisory group across Mayo's three campuses, adds: "We were concerned this valued heritage not be lost amid constantly changing diagnostic and treatment technologies, public expectations of healthcare, government and regulatory requirements, and the financial challenges of healthcare delivery." Dr. David Herman, former chair of the clinical practice committee for the Rochester campus, explains its use: "We use the document as a country would use a constitution. It is the articulation of the principles that make Mayo Clinic the Mayo Clinic. It is a rare meeting of the executive board or the clinical practice committee [in which] the document is not specifically mentioned." Dr. Milliner calls it a "touch point."[5] As the opening letter of this chapter shows, patients clearly recognize the attributes of this model in their experience in Mayo Clinic and its hospitals. They appreciate time with physicians and other team members to fully tell their medical stories. They realize that the physicians whom they see are in clear and open communication with one another.

Most new service employees learn their job by observing others do it. The experience is inherently social and creates a rich opportunity to transmit informally an organization's values and culture. Nowhere is this truer than in healthcare, where the training and orientation programs are long. More than 62 percent of Mayo Clinic physicians have received some or all of their training at Mayo, so in a sense, they have had "job interviews" that have lasted for years. In addition to assessing the technical and cognitive skills required to become Mayo Clinic physicians and surgeons, physician mentors also look for evidence of commitment to the Clinic's values. As we discuss in Chapter 5, Mayo Clinic is a physician-led organization, so the understanding and practice of patient centricity among the medical staff is essential if this value is going to survive.

All registered nurses, even experienced nurses, who are new employees undergo an extensive orientation. According to Elizabeth Pestka, RN, the director of the orientation program in Rochester, the values are an important component of this program—it is not a lecture per se but rather a concept woven into the orientation experience. Recently, the program has added a "reader's theater" activity featuring the roots of nursing at Mayo Clinic.[6] The readers, who are the orientees, are cast as the Drs. Mayo, Franciscan sisters, and Edith Graham, who was the first professionally trained nurse in Saint Marys Hospital. One scene portrays the first day on the job for the young Franciscan, Sister Mary Joseph, who recalls:

> *One of my first nursing duties was to assist at the examination of a male patient whose entire body had to be uncovered for observation. While one of the doctors and Miss Graham worked with him, I stood off in the corner, my back turned, quivering with outrage and shame. After the examination I protested to Miss Graham and asked to be returned to my teaching duties. I was told that taking care of all patients, both women and men, was my responsibility and that prudery among sisters could lead to neglect in nursing. I learned to meet the needs of all patients. . . .[7]*

This Franciscan sister went on to serve as the administrator of Saint Marys Hospital for more than 47 years and "was always on guard against prudery among the sisters where it might lead to neglect in nursing."[8]

Preserving the patient-first value is a focus of "Mayo Clinic Heritage Days," a week-long celebration that is held each October. The celebration originated on the Rochester campus as a way to reinforce the historic collaboration among Mayo Clinic, Saint Marys Hospital, and Rochester Methodist Hospital, as those hospitals had operated separately from Mayo Clinic until the mid-1980s. In 2000, a consulting anthropologist studied Mayo Clinic culture on each of its three campuses and recommended extending Heritage Days to the two newer campuses—the three-campus program began in 2001.

Heritage Hall, which opened in 2004, is a museum dedicated "to telling the great stories of Mayo Clinic," according to Director Matthew Dacy. Although it was first opened in Rochester, today similar museums are located in Jacksonville and Scottsdale/Phoenix. Some exhibits rotate among the sites. The museums, says Dacy, show that "patient care is the first and greatest story of all." The original museum was founded by two benefactors, loyal Mayo Clinic patients John and Lillian Mathews. In establishing the gift, the donors said that their goal was "to add more voices to the Mayo Clinic choir." Heritage Hall creates an additional voice to reinforce for patients and employees alike that the great men and women of the past first created solid values and then the great organization, the great reputation, the great brand—Mayo Clinic—where the needs of the patient come first.

In the historic 1928 Plummer Building on the Rochester campus, the offices of the founding brothers are preserved in much the same state as they were when the brothers last occupied them in the 1930s. Also in this historical suite is the room where the board of governors convened for several decades. Framed honors bestowed upon the Mayo brothers cover the high walls—honorary doctoral degrees, memberships in medical societies around the world, awards for public service. Visitors to this room realize that the Mayo brothers were genuine medical pioneers and not a product of a marketing campaign or good press agents. This preservation of the past reminds succeeding generations of employees that they must perform with a technical, professional excellence and a spirit of humanity that preserve the reputation that created the 100-year brand. It also is an antidote to smugness in individual achievements.

A statuary park, situated across the street from the main entrance to the Gonda Building, was added to the Rochester campus in 2004. Statues of William Worrall Mayo, whose sons founded Mayo Clinic, and Mother Alfred Moes, founder of Saint Marys Hospital, stand near each other at one end of the park. At the other end, the brothers William J. and Charles H. Mayo, rendered in bronze, sit on steps in a casual pose with the main entrance to Mayo Clinic behind them. The pose is based on a photograph of the brothers in their prime sitting on the front steps of a family home, but in the statuary park they sit on the front steps of the Clinic that bears their name a century later. Artistic license has turned the wooden steps into marble and extended them in a large arc. It is a sculpture and setting that invites photographers. Mayo Clinic work groups pose on the steps with the founding brothers who are cast in life size, neither rendered in an exaggerated scale nor elevated on high marble pedestals. Casual photos of physicians in training at Mayo Clinic show them sitting shoulder to shoulder with the brothers—yes, sometimes even clowning. Guests and patients also capture in photos their connection with the healing legacy of Mayo Clinic.

In the end, the formal initiatives—employee orientation, educational courses, Heritage Days, the museums, and the statuary park—are complements. The core force in preserving the value is the on-the-job living of the patient-first value by employees throughout the enterprise.

The Authority to Serve

When a value becomes "part of an employee's DNA," it guides not only the way the day-to-day work is performed, but it also gives employees the power and moral authority to act in unique situations. Explicit permission is not needed when an employee sees a patient need that requires action. If the employee's choices are either getting back to work on time or taking 10 minutes to get a wheelchair for a patient who seems unsteady, the patient will most likely get a wheelchair. Exceptional service frequently results when employees invoke values-based authority.

Matthew McElrath, formerly chair of human resources for Mayo Clinic Arizona, shares this story of employee empowerment:

> *I... ended up as a patient in the ICU at Mayo Clinic Hospital. Dr. Trastek [CEO of Mayo Clinic Arizona] and his wife were returning to Arizona from a trip to Rochester and learned of my being hospitalized and came to the hospital to visit me.*
>
> *What was remarkable wasn't that they came to visit me—I was deeply touched that they wanted to come and see me, but what made it so remarkable was that... the nurse let me sleep and turned Dr. Trastek away at my door.*
>
> *When I woke later that day, she said to me, "You had some visitors, but I turned them away. I hope you don't mind—but one in particular I feel a little strange about."*
>
> *I asked, "Why?"*
>
> *And she said, "Dr. Trastek and his wife came by to see you... I told them that you were sleeping, and I really wanted you to sleep."*
>
> *I said, "Thank you very much, it's the best thing, I'll catch up with him later."*
>
> *And she was like, "Is that OK—you don't mind?"*
>
> *And I said, "Absolutely." I thought to myself, "Here was a great example where the nurse asked herself, 'What is the best thing to do for the patient?' and that's what she did." She knew that the best thing for me was to sleep even if it meant her shooing away the CEO from my door.*

A clinical assistant, whose primary task is scheduling follow-up medical appointments, goes into extra-effort mode when the appointment system creates full-day gaps in patients' progress through the Clinic. Showing determination and pride in patient-first service, she spends considerable time in structuring appointments based on patients' particular needs. Patients probably will never know about the clinical assistant's behind-the-scenes special effort, which gives the institution—rather than the assistant—the credit for patient-first service. The reward for this employee is the personal satisfaction that comes from helping Mayo Clinic deliver on "the needs of the patient come first."

Empowerment is most important when any employee observes a patient in trouble, a patient whose medical condition appears to be deteriorating. The Joint Commission, which accredits hospitals and clinics, recently identified poor communication as a major cause of detrimental events and put "improving the effectiveness of communication among caregivers" near the top of its 2007 national patient safety goals. Mayo Clinic was ahead of the curve in Arizona, as leaders there initiated in 2005 a program called Plus-One. This program is designed to ensure that critical information is accurately and persuasively communicated when "the clinical needs of the patient" are possibly not being met. The program makes explicit the responsibilities to exercise Mayo's historic primary value. Plus-One refers to the expectation that any one person can consult an additional person up the chain of command to get what is needed for a patient. Often a supervisor or manager is the one additional person, but sometimes it is a peer. For instance, the nurses working together usually can concur quickly that the on-call physician should or should not be called even if it is 2:00 a.m. Likewise, if a caregiver senses that his observations about a patient do not match those of others, Plus-One can be initiated to determine the best course of action for the patient at that time. Any person on the care team—a nurse, a technician, a physician—can use this tool to ensure that the needs of the patient are being appropriately met in a timely manner.

Dr. Annie Sadosty, a Mayo Clinic emergency physician, recounts a service episode that is sometimes used in Clinic educational sessions. The driver of a big-rig transport truck became ill while driving through Rochester and proceeded to Mayo Clinic's Saint Marys Hospital, parked her big rig right in front, and made her way to the emergency department (ED). The doctors strongly advised that she be admitted to the hospital immediately, but she resisted. After some probing questions, the staff learned that the driver was very concerned because her truck was parked on the street and her dog was locked in the cab. At this point, the patient's ED nurse volunteered to handle the truck and the dog, accepting the responsibility though it was not his job to do so. The patient gave him the truck keys, and, he says, "I was a little surprised to find that it was a Kenworth with a 53-foot trailer." Then he recalled that a nurse colleague in the ED had been an over-the-road truck driver and had maintained his commercial driver's license. This second nurse moved the patient's truck, but parking it for a few days was another matter. He called the management of a local shopping center, as well as the Rochester Police Department, and received permission to park in the mall lot. The first nurse looked after the patient's dog.

These nurses were volunteering to honor "the needs of the patient" not only in the ED but also through their personal efforts beyond assigned work responsibilities. The nurse who took the dog not only kenneled it but also took care of the dog's medical needs. He reports, "Both the dog and the patient got better and were reunited in a few days." Dr. Sadosty concludes, "All of this was done in an effort to be sure that what needed to be done for the patient was done. It is an incredible story. The people are incredible, and I know these stories are created every day."

Armando Lucchesi, housekeeping manager for Mayo Clinic Arizona's Scottsdale campus, invites his staff to call him any time during their day or late night shifts. These calls illustrate how he has managed to instill the patient-first value among his employees and then how they feel empowered to make a difference in the patient experience, even though most of them work at night when most patients are gone. One employee who was out on sick leave called Lucchesi from home to share that during a medical exam at the Clinic that day she had noticed that a tile had fallen from the ceiling of the exam room. The employee wanted to ensure that no more patients would see this. These housekeeping employees often come to Mayo Clinic with virtually no knowledge of the organization. "I tell my staff about the history of Mayo Clinic, about the expectations people have when they come here. That makes us proud," Lucchesi says. "Our traditions and the Mayo brothers inspire us. We want to be part of the team that provides the very best to patients."

Mayo Clinic employees are Mayo's most critical patients; they give lower patient satisfaction scores than any other patient segment. Their standards are extremely high, and they are among the first to identify even the little failures in patient-centric service. Dr. Edward Rosenow III, a retired Mayo physician, volunteers to talk about Mayo Clinic's service culture to current employees; he relates this recent experience: a 15-year Mayo Clinic employee was diagnosed with breast cancer and had come to the department of radiology for a follow-up X-ray. She was called from the waiting room by a clinical assistant. The patient noticed that the clinical assistant was yawning. The employee-patient, carrying the burden of great anxiety about her disease, was offended. She complained to Dr. Rosenow, "I have breast cancer, and the woman helping me appeared tired and bored." The empowered employees set a very high standard for one another, even on seemingly little things.

Dr. Robert R. Waller, an ophthalmologist who retired as president and CEO of Mayo Clinic in 1999, also makes the point that "the needs of the patient" often involve simple matters but are never unimportant. He recalls, for instance, a phone conversation with an internist colleague late on a Friday afternoon. The internist was seeing a patient who needed to leave soon to catch a plane. The patient, a diabetic, had concerns about his vision but had not been able to fit in an ophthalmology appointment. This patient needed only to have his mind put at ease, so Dr. Waller agreed to consult with the patient—"It only took five minutes," he notes. In this case, he could reassure the patient by suggesting that a detailed exam could safely be postponed until a later visit. Dr. Waller observes, "Not only is the patient satisfied and at ease, but physicians get great joy from providing this type of service."

In September 2005, several patients were evacuated from hurricane-ravaged New Orleans to Mayo Clinic's hospital in Jacksonville, Florida. While caring for one of those patients, a doctor in the emergency department noted that it was the patient's birthday. Then he discovered that she had no family in Jacksonville to celebrate with her and, in fact, had no living relatives anywhere. He called his wife at home and asked her to bring a birthday cake and their young children to the emergency room where a celebration took place. This simple, humane act brought needed joy into the soul and spirit of a patient who had lost everything but her life.

When stories like these are shared inside Mayo, people are inspired to create more. An administrator tells how nurses, who were caring for a young woman who was dying of cancer, pooled their own money to buy a ticket to bring her husband from a thousand miles away to the patient's bedside. In another instance, the patient comments, "I had not realized the value of 'touch' until being placed in the stress that goes with a cancer diagnosis and surgery. Thank you for taking care of me physically and mentally." A final example from the hundreds collected through Mayo's comment card system: the nursing unit staff turned a two-patient room into a private room for one night so the spouse of a 37-year-old man could be with him following surgery for what they thought was a "benign" tumor. After the surgical biopsy revealed osteosarcoma—a bone cancer—the spouse wanted to be near.

Patient centricity also functions in deliberations in the committees and governing boards. During Dr. Waller's years on the board, he and his colleagues frequently faced complex decisions. When it was difficult to achieve unanimity, someone would invariably ask, "Yes, but what is best for the patient?" Shirley Weis, chief administrative officer of Mayo Clinic, echoes Dr. Waller, "Our value of patient-needs-first helps cut through a lot of chatter in meetings. Just ask. 'Is this right for the patient or not?' And that gets you centered properly on the issue." She illustrates with an example dealing with the electronic medical record in which the issue concerned how much time should elapse before physicians would need to sign on again. Sign-on is an annoyance, of course. However, when one physician asked what patients would feel best meet their needs for privacy, a decision was quickly reached that favored patients' needs.

Mayo Clinic buildings are impressive—large, clean, efficient, and accessible. The museums, statuary park, and landscaping are designed to be inviting and comforting. But in the end, the real

Mayo Clinic is not tangible—it is a service, not bricks and mortar and marble. As a service organization, Mayo Clinic is only as good tomorrow as its service is today. The Mayo Clinic that patients talk about to friends and family is the humane medical and personal service created on the fly every day by staff interacting with patients and their families. Broad employee empowerment is required to achieve the long-term success that Mayo Clinic enjoys.

Generous Acts Strengthen the Core

From the beginning, the "needs of the patient come first" value has frequently had an underlying financial dimension. Dr. Hugh Butt, one of the last living physicians personally trained by Dr. William J. Mayo, recounted doing a three-month clinical rotation with Dr. Mayo in 1936. Dr. Will, who gave up his surgical practice in 1928 and retired from the board of governors in 1932, remained active in the affairs of the Clinic. Dr. Will instructed the young Dr. Butt, "I only want to see the following patients, the very sick and the very poor, None others. Do you understand?" Dr. Butt soon found a patient who was both very poor and very sick, perhaps at the door of death. His bed was on an open eight-patient ward where Dr. Butt and Dr. Mayo examined him. Dr. Butt recalls that as they walked away, Dr. Mayo spoke, "Well, I agree with you, he is very sick, and you say he is poor." Dr. Butt's story continues:

> Dr. Will gave me $400! ... Then he said, "You go upstairs and give it to the cashier. Don't tell him where the money came from and move him [the patient] up to a private room with a nurse. Be sure there is an ice tub and fans to keep him cool"—that is the only kind of air-conditioning we had. He did this time and time again, helping these people and no one ever knew it was Dr. Will who had them moved up to a private room.

The founders of Mayo Clinic lived the value more than they talked about it. Sometimes the need was clinical, but, as in the preceding example, the very ill patient and his family just needed privacy, comfort, and dignity, which the money would buy.

The Mayo brothers insisted that every patient receive the same highest level of care. For much of its early history, Mayo Clinic did not have a standard "charge master;" rather, patients' charges were based on their perceived ability to pay. During World War II, for instance, the young wife of a U.S. soldier who was serving in Europe came to Rochester for treatment of severe multiple sclerosis. She and her mother lived in an apartment for several months, and the daughter had nearly daily treatments. Their first and only bill was presented as they were leaving. "It was about $28 for all the examinations, medications, and treatments combined," the elderly husband recently recalled. "That figure was chosen because it was equal to one month of my pay from the U.S. Army." Clearly, this patient's needs were addressed at a significant financial cost to the Clinic.

Dr. Waller remembers a conversation in the late 1980s with a cardiologist who faced a patient decision that had financial implications for Mayo Clinic. The patient needed a pacemaker implanted. Option A was a Medicare-approved pacemaker model that required a relatively involved surgery and several days of postoperative hospitalization with risks of complications. Option B was a new pacemaker model that could be implanted in a simple surgery with no more than one day of hospitalization. However, the Option B pacemaker was not yet Medicare-approved, and Mayo would receive no reimbursement. Dr. Waller recalled, "This was a no-brainer—use the pacemaker that is best for the patient."

Today, insurance contracts and public policy no longer allow Mayo Clinic to administer a "social contract" in which the rich and the poor both pay according to their means to a benevolent organization that treats all equitably while earning enough to sustain its mission. As a twenty-first century not-for-profit organization with more than $7 billion in annual revenue in 2007, Mayo Clinic expresses its charity and community citizenship somewhat differently from the way its founders did. There is still considerable focus on the needs of individual patients: in 2007, Mayo Clinic provided care valued at $55.6 million to patients who were unable to pay. In addition, unpaid portions of Medicaid and other indigent care programs totaled another $127.1 million of unreimbursed care. Thus, in 2007 more than $182 million of unpaid medical care was provided directly to patients in need. But Mayo Clinic also serves large groups of patients by training new physicians and other healthcare providers as well as through support of medical research seeking cures or relief from disease. In 2007, Mayo Clinic provided $346 million to support its medical education and medical research missions. The broad community benefit in 2007, therefore, totaled more than $500 million. In the end, all net operating revenue is reinvested in medical research and medical education for the benefit of future generations.

New Service Needs Identified

Viewed through the eyes of the modern consumer, some traditional elements of Mayo Clinic service would not be considered patient-centric. Appointment calendars are an example. For many years, most of the outpatient clinical desks offered just two appointment times: 8:00 a.m. and 1:00 p.m. This meant that one of the four patients normally scheduled for the morning would be seen immediately and the other three might wait for one, two, or three hours before seeing the physician. The system was physician-centric in that it ensured that the physician would not have to "waste time" between patients. Robert Fleming, who retired as chief administrative officer in 1993 after a 43-year administrative career at Mayo Clinic, explained, however, that there were some patient-centric aspects to this scheduling system. Most importantly, it provided an opportunity for the physician to spend as much time as needed with each patient, a critical Mayo Clinic commitment. For instance, patients faced with a grim diagnosis and complex treatment options could require much more time than the normally allotted 60 minutes. The patient's need to maximize personal time brought this scheduling system to a final end in the early 1990s. Today, the appointment system schedule is built for each patient with the goal of no more than a 15-minute wait.

In recent years, Mayo Clinic has become more sensitive to patient needs beyond on-campus care. Dr. Eric Edell has for the better part of a decade been working on improvements. He observes, "We do a fantastic job of managing the patients once they get inside Mayo, but we have dealt with our high demand for appointments by creating a fortress around ourselves. If you're outside the institution, it's hard to get in, and the service has sometimes been poor." Dr. Edell reports some improvement in appointment access. For instance, in cases where medical review is required before an appointment request is granted, the current service standard is to reach a decision within 24 hours. Before this standard was applied, patients might not have heard for a week or more and sometimes never. Now, if the appointment office has not heard from the clinical reviewers after 24 hours, the default is to grant the appointment. Dr. Edell also notes, "In the past, we'd announce the appointment by letter or phone—'You can come, at 2:00 p.m. on Tuesday, March 3.' We realized this was insensitive as Mayo was asking patients to arrange their lives for our convenience. Now we ask the patients their preferred timing, and we are trying to accommodate them."

The greatest service challenge in addressing patient needs, perhaps, can never be resolved, because it concerns denied appointment requests. For more than a century, former patients' stories have positioned Mayo Clinic as the "court of last resort"—a position the Clinic has never claimed for itself. An individual in physical or emotional pain or living with a devastating diagnosis often sees access to Mayo Clinic as the last hope. Appointment denials are sometimes received as harsh rejections that dash hopes. Judgments typically rely on an assessment of the perceived needs of the patients with the probability that care at Mayo Clinic would make a difference. Those judgment calls sometimes cause sadness.

The central focus of "the needs of the patient" is the medical—the clinical—needs of the patient. However, Mayo Clinic has evolved to include the "customer service" needs and expectations in an age of medical consumerism, which encompasses the aesthetic and spiritual needs of patients.

Whole-Person Care

For most of the last century, the clinical and public spaces of Mayo Clinic have used architectural and interior design to address patient needs that medical science cannot fulfill. The architectural intent has been to create a sense of substance that justifies patient confidence. "Patients immediately need to feel that they have made a good choice in coming to Mayo Clinic," states James Hodge, vice chair of development and chair of Mayo Clinic's art committee. Even today, the 1928 Plummer Building, a fine example of the Romanesque art deco style, provides rich design elements that offer patients a refuge from the sometimes painful and frightening realities of medical diagnosis and treatment. Cesar Pelli, design consultant for the Clinic's 2001 Gonda Building, describes his approach: "I wanted to design a building where the healing process begins the moment a patient enters the front door." Indeed, a seriously ill new patient stated in a focus group, "I felt better the moment that I stepped on campus." She was not suggesting that she had been miraculously healed, rather that she had arrived at a place that presented itself as a solid and successful organization that offered her a haven and hope.

In more recent years, benefactors have helped Mayo understand even better the importance of beauty in art, music, architecture, and landscaping in the healing process. Serena Fleischhaker, who at age 93 donated the large Chihuly chandeliers for the Gonda Building lobby, stated her intent in remarks to Hodge as well as at the dedication ceremony on October 8, 2001. Hodge recalls her message:

> *Not all patients who come to Mayo are cured; some come and are told very bad news, some come in the storms of their lives. I want the Chihuly glass chandeliers to pleasantly distract people, to cause them to raise their eyes towards the heavens, to pause in the anxious interludes between appointments, to have a tiny respite from their suffering.*

A grateful patient wrote, "When I came to Mayo I expected good medicine well practiced. What I did not expect was a beautiful artful environment—Miros, Calders, and Rodins. Thank you for caring for my soul as well as caring for my body."

Atop the Plummer Building is a three-octave set of carillon bells purchased by Dr. William J. Mayo on a trip to England in the mid-1920s. Since the dedication of the bells in 1928, Mayo Clinic has employed a carillonneur who plays regularly scheduled concerts six times per week—at noon and in the early evenings as patients and employees are outside the buildings. Jimmy Durmmond, who held the position from 1928–1957, eloquently described how he felt his work fit into Mayo Clinic: "Here science serves, enthroned in architecture and crowned in music."[9]

"The art program at Mayo Clinic is very deliberate," notes Hodge. "Mayo Clinic practices the art of medicine within the art of architecture complemented with paintings, sculpture, glass, fabrics—most of the forms and media of art are present." This atmosphere is part of the healing environment. "It addresses needs of the mind and soul within the bodies here for diagnosis, treatment, and healing."

In recent years, donors have given many new musical voices to Mayo. Grand pianos stand in public areas on all three campuses, and most are open to any patient or visitor who wishes to play. Hodge notes, "It is rare that someone is not playing the piano in the Gonda lobby. I've seen patients and visitors join in a sing-along—once patients and visitors were dancing. Another time a diva of opera paused and spontaneously sang. On another occasion, a well-known pop musician sang while a volunteer accompanied him on the piano." Donors and the volunteer musicians have made their gifts because they see them as meeting the needs of patients who are experiencing the pain and fear and hope that the donors themselves know personally.

Mayo Clinic recognizes the importance of whole-person care and has expressed concern for the spiritual needs of patients since Saint Marys Hospital opened in 1888. The Clinic, however, was marginally involved as the chaplains were employed by the hospitals and served only inpatients. Chaplains became employees of Mayo when the ownership of the hospitals changed to Mayo Clinic in 1986.

Then a decade later, for the first time, chaplains began serving the spiritual needs of outpatients, starting with cancer patients. Today more than 30 Mayo-employed chaplains are available in the four hospitals and the Clinic operations as well. These employed chaplains come from Christian, Muslim, and Jewish traditions. The spiritual program encourages all patients to seek spiritual support through their own traditions, rituals, faith, and beliefs. To that end Saint Marys Hospital opened a meditation space in 1998 that includes private prayer areas for people of all faiths.

Articulating the Value for a Time of Change

Robert K. Smoldt, who served as chief administrative officer of Mayo Clinic and retired from the Clinic in 2008, observed a consistent emphasis on "the needs of the patient" throughout his nearly 36-year administrative career. The robust Mayo Clinic culture kept the value alive and immediate, but its leadership recognized the risk that this value could be lost with the expansion to Jacksonville and Scottsdale in the mid-1980s. In addition, Dr. Waller, who was chair of the board of governors at that time, explains that the leaders wanted to ensure that Mayo Clinic would retain its values and successful course as it navigated the uncharted seas of "healthcare reform" that was anticipated in the early years of then U.S. President Bill Clinton's administration. Although the clinics in Jacksonville and Scottsdale had been controlled by Mayo, both the market forces and the political forces shaping healthcare policy were beyond its reach. At best, Mayo Clinic might influence the change.

In response to these forces, Mayo Clinic formally identified "the needs of the patient come first" as its "primary value." This prominence guides internal communications where the message has become the underlying theme. At times it is front and center as demonstrated in Exhibit 2-2 where Dr. Denis Cortese, president and CEO of Mayo Clinic, celebrates empowered employees who apply the value in their work.

Exhibit 2-2
A Single Focus—A Message from Dr. Cortese

July 21, 2005

Dear Colleagues:

Thirty-five years ago when I joined Mayo as a new clinician, I was unaccustomed to having a desk attendant tell me, a physician, that I needed to adjust my schedule to see a patient right away. One of the older clinicians soon set me straight. He shared a phrase and a philosophy with me— "Don't mess with the desk attendants"—meaning that when a desk attendant needed help with a patient, I was expected to respond. He explained that at Mayo Clinic, the focus is always on the patient. And, whichever member of the staff is interacting with the patient deserves our full support.

I learned to trust the desk attendants. The one who asked me to change my schedule had years of experience and she knew how to listen to patients. She knew that a five-minute change to my schedule would make a world of difference to that patient.

I've never forgotten that lesson. As I've moved through my career and now as CEO, I've always known that my job comes down to one thing— making sure that all of the resources of Mayo Clinic are focused on supporting our interactions with patients. From the landscaping and the architecture to the plumbing and the computer systems, from the teaching in our classrooms and mentoring in the clinic to the cutting-edge research in our laboratories—every resource at Mayo needs to be focused on our patients.

Thirty-five years ago, that desk attendant used all of her experience and knowledge to serve the patients at her station and it was my job to help her. Nothing much has changed. It is still my job—it's all of our jobs—to serve patients directly, or provide support for those who are serving patients. And after thirty-five years, it is still a privilege.

Denis Cortese, M.D.
President and CEO
Mayo Clinic

Source: Internal e-mail letter from Dr. Cortese to Mayo Clinic physicians and leadership, July 21, 2005.

Lessons for Managers

The story of Mayo Clinic's primary value shows that it is a "working value" in the sense that it functions every day in the experience of virtually all employees at every level of the organization. Clearly, this value focuses the workforce and drives individual and institutional decisions large and small. Employees' high level of awareness of this value plays a crucial role in the success of the Clinic and the durability of its brand strength. The Mayo Clinic story can be instructive for managers of all types of organizations.

Lesson 1: The real values of an organization are the values lived.   Espoused values are hollow words—just a pin on a lapel—until brought to life by human interaction between the organization's employees and its customers. The freeing energy and pride fueled by the primary value creates much of the extraordinary service that surprises patients at Mayo Clinic. But the living value that patients directly experience is just part of what actually happens in the organization. The value at Mayo Clinic is not just a frontline phenomenon. It permeates the entire organization, encouraging a behind-the-scenes clinical assistant to find a way to save an out-of-town patient from waiting extra days for the next open appointment, for example. The primary value centers the organization on its "reason for being." It clarifies the correct course in otherwise complex decisions and offers perspective during difficult periods, which all organizations—and the people who work for them—experience. Values are sustained by actual behavior.

Lesson 2: A humane value resonates.   "The needs of the patient come first" resonates with all players in the value chain, both inside and outside the organization. Clearly, patients and their family and friends applaud when they experience the value. Most people choosing careers in healthcare also find personal fulfillment in living this value. If any player in the value chain—patient, family, physicians, nurses, transcriptionists, grounds staff, custodians—feels exploited by the organization, a stated value is at risk of disintegration. The Mayo value statement is humane. The value statement's basis of moral authority does not come from any one ethnic, political, or religious tradition, so employees are able to create personal connections between the value and their own belief systems and traditions.

Lesson 3: Substance trumps rhetoric.   Mayo Clinic's seven-word value statement uses one syllable words, except for "patient." Most significantly, the focus of the value is on the individual patient—"patient" is a singular noun, not a plural. The expectation is that each individual patient must be well served. Grammatically, this value is rendered as a simple declarative sentence—a populist distillation of Dr. Will's oratorical declaration. The sentence has just four content words: "needs," "patient," "come," and "first." The words are not modified in any way that could render them meaningless by suggesting they are in any way conditional. This statement is easily remembered because its subject, "the needs of the patient," is constantly before the eyes of the entire workforce. All who work in clinics and hospitals live constantly with fresh images of patients and their needs. Even those whose work does not involve direct patient care see patients in the halls, lobbies, and parking lots. As they head into their work spaces, secretaries, administrators, and lab technicians carry images of patients they have just seen—cancer patients wearing hats and scarves, a child of less than 10 years of age maneuvering his power wheelchair through the human traffic of the lobby, or a middle-aged woman guiding her disoriented mother as if she were a child. This value is memorable to Mayo Clinic employees because it speaks to the human needs seen in flesh and blood. The verb phrase of the value statement—"come first"—is the least that any employee could do. How could anyone not remember that?

Lesson 4: Core values rarely change but their effective implementation requires change.   Mayo's primary value has not changed in a century. Nevertheless, the understanding of the patient's needs has evolved. The Drs. Mayo wanted each patient to receive the best in clinical care—this remains. But today Mayo Clinic must also provide "customer service" needs such as an efficient access to information on the Internet, as well as on-campus accommodations such as short waiting times at appointments, clear signage to give directions, and spiritual and psychosocial support.

Summary

The "needs of the patient" value first and foremost must be experienced in the clinical care Mayo Clinic provides for each patient. Patients must be able to tell their medical histories to caregivers who process them seriously. Each patient must receive a thorough and respectful examination. But some of the magic associated with Mayo Clinic and its brand comes also from unexpected service from Mayo Clinic employees who sense a special need, such as moving a truck, caring for a dog, or celebrating a birthday.

The century-old Mayo Clinic brand thrives today, not only because one of its founders defined its values in 1910 but also because those values are renewed every day in surprisingly sensitive service delivered to thousands of patients and their families. The stories of great service also touch the hearts of Mayo Clinic employees and give meaning to their work—a bonus of personal significance added to the biweekly salary deposits in their bank accounts.

NOTES

1. Letter, September 5, 2006.
2. Helen Clapesattle, *The Doctors Mayo* [abridged] (Rochester, MN: Mayo Foundation for Medical Education and Research, 1969), pp. 136–140. This authorized biography of the family was originally published in 1941 by the University of Minnesota Press. Mayo Clinic purchased the rights to the book and has kept the abridged version in print since 1969.
3. William J. Mayo, "The Necessity of Cooperation in Medicine," address delivered at the Rush Medical College commencement, June 15, 1910, originally published in the *Collected Papers* by the Staff of Saint Marys Hospital, Mayo Clinic, 1910; 2: pp. 557–566; and reprinted verbatim in *Mayo Clinic Proceedings*,

vol. 75, 2000, pp. 553–556. The quote used in this chapter appears on p. 554 of the *Mayo Clinic Proceedings* reprinting.

4. Robin Finn, "Public Lives; New Man in the Hot Seat of State Health Commissioner," *New York Times*, February 2, 2007.

5. Leonard. L. Berry and Kent D. Seltman, "Building a Strong Services Brand: Lessons from Mayo Clinic," *Business Horizons* 50, 2007, pp. 203–204.

6. Elizabeth Pestka, "Nurses Built the Hospital: A Readers' Theatre Used in Nursing Orientation," forthcoming in *Journal of Continuation Education in Nursing*.

7. Reader's theater script quotes from Sister Ellen Whalen, O.S.F., *The Sisters' Story* (Rochester, MN: Mayo Foundation for Medical Education and Research, 2002), p. 60.

8. Clapesattle, p. 145.

9. Harold Severson, "After 30 Years and 4,355 Recitals, Drummond to Retire as Carillonneur," *Rochester Post-Bulletin*, December 24, 1957, p. 10.

CHAPTER 3

PRACTICING TEAM MEDICINE

I returned from a conference on an earlier flight than scheduled to see my wife and daughter before bedtime that Friday night. I had been home for 45 minutes when I received an emergency call from the operating room. One of our surgeons was in trouble with a young man who had a collagen vascular disease that made his blood vessel walls weak and prone to forming and rupturing aneurysms. The young man was driving home with his rented tuxedo for his wedding the next day when he developed acute abdominal pain and collapsed. He was taken to a nearby hospital in Flagstaff, and then his heart arrested. Following resuscitation, he was transported to Mayo where he arrested again before being rushed into surgery. After 23 units of blood, they still couldn't control his ruptured left hepatic artery aneurysm.

When I got the call, I rushed to the hospital and was able to gain control of the artery without sacrificing the right lobe of the liver. The next day the patient was off the ventilator and talking with the nurses in the unit like nothing had happened. The following day, our chaplain performed a wedding for the couple in the hospital intensive care unit. The patient was discharged the next week with no problems.

What a great feeling to help that patient. If an opportunity arises to collaborate on a difficult case, there is no hesitancy in jumping in to help.[1]

Stories like this one—told by Dr. David Mulligan, chair of transplant surgery at Mayo Clinic Arizona and a liver surgery specialist—capture Mayo's culture and core competency of teamwork. Mayo employs highly capable doctors and other caregivers, but so do other healthcare organizations. What helps distinguish Mayo is effective medical staff teamwork. The Clinic excels in *pooling* talent for the benefit of patients.

Mayo Clinic is a collaborative organization, a pliable institution that assembles the expert care teams for individual patients. Imagine a huge store that sells everything, with experts in every department who work together to help customers. This is how Mayo Clinic is designed for medical customers. Patients don't get just a doctor; they get, in effect, the "whole company." Some patients see more than one Clinic physician. Typically, the first doctor to treat a patient is responsible for coordinating the care plan with other Mayo clinicians and the patient's hometown physician. Most Mayo patients see only one physician who, in turn, may informally consult with other clinicians on staff to reach a diagnosis or develop a treatment plan. Depending on an individual patient's needs, a surgeon and surgical nurses and technicians, nurses with specialized training, a dietician, a physical rehabilitation specialist, a social worker, and others may join the team. Once the care is provided to a particular patient, staff members reconfigure to serve other patients.

In another story of teamwork, Dr. Mulligan illustrates how the Mayo system is designed to work:

> One of our oncologists called to review some films taken on a patient he saw with metastatic colon cancer to the liver. We both sat in front of computer screens (he at the Clinic and I at the hospital) and looked at the films simultaneously. Then, I conferenced in with one of our radiologists to obtain his detailed opinions on some nuances of the images. We then made plans for the patient to have a surgical procedure to resect the majority of the metastatic lesions and perform radiofrequency ablation on the others that could not be resected. I would then install an intra-arterial catheter and pump which the oncologist could access a few weeks after surgery to infuse chemotherapy to reduce the chances of recurrent metastatic cancer to this patient's liver.

The Mayo system of integrated, multispecialty, outpatient and inpatient medical care does not always work as well as intended. But it does work well most of the time and represents the Clinic's most important competitive advantage.

This chapter explores the meaning and application of Mayo Clinic's primary "how" value of collaborative medicine, a natural corollary to the Clinic's primary "what" value: "The needs of the patient come first" (see Chapter 2). Core values embody the standards an organization cherishes—its central ideals, its foundational principles. In Dr. William J. Mayo's commencement address to Rush Medical College in 1910, he proclaimed that the "union of forces" was the best way to serve patients. A passage from the speech elaborates on this point: "It became necessary to develop medicine as a cooperative science; the clinician, the specialist, and the laboratory workers uniting for the good of the patient, each assisting in the elucidation of the problem at hand, and each dependent upon the other for support."[2] Dr. Will articulated Mayo's two primary core values: an aspirational value (the good of the patient) and an implementation value (medicine as a cooperative science). The Clinic not only has survived but has prospered for more than a century because its founders' core values continue to energize the spirit and guide the functioning of the enterprise. The Clinic epitomizes the phrase "values-driven organization." Should it ever lose its core values, it is destined to become an ordinary institution.

Thomas Watson, Jr., the renowned former CEO of IBM and a member of the Mayo Foundation's board of trustees for eight years in the 1970s and 1980s once wrote: ". . . the basic philosophy, spirit, and drive of an organization have far more to do with its relative achievement than do technological or economical resources, organization structure, innovation, and timing. All these things weigh heavily in success. But, they are . . . transcended by how strongly the people in the organization believe in its basic precepts and how faithfully they carry them out."[3] We know of no organization that better reflects this statement than Mayo Clinic. For a long time, it has embraced not only *what* it wished to be but also *how* to be through teamwork.

Teamwork Isn't Optional

"Teamwork isn't optional"—a line from a *Fast Company* article[4] about Mayo Clinic—is true. Many excellent clinicians would not fit in at

Mayo, including those who prefer to work independently, covet personal acclaim, lack interpersonal competencies, or seek to maximize their income. Mayo is well known within the academic medicine community for what it is—and is not. Self-selection influences who works at Mayo. Gastroenterologist Dr. Jonathan Leighton says: "The Mayo culture attracts individuals who see the practice of medicine best delivered when there is an integration of medical specialties functioning as a team. It is what we do best, and most of us love to do it. What is most inspiring is when a case is successful because of the teamwork of a group of physicians from different specialties; it has the same feeling as a home run in baseball."

The Clinic ardently searches for team players in its hiring and then facilitates their collaboration through substantial investment in communications technology and facilities design (see Chapters 6 and 9). Further encouraging collaboration is an all-salary compensation system with no incentive payments based on the number of patients seen or procedures performed. A Mayo physician has no economic reason to hold onto patients rather than referring them to colleagues better suited to meet their needs. Nor does taking the time to assist a colleague result in lost personal income (see Chapter 5).

Mayo staff members are immersed in the core value of collaborative medicine from their first day on the job. Dr. James Li, an allergy and infectious diseases specialist, says: "Our culture is fundamentally unchanged over the more than 20 years that I've been here. I was acculturated in the Mayo way during my first year, and it has been reinforced ever since." Perhaps the Clinic's most remarkable achievement through the years is bringing thousands of new staff members into an increasingly complex organization while connecting them to each other and to the mission.[5] As a British surgeon who trained at Mayo commented: "The most amazing thing of all about the Mayo Clinic is the fact that hundreds of members of the most highly individualistic profession in the world could be induced to live and work together in a small town on the edge of nowhere and like it."[6] Indeed, as historian Helen Clapesattle wrote in 1941: "As an experiment in cooperative individualism, the Mayo Clinic deserves watching—and not by doctors alone."[7]

I Am a Better Doctor Here

Providing healthcare services is unusually demanding work. Both the physical and emotional stress can be daunting. Patients expect their healthcare providers to know everything, never make a mistake (because the consequences can be catastrophic), and, if necessary, perform miracles. Practicing medicine at Mayo Clinic adds pressure because the institution attracts so many patients with severe, complex illnesses. It is common for a new Mayo patient to tell his or her doctor: "You are my last hope."

Not only does the Clinic's strategy of integrated, multispecialty medicine require teamwork, but so does the complexity and severity of illness that patients present. The spirit of collaboration that defines Mayo is a potent teaching mechanism. Doctors become better at Mayo, a necessary development in order for them to function effectively in this institution. The same type of personal growth occurs with other clinical staff and employees in general. At Mayo, more is expected, and teamwork helps deliver the more.

The Clinic is a teaching institution in the traditional sense; it trains new doctors. However, it also is a stellar teaching institution in the way Mayo staff members instruct one another. As Dr. Kirk Rodysill, an internist, says, "The clinical notes as well as the test and medication orders that I write in the record are read every day by experts in about every field of medicine. And if something that I wrote is not quite right, I'll get a phone call from which I learn something. Perhaps, a test or prescription that I've ordered is last year's or even last week's state-of-the-art." He concludes, "This makes me a better doctor than I was in my last position."

Dr. Nina Schwenk, also an internist, was asked if she was a better doctor at Mayo Clinic than she could have been elsewhere. She answered: "Hundreds of times better because of the support system. It's like you are working in an organism; you are not a single cell when you are out there practicing. As a generalist, I have access to the best minds on any topic, any disease or problem I come up with and they're one phone call away." Adds endocrinologist Dr. Robert Rizza: "I never feel I am in a room by myself even when I am."

I Need Your Help

The Clinic's culture is notable in that it not only gives staff members permission to ask for help, but it encourages them to do so. Not asking for assistance when needed can be career-damaging; asking for assistance is expected behavior. As Elaine Gustetic, a transplant surgery social worker, states: "I can call anybody, anywhere, to do whatever is needed for the patient."

Dr. Eric Edell, a pulmonologist, recounts how Dr. Will taught the value of medicine as a cooperative science through his own behavior: "If Will saw patients and needed Henry Plummer, he'd pick up the phone and say, 'Henry, get yourself over here. I need some help figuring this out.' He may not say it in front of the patient, but they'd be stepping outside, and they'd be working together. And then Will would go back in the room."

On hospital rounds one day, gastroenterologist Dr. Russell Heigh had 13 patients to see. He planned his visits so that he could see the sickest patients first. However, the reality was that most of the patients were really sick. Dr. Heigh's first patient was a 94-year-old female with sudden onset of acute abdominal pain among other symptoms. He immediately consulted with two other physicians, including a surgeon. As he commented to one of us: "This kind of case gets me nervous because this is a life-threatening situation. This is a 94-year-old person. The real question is whether she gets an operation or not. The surgeons and I don't want to operate on a 94-year-old unless we absolutely have to."

After seeing several more difficult cases, Dr. Heigh was asked about all the tough decisions he was having to make and how he copes with the stress. His response: "I have great colleagues, and I get input. When the going gets tough, I share my stuff. The specialists I can turn to on tough cases make me more effective."

Dr. Keith Kelly, a retired Clinic surgeon, shared a revealing story that would not have occurred at many medical institutions:

A Mayo surgeon recalled an incident that occurred shortly after he had joined the Mayo surgical staff as the most junior member. He was seeing patients in the Clinic one afternoon when he received a page from one of the most experienced and renowned surgeons on the Mayo Clinic staff. The senior surgeon stated over the phone that he was in the operating room performing a complex procedure on a patient with a difficult problem. He explained the findings and asked his junior colleague whether or not what he, the senior surgeon, was planning seemed appropriate. The junior surgeon was dumbfounded at first that he would receive a call like this from a surgeon whom he greatly admired and assumed had all the answers to even the most difficult problems. Nonetheless, a few minutes of discussion ensued, a decision was made, and the senior surgeon proceeded with the operation. The patient's problem was deftly managed, and the patient made an excellent postoperative recovery. A major consequence was that the junior surgeon learned the importance of intraoperative consultation for the patient's benefit even among surgeons with many years of surgical experience.

Dr. Victor Trastek, CEO of Mayo Arizona, continually reinforces the principle of "teach, don't blame." When something goes wrong, when a mistake occurs, it should be viewed as a teachable moment, an opportunity to get better. Does constructive teaching always supplant blaming? No. However, Dr. Trastek is relentless in articulating a principle that strengthens self-confidence and self-esteem, which paves the way for true collaboration.

This Is What We Do

Most service jobs involve discretionary effort, which is the difference between the maximum amount of energy an employee can bring to the service role and the minimum necessary to avoid penalty, such as a reprimand, less merit pay, or even termination. The difference between this maximum and minimum energy investment is discretionary for the individual employee—it is voluntary. Truly excellent service organizations get more "volunteerism" from their employees than most organizations, and this extra effort directly contributes to the organizations' excellence.[8]

Mayo Clinic and its patients benefit from a high level of volunteerism from the staff. Extra effort—for patients and for the team—is embedded in the essence of the culture. Most Mayo employees volunteer hard. Their day-to-day volunteerism is not always in dramatic, life-saving contexts such as is reflected in the opening story of this chapter. But extra effort played out in thousands of ways every single day transforms the strategy of team medicine into the reality of team medicine. Elena Henderson is a front-desk supervisor for orthopedics and has been with Mayo for more than 25 years. When asked what she considers the best part of working at Mayo Clinic, she replied: "Going home every night and knowing that I have reassured or helped a patient. It is exciting. Appointment availability in orthopedics is a real challenge. Sometimes we will sneak an extra patient in, and the doctor doesn't mind—or even notice."

Not all Mayo staff members have a volunteering spirit of course, but Mayo actively seeks out such people. As transplant social worker, Elaine Gustetic, who participates in hiring decisions in her unit, puts it: "I'm looking for people who can feel what the patient feels, and I want people who will finish the job rather than look at the clock." Gustetic, who is in the organ transplant group on the Jacksonville campus, works with very sick patients and their families. She has many stories, one of which concerns an elderly male patient (we call him Ted) who had been turned down at other transplant centers. He needed a lung transplant and came to Mayo where he was evaluated and then approved. The family then had to move to Jacksonville. Ted got his transplant and did well for several months. Then all of a sudden there was, in Guestetic's words, "... a problem, not just a bump, but a big problem." Ted developed cancer in the other lung and died within a few months.

Gustetic helped organize a memorial service for Ted as she does for other patients. "We hold a memorial service for our patients who die. We get close to the families and they to us, and it seems like the families need to come back here specifically to have the memorial service in our hospital chapel. The staff and physicians attend, a physician speaks, and there is a reception afterwards. This is important, and people who aren't emotionally connected to their work don't do these kinds of things."

As mentioned in the opening story, the Clinic performs weddings. Another wedding occurred when a critically ill patient was admitted to Mayo's hospital in Phoenix shortly before her daughter was to be married, and she was unlikely to live to see the wedding. The bride told the hospital chaplain how much she wanted her mother to see her get married, and he conveyed this to the critical care manager. Within hours, the hospital atrium was transformed for a wedding service, complete with flowers, balloons, and confetti. Staff members provided a cake and a pianist, and nurses arranged the patient's hair and makeup, dressed her, and wheeled her bed to the atrium. The chaplain performed the service. On every floor, hospital staff members, other patients, and visiting family and friends ringed the atrium balconies "like angels from above" to quote the bride. The wedding scene provided not only evidence of caring to the patient and her family but also a strong reminder to the staff that the patient's needs come first.[9] The event reflects the Clinic's spirit of volunteerism at its best.

Hospital memorial and wedding services are not daily occurrences. Matthew McElrath, who chaired human resources for the Arizona Clinic for 16 years, tells a story of Mayo volunteerism that is far more common:

My father-in-law was hospitalized here on an emergency basis. He's from California and came in through the emergency department. He went into the ICU. It was late at night, and my wife and I went up to the ICU and there were literally eight nurses in the room getting him settled in. We asked who his nurse was, and one of the nurses turned around and said, "None of us is his nurse." And I said, "What do you mean?" She said, "Oh, she's in the next room taking care of another patient, and we're here helping her get set." It's like 2 a.m., and all of these nurses came from around the unit to help get this brand new patient settled in and everything done. Fifteen minutes later, when everything was set up and done, his nurse came into the room. I was amazed, but this is what we do.

The Power of Respect

"Mutual respect is important here," asserts Bridget Jablonski, a nurse team leader for an oncology and transplant unit in Mayo's Phoenix hospital. "There is an expectation that you treat everyone with respect whether it's your patient or colleague, physicians, house-keepers, everyone. You incorporate them as a member of the team. None of us could do our job without the contributions of others."

Mayo's culture leverages the inherent power of respect. Feeling respected is a universal need in the workplace. To be respected on the job means to be trusted, to be listened to, to be included, to be treated as a contributor, to be treated fairly. Teamwork cannot be sustained without mutual respect, for teamwork depends on trust, listening, inclusion, teammate contribution, and fair treatment—the attributes of respect.

A respectful organizational culture injects esteem into one's work; it underscores worthiness. Respect uplifts the human spirit, helping to generate the extra energy needed for volunteerism. Respect contributes to self-confidence, which contributes to motivation, which contributes to team acceptance.

Dr. Annie Sadosty, an emergency physician, doesn't use the term "respect" in characterizing team medicine at Mayo, but it is central to her description:

> It's a lot of people with varied talents coming together for a common mission, and those people may or may not be directly related to patient care. They may actually never see the patient themselves, but they all have unique expertise, and they apply that expertise to optimize the care of the patients. And it is not just within the clinical group; it's the administrative staff, the paraprofessional staff, the allied health staff, and the custodial staff. If the custodians don't do their job well, it impacts my ability to care for a patient in a sanitary or timely way. I know by name the custodians that work in the emergency department, and I appreciate them as much as I appreciate my physician colleagues.

Adds nurse team leader Bridget Jablonski:

On our floor we have daily bone marrow transplant rounds where we all come together to discuss the progress of our patients. Each person offers a different perspective reflecting their area of expertise. The physicians, nurse practitioners, transplant coordinators, case managers, social workers, dieticians, pharmacists, chaplains, physical therapists, and the primary nurse caring for the patient—they all put their knowledge together to develop the best plan for the patient. Everyone's opinion is respected, and it ultimately leads to better patient care and better outcomes.

Importantly, an emergency department and a transplant unit are relatively defined units in that it's usually the same group of people who interact. Defined work groups offer familiarity and facilitate friendships. However, as discussed previously, much of Mayo's work relies on teamwork across units and geography, where the benefits of familiarity and friendship are not always present. The Clinic's cultural commitment to mutual respect must be sufficiently strong to transcend different job titles and organizational units, different campuses, and lack of familiarity. Being a colleague at Mayo Clinic—even among colleagues who have never met before—must offer an assumption of high competence and collegiality when newcomers appear as a new team member. Further, mutual respect must be as strong vertically (e.g., doctors and nurses) as horizontally (doctors and doctors).

Respect is a strength of the Clinic, but the organization must be decisive in addressing disrespect when it occurs at all employee levels. Sometimes it is, but not always. The stakes are high because Mayo Clinic cannot be Mayo Clinic without the consistent presence of respect. Team medicine depends on it.

Practicing Medicine in a Goldfish Bowl

From the early days of their practice, both Drs. Will and Charlie maintained medical records of the examinations and treatments of their patients. The records were handwritten separately by each physician in large ledger books kept in his own office. Initially, these records sufficed, and they became the basis of many papers the two doctors published in the scientific literature. But as the number of patients and medical staff members grew, the limitations of the system became readily apparent. Sometimes, a return visit to the same doctor would result in a note written in the margin of the previous visit; this complicated searching for a record chronologically. If two or three different doctors saw or treated the patient, the patient's medical history was spread across two or three different ledgers stored in different offices.

Dr. Henry Plummer, soon after he was hired in 1901, asked permission to overhaul the ledger system. Doctors were making medical decisions without access to all the relevant patient information that was available somewhere in the ledgers. With the endorsement of the Mayo brothers, Plummer sought a better system. He benchmarked the record systems at other clinics and hospitals as well as industries outside of healthcare. Plummer developed the unit medical record so that all medical information about a patient, such as prior surgeries at the Clinic and diagnosis and treatment records provided by an outside referring physician, would be available when needed. This integrated patient record system was implemented in 1907 and is still in use at Mayo Clinic a century later, although it has been modified over time and is now in electronic format.

Key to the system was organizing the records by patient rather than physician. Each patient receives a unique patient identifier, which is basically a simple numbering sequence beginning with number 1, which was assigned to a patient in 1907, and is now approaching 7 million. The ledger books were replaced by patient-specific folders where the collected information was stored.

The concept of a current, comprehensive medical record for each individual patient was a breakthrough idea a century ago and is universally used now. But the integrated clinic and hospital record is, even today, rarely found except in highly integrated institutions, many of which were created by Mayo Clinic alumni. Mayo Clinic began migrating from the paper medical record to an electronic medical record in the mid-1990s, and today the record is totally electronic.

Through the years, the unit (or integrated) medical record has proved to be a powerful driver of quality at Mayo. It facilitated the vision of Dr. Plummer and the Mayo brothers for improving diagnoses and treatment through better information. However, it likely has contributed far more good than they imagined. The electronic medical record functions as a primary teaching tool, as discussed earlier. It also opens a window within Mayo that reveals the quality of medical care being provided. As Dr. George Bartley, the CEO of Mayo's Jacksonville campus, wrote in a 2004 New Year's letter to his staff: "Our communal medical record leaves little place to hide one's mistakes."

The combination of an integrated medical practice (in which multiple clinicians may care for one patient), an integrated medical record (in which these clinicians all use the same set of patient records), and the reputation of Mayo Clinic creates strong peer pressure to practice quality medicine. A doctor's skills and knowledge are continually on display internally. The peer pressure to keep learning—or leave—is real. In effect, the medical record is both a tool for learning—an electronic medical textbook—and an incentive for learning.

Dr. Hugh Smith, a cardiologist who retired as CEO of the Rochester campus in 2005, captures the unspoken role the integrated medical record plays as a quality control system:

When I see a patient, I do a history and a physical. I come up with a differential diagnosis, think of the tests that help prioritize things and sort them out, and confirm the diagnosis. And it's all in the medical record for my colleagues to see. So my colleagues read my notes about this patient, and they have the chance from their unique point of expertise to examine the patient. They see my competency as a physician. Did I do a thorough history? Was I on target with my physical exam? Was I complete with my differential diagnosis? Had I prioritized things correctly? Had I used tests appropriately and wisely? Had I called in other resources as well? Did I do the effective follow-up and

*get things through to completion, and was the patient fully informed
of that? In other words, I practiced at Mayo my whole life in a
goldfish bowl.*

A team medicine model cannot work effectively unless the players
on the team have confidence in their teammates. Dr. Plummer's idea,
much refined, strengthens confidence. Dr. Sadosty explains that what
differentiates Mayo from other healthcare organizations for her is
her confidence in the team:

> *I never have to worry when I admit a patient from the emergency
> department to the hospital about the quality of care they will receive.
> Whether the patient is going to the surgical service, the medical
> service, or the intensive care unit, my confidence in the other care
> providers and the rest of the team is such that I can say earnestly to a
> patient, "We're going to take wonderful care of you, don't worry. . . ."
> If I were to get sick or a loved one were to get sick, there is no
> question in my mind where I would want us to go.*

Lessons for Managers

Mayo Clinic is remarkable for the durability of its success and the
core values that have made that success possible. It is refreshing and
revealing to learn so much from a world-renowned institution that
started with two primary values more than 100 years ago and continues to rely on them today. Among the managerial lessons that
emerge from this chapter are the following:

Lesson 1: Act small even if big.   Mayo Clinic is a large enterprise
that at its best acts like a small one. Organizational bigness, to be
sure, has its competitive virtues, such as more complete service lines,
broader distribution, and an expansive operational support infrastructure. The problem with scale is its common side effects,
for example, bureaucracy, poor internal communication and coordination, and impersonal service. The key for larger organizations

is to maximize the advantages of bigness while minimizing the disadvantages. Despite its bureaucratic quirks (see for example the discussion of the Clinic's committee system in Chapter 5), Mayo benefits simultaneously from the virtues of bigness and smallness, and so can other organizations.

Acting small with customers means to act quickly, efficiently, responsively, flexibly, and personally. It means finding ways to come through for customers with unusual needs, as Mayo Clinic demonstrates in assembling a unique team to meet the needs of patients requiring diversified expertise. It means extra effort, being creative, and "finishing the job rather than looking at the clock."

Acting small with employees means creating a sense of community, a shared vision, a collaborative spirit. It means creating individual and collective accountability. It means creating a trust-based culture, a can-do mindset, and a feeling of ownership.[10]

Of course, organizations that are actually small do not always capitalize on the advantages their size provides. Acting small is reflected in the attitudinal and behavioral manifestations of an organization's values and strategies and the investments it makes to strengthen them. Mayo teaches this lesson. Its value ("the needs of the patient come first") personalizes and customizes the patient's service experience even though more than 13,000 individual patients may be served by the Clinic in a single day. Its value ("medicine as a cooperative science") leads to the assembling of a team to care for each patient. The team becomes the face of the Clinic—a tiny company within a huge company. Supporting the team is a big-company investment in the tools, technologies, and systems to provide high-quality, individualized service, not the least of which is the supporting role played by the Clinic's patient-specific integrated medical record. Big companies that effectively act small invest in both high-touch and high-tech capabilities. Mayo Clinic does this well.

Lesson 2: Encourage boundarylessness.   Mayo's story reveals the positive effects of boundarylessness, a term popularized by General Electric's former chief executive Jack Welch.[11] Boundarylessness is cultural encouragement to employees to step out of the organization chart box in which they work to connect with people in other parts of the organization whose expertise can add value in addressing the problem at hand. Whereas tightly bounded work relies on strict role definitions, lines of authority, and physical separation of different functions to organize work, boundarylessness relies on breaking down artificial barriers to collaboration, proactively seeking multiple perspectives, using distributed information technology, and forming ad hoc groups (such as teams, task forces, and study groups).

Boundarylessness opens up an organization, freeing its capabilities and resources for best-use applications. Boundarylessness creates the opportunity for teamwork across the organization rather than just within set organizational boundaries. Mayo Clinic demonstrates the power of "no-boundary" teamwork versus "within-boundary" teamwork. The specialized talents and knowledge available within the Clinic's vast medical department store can be tapped on an as-needed basis. Boundarylessness means removing the walls in the department store so talent and knowledge can converge where it is needed. Many larger organizations in various industries are department stores too in that they have specialized expertise spread throughout their workplace. But the expertise of various work groups may not be optimized; the opportunity for a "union of forces" to solve problems and provide cross-boundary teaching may not be fully realized.

At Mayo Clinic, it is more than okay to ask for help; in many organizations asking for help may be viewed as a sign of weakness. One of the Clinic's greatest cultural achievements is making requests for assistance normal, expected behavior.

Mayo's open culture has prepared the institution to "play rugby." "Rugby is a flow sport," states Professor Noel Tichy. "It looks chaotic, but it requires tremendous communication, continuous adjustment to an uncertain environment, and problem solving without using a hierarchy."[12]

Lesson 3: Value "how," not just "what."   Mayo Clinic's two primary values—"the needs of the patient come first" and "medicine should be practiced as a cooperative science"—reign over all others. These truly are cherished principles of the Clinic, defining what it wishes to be and how, from its beginnings to the present day. That one of the values is aspirational and the other concerns implementation is instructive. We believe a lesson for other managers is embedded in Mayo's multidimensional core values framework.

The conventional wisdom in business is that a company's core values remain stable while its strategies and tactics change with the times. However, Mayo Clinic teaches that excellent organizations can have one or more strategies that are so central to their belief system, so integral to who they are, that they rise to the level of a core value. The pooling of talent is integral to *how* Mayo serves the needs of its patients. It is both core value and core strategy. The Clinic's enduring success stems not only from an enduring aspirational core value, but from an enduring implementation core value. The original Clinic framed how it wanted to conduct business for the ages, and it has remained true to its vision while evolving into a modern healthcare organization.

Summary

Collaboration, cooperation, and coordination are the three dynamics supporting the practice of team medicine at Mayo Clinic. These dynamics drive the delivery of personalized care for patients, although staff members care for thousands of patients each day. Individual staff members—from physician to custodian—become active team players to serve patients' needs because treating complex illnesses requires the diverse expertise available from all personnel and the supporting infrastructure. To work at Mayo is to be on the team. Organizations in any field must determine the what and the how of their existence. The Mayo model offers principles and practices worthy of emulation by businesses both in and outside healthcare.

NOTES

1. This story, one other, and several paragraphs in this chapter are drawn from Leonard L. Berry, "The Collaborative Organization: Leadership Lessons from Mayo Clinic," *Organizational Dynamics*, No. 3, Fall 2004, pp. 228–242.

2. William J. Mayo, "The Necessity of Cooperation in Medicine," speech delivered at the Rush Medical College commencement, June 15, 1910, originally published in the *Collected Papers* by the Staff of Saint Marys Hospital, Mayo Clinic, 1910, vol. 2, pp. 557–566, and reprinted verbatim in *Mayo Clinic Proceedings*, vol. 75, 2000, pp. 553–556. The quote used in this chapter appears on p. 554 of the *Mayo Clinic Proceedings* reprinting.
3. Thomas J. Watson, Jr., *A Business and Its Beliefs: The Ideas that Helped Build IBM* (New York: McGraw-Hill, 1963), pp. 5–6.
4. See Paul Roberts, "The Best Interest of the Patient Is the Only Interest to Be Considered," *Fast Company*, April 1999, pp. 149–162.
5. Matthew Dacy, "Aspects of Integration—The Spirit and Systems that Hold Mayo Clinic Together," *Mayo Today*, January–February 2007, p. 20.
6. As quoted in *Teamwork at Mayo: An Experiment in Cooperative Individualism*, a publication of the Mayo Center for Humanities in Medicine, Mayo Press, 1998, p. 6.
7. Helen Clapesattle, *The Doctors Mayo* [abridged] (Rochester, MN: Mayo Foundation for Medical Education and Research, 1969), p. 423. Based on the original volume published in 1941.
8. Daniel Yankelovich and John Immerwahr, *Putting the Work Ethic to Work* (New York: Public Agenda Foundation, 1983), p. 1. and Leonard L. Berry, *Discovering the Soul of Service: The Nine Drivers of Sustainable Business Success* (New York: Free Press, 1999), pp. 13–14.
9. Leonard L. Berry and Neeli Bendapudi, "Clueing in Customers," *Harvard Business Review*, February 2003, pp. 100–106. The wedding story appears on pp. 102–103.
10. Berry, *Discovering the Soul of Service*, Chapter 9.
11. See Noel M. Tichy and Stratford Sherman, *Control Your Destiny or Someone Else Will* (New York: Currency Doubleday, 1993), pp. 234–235.
12. As quoted in Frank Rose, "A New Age for Business," *Fortune*, October 8, 1990, p. 162.

CHAPTER 4

PRACTICING DESTINATION MEDICINE

"*My mother injured her back weeding my garden, but, of course, she didn't tell me," reports a Mayo Clinic physician. "And then she flew three hours back to her home, but she could hardly walk off the plane—pain was going down her leg, and it was numb." After three days, the Mayo physician had a phone call from her mother to report that she was not getting any better. "I told her she had an extruded disc in her back, and told her to see a doctor. Tell him you need a spine evaluation." The mother followed her daughter's orders. Her doctors were associated with one of the best-known hospitals in the country, "But after five weeks of running around and nobody really listening to her, they injected her knee, because that's where her pain was. And I'm thinking what on earth? Her problem is her back. She's got a disc problem, and they're injecting her knee." The doctors prescribed narcotics for the pain when the knee injection failed to help her. "When I was talking to her on the phone, it was clear she was overmedicated; she wasn't speaking English anymore—she reverted to her native language. She was not making sense, and she was slurring her words."*

The Mayo physician asked her sister to put their mother back on a plane bound for Mayo. "She came here, she saw the neurologist the next morning, she saw the neurosurgeon that afternoon, and we put her in the hospital that night. They operated on her back the next day; she was pain free and out of the hospital in four days. Three weeks later, we took a safari to Africa, rode in a jeep, and she was fine!"

This story reflects Mayo Clinic's business strategy working the way it is intended to work for all patients—one does not need to be the mother of a Mayo physician to receive expedited service.

A young business consultant first noted weakness in his left hand while still in graduate school. Beginning with the student health service, he sought help from more than a dozen specialists—hand surgeons and neurologists—in four cities over the next four years. One doctor literally threw up his hands, saying, "I give up—we can't find anything." A hand surgeon in another city made an incision from the young man's wrist to the elbow in an attempt to relieve what he thought might be pressure on a nerve that could account for the weakness. Postsurgery, the symptoms remained the same. Then the other hand became weak.

A neurologist in yet another major city tentatively diagnosed multifocal motor neuropathy with conduction block (MMN), except that it did not manifest "conduction block." The patient reports, "He could not get enough evidence to definitively call it MMN, so he was not willing to take off the table other frightening and grim possibilities like ALS." (ALS—amyotrophic lateral sclerosis—is also known as "Lou Gehrig's disease.") The low-risk treatment for MMN, if it manifests conduction block, is intravenous immunoglobulin (IVIG), so the patient underwent six months of treatment even though there was no evidence of conduction block. "The optimistic hope was that the IVIG would have immediate and recognizable impact. And the long story short is that it had none," he laments.

Finally, the young man self-referred to Mayo Clinic and flew halfway across the United States for the appointment. His five days at Mayo Clinic changed his life. "What it did was condense a whole lot of diagnostics into a very short period of time with a quick turnaround of results, which allowed the doctor to ask for other tests that really helped us drive to the diagnosis quickly and efficiently," he reports. He has what he accepts as a definitive diagnosis: *multifocal motor neuropathy* without *conduction block*. It is rather rare that MMN manifests *without* conduction block, but the Mayo Clinic neurologist had seen other cases. The young man says, "The most

important thing he did was look me in the eye and tell me definitively that it was not ALS." He continues his story:

> *The doctor actually did one of the studies himself, and as he listened
> during the electrical studies of the nerves, he said, "This is really
> interesting! It almost looks like you have polio, and let me tell you that
> you don't have polio." Then the doctor pointed to the extremely high
> creatine kinase levels, and he said, "If I didn't know the rest of the
> picture, I might even say that you had muscular dystrophy, but let me
> say that you don't have muscular dystrophy. But what that tells us is
> that you are overworking the muscles, and this is not just in your left
> hand, this is all over your body. You are creating undue stress on your
> muscles all across your body. What you need to do, young man, is ramp
> down your physical activity." That's extremely helpful to know. If I
> hadn't made it to Mayo, I would still be playing competitive soccer
> and, unknowingly, doing a lot of unnecessary damage to my body.
> And I also would still be losing sleep every single night wondering
> if I had ALS.*

The patient is pleased: "He was the finest doctor I'd ever seen, in
terms of the way he went through the assessment, the way he conducted himself with us, the way he communicated his messages; he
was truly the finest doctor I've ever seen." As satisfied as he is with
his experience, however, the young business consultant does not
expect that he will return to Mayo Clinic. In five days he received
guidance that he believes will serve him for years to come. So, he
concludes, "As it stands right now I have an expectation of what will
happen, I have some parameters around which I can live my life
more healthfully. And I really feel like I know what I need to know,
and I don't need to waste any more time hooked up to an IV on my
weekends, and I can go about the rest of my life." He has experienced "destination medicine." And, yes, he would return to Mayo
Clinic if an unexpected or serious medical problem arose.

Destination medicine provides an integrated system of comprehensive care that addresses the patient's medical problem(s)
in an efficient, time-condensed manner. The practice of destination

medicine enables patients and families traveling from long distances as well as nearby patients to receive medical care comprehensively and expeditiously. Destination medicine could include highly focused services such as joint replacement, cosmetic surgery, or hernia repair. Mayo Clinic, however, is not a single-specialty boutique but rather a department store of medical care capable of addressing virtually all medical needs from cancer care to cosmetic surgery to joint replacement to organ transplantation.

Our two patient stories illustrate the nature of the destination medicine practice of Mayo Clinic and show Mayo Clinic functioning at its best. In the first instance, the service is delivered promptly and efficiently. In the span of about 24 hours, the diagnosis is completed and the surgery begins—next-day surgery is commonly offered to patients at Mayo. In his story, the young consultant expressed the essence of "destination medicine" when he observed that in the five days while he was at Mayo Clinic, his lead doctor was able to "condense a whole lot of diagnostics into a very short period of time with a quick turnaround of results, which allowed the doctor to ask for other tests that really helped us drive to the diagnosis quickly and efficiently."

Each year more than 140,000 patients travel more than 120 miles—two hours—from their homes specifically for care at Mayo Clinic. Healthcare is the primary object of their journey, and they typically stay in hotels for the three to five days they are undergoing diagnosis. The stay may be longer if they are hospitalized. The Clinic expects these patients to have a doctor—or doctors—at home who will provide their ongoing care. Not all patients take journeys through Mayo that are as smooth or as definitive as the doctor's mother or the young business consultant. On the other hand, their cases are not unusual. Indeed, the word-of-mouth recommendations from such patients sustain Mayo Clinic.

In this chapter, we look behind Mayo's clinical services in order to understand the role of systems engineering in designing the structures and systems that support Mayo's delivery of efficient and individualized service to patients. We examine first the nature of Mayo Clinic's integrated practice where all employees—including all physicians—and all inpatient and outpatient services are part of a single organization. Then we turn to the important role of the integrated medical record in providing efficient and effective care. Next we discuss the complex infrastructure required to schedule thousands of customized patient appointments each day. Then we explore how Mayo uses its data to manage growth to meet anticipated demand. Finally, we look at the timely completion of reports needed to facilitate the rapid pace of clinical care at Mayo. We begin, however, with the origin of destination medicine in Rochester.

Destination Rochester

The reputation of the Drs. Mayo made Rochester, Minnesota, a medical destination more than two decades before their practice became known as Mayo Clinic in 1914. Beginning in the late 1880s, many new settlers in the Dakotas came by train to Rochester for their serious medical needs. Most had passed through Rochester when they had migrated west, and the stories they heard from others convinced them to seek treatment by the Drs. Mayo. Awareness was spreading by word of mouth, so by 1893 patients at Saint Marys Hospital came from 11 different states: Minnesota, Illinois, Kansas, Missouri, Nebraska, New York, Ohio, Wisconsin, South Dakota, North Dakota, and Montana.[1] For more than 100 years, Mayo Clinic in Rochester has been a major medical destination.

On display in Heritage Hall is an ornately lettered rendition of a "marketing" aphorism attributed to Ralph Waldo Emerson: "If a man can write a better book, preach a better sermon, or make a better mousetrap than his neighbor, though he build his house in the woods, the world will make a beaten path to his door." It hung for many years on the wall of Dr. William J. Mayo's last office. This artifact suggests that the Drs. Mayo recognized that their practice in the small town of Rochester, Minnesota, was a realization of Emerson's challenge to nineteenth-century America. Rochester seems an unlikely location for a medical mecca. But in the late nineteenth century, few competitors seemed to offer results as positive and definitive as the Drs. Mayo—they were the vanguard of modern surgery in the eyes of much of America, including many physicians. Even though their clinic was inconveniently located, patients did beat a path to their door.

A century later, however, the competitors are many. Sophisticated health services are available to most Americans in local or regional medical centers. And still, thousands of patients from all 50 states and approximately 150 countries travel to Mayo Clinic each year. The patients do not all come to Rochester of course, as Mayo Clinic's campuses in Florida and Arizona attract respectively about 20,000 and 25,000 national and international patients each year. Rochester, a small city of about 100,000 residents, has more than 5,000 hotel rooms. About 65 percent of the hotel capacity is filled by the 95,000 patients and their families that annually come to Mayo Clinic from more than 120 miles away.

Mayo Clinic has created service systems that provide expeditious and efficient care delivery to patients traveling for serious medical needs. But Mayo Clinic president and CEO Dr. Denis Cortese emphasizes that local patients should not have long, anxiety-filled waits for definitive answers even though they can go home at night and sleep in their own beds. For the most part, all patients at Mayo Clinic receive efficient, time-compressed care that can usually provide a definitive diagnosis and sometimes initial treatment—including major surgery—within three to five days.

After hearing spontaneous comments about the unexpected efficiency of Mayo Clinic in patient focus groups, Mayo's marketing division added a question about efficiency to its ongoing patient satisfaction surveys. The results show that the systems and processes that efficiently control the flow of the patient experience are as important as the care provided to patients' overall satisfaction with Mayo. Based on more than 36,000 surveys, efficiency is just as highly correlated with patients' overall satisfaction with Mayo Clinic as is their relationship with the physician or even the outcome of the care provided. This was not a surprise to Laurie Wilshusen, the Mayo Clinic marketing director responsible for Mayo's patient satisfaction surveys. She says, "Patients may not be able to judge physician skill or the accuracy of a test, but they can evaluate their experiences with a system that delivers what they need and respects their time. The better we can perform in terms of efficiency, the greater trust patients can place in our ability to take care of the things they cannot assess."

Under One Umbrella

"Mayo Clinic is an idea—it's the concept that the patient is the center of what we do. And we've built everything else around the patient with this idea in mind," explains Dr. Cortese. As described earlier, Mayo has built a group practice comprising medical experts in virtually every known medical specialty or subspecialty. All those doctors are integrated into a single umbrella organization run by physicians. The physician-led organization operates all the outpatient clinics and diagnostic laboratories. The hospitals are integrated into the organization as well. Each patient has a virtual medical group built up around him or her to address personal medical needs. In this single organization, all operations revolve around serving patients efficiently, not just effectively.

Craig Smoldt, chair of the department of facilities and support services in Rochester, makes the point that Mayo Clinic can offer efficient care—the cornerstone of destination medicine—because it functions as one integrated organization. He notes, "The fact that everybody works under the same roof, so to speak, and is on the payroll of the same organization makes a huge difference. The critical mass of what we have here is another factor. Few healthcare organizations in this country have as many specialties and subspecialties working together in one organization." So Mayo Clinic patients come to one of three locations, and virtually all their diagnoses and treatment can be delivered by that single organization in a short amount of time.

Most U.S. healthcare is not delivered in organizations with a comparable degree of integrated operations. Rather than receiving care under one roof, a single patient's doctors commonly work in offices scattered around a city. Clinical laboratories and imaging facilities may be either in the local hospital or at different locations. As a report by the Institute of Medicine and the National Academy of Engineering notes, "The increase in specialization in medicine has reinforced the cottage-industry structure of U.S. healthcare, helping to create a delivery system characterized by disconnected silos of function and specialization."[2]

Dr. Cortese, who served on the committee that developed this report, illustrates this absence of integration with a hypothetical patient in Philadelphia: "Suppose the patient has four medical problems. That means she would likely have at least five different doctors." For instance, this patient could have (1) a primary care doctor providing regular examinations and treatments for general health, (2) an orthopedist who treats a severely arthritic knee, (3) a cardiologist who is monitoring the aortic valve in her heart that may need replacement soon, (4) a psychiatrist who is helping her manage depression, and (5) an endocrinologist who is helping her adjust her diabetes medications. Dr. Cortese then notes, "With the possible exception of the primary care physician, most of these doctors probably will not know that the patient is seeing the others. And even if they do know, it is highly unlikely they know the impressions and recommendations the other doctors have recorded in the medical record, or exactly what medications and dosages are prescribed." If the patient is hospitalized, it is probable that only the admitting physician and the primary care physician will have that knowledge.

Mayo Clinic is the antithesis of this model. Its service system surprises many patients because it is so unlike what they are accustomed to receiving. For instance, the owner of a bed and breakfast establishment in the Midwest has lived with fibrocystic breast disease for a number of years. So she was an experienced patient when she recently detected a new, large lump. Alarmed, she came to Mayo Clinic—several hours by car from her home on a drive that took her past a local hospital 30 minutes from home and a regional medical center that was an additional 60 minutes down the road. She came to Mayo Clinic because she thought that it would be more convenient. And it was.

She had used the local hospital years earlier in the first episode of her disease. But its service fell short when radiologists began collecting the entire day's mammograms for interpretation in the evening, even though a radiologist was in the facility. Because no radiologist checked the image quality shortly after it was first available, she was once called back after a few days for a second mammogram. The final straw came when she was billed for the additional mammogram even though it was required because the initial images were inadequate. This ended her care at her local hospital.

The regional medical center 90 minutes away had provided better service. The patient had worked out an arrangement with a gynecologist based there so that she could get a mammogram shortly after seeing her doctor. When requested, as it usually was, a sonogram of the breast sometimes could also be completed on the same trip. But this service model was the result of the patient's initiative; it was not a standard service protocol for breast patients.

She came to Mayo Clinic when she learned that her physician in the regional center was on vacation and that she would have a "luck of the draw" physician see her through the evaluation of the new lump. Because a new physician would be involved, the odds for arranging convenient follow-ups in radiology seemed small. She elected to seek care at Mayo Clinic. As a patient in the breast clinic, she began with the internist/breast specialist who took the medical history and performed an exam. The mammogram followed in the nearby breast imaging center. The breast ultrasound, ordered to evaluate a specific area on the breast, was done immediately after the mammogram.

The breast radiologist who performed the ultrasound had all the medical history and impressions of the other doctors available in the electronic medical record (EMR). The ultrasound confirmed that the lump was a simple cyst, not a cancer. The radiologist shared this information with the patient and offered her an aspiration of the cyst that would draw off fluid if the cyst was painful. But comforted with the diagnosis of the simple cyst and with the fact that it was not painful, the veteran patient declined the aspiration. Within an hour of completing the breast imaging, the radiologist communicated to the breast specialist a "verbal report" of the imaging findings. The patient returned to the internist/breast specialist who then had a wrap-up visit with the patient and recommended follow-up care. This patient's care at Mayo was completed in three and one-half hours—before lunch.

Similar stories of efficient service are told again and again by Mayo patients and family members. The owner of a small business in a large Midwestern city explained to a Mayo administrator why she came several hundred miles with her elderly parents to Mayo for guidance with their complex medical care. "I can block out a week in my calendar, and we can get everything needed done for both my mother and my father in that week," she said. "If we tried to get this care at home, we would have to go to many different doctors' offices. Each one would require that I take at least a half-day off work. It would require more time off work if I stayed at home. But even more frustrating is the fact that this would be spread over two to three months." Mayo Clinic's efficient care systems enabled this business owner to be more productive in her own business.

Cables, Lifts and Chutes, and Computers

The accolades such patients and family members offer have not been earned by chance. They have not come about just because the Clinic tries to hire the right people. High levels of service satisfaction result in part from the strategic investment of millions of dollars each year in industrial engineering to create the processes and infrastructure that facilitate clinical quality and safety as well the efficient delivery of care.

Dr. Henry Plummer faced a major hurdle in instituting integrated medical records (see Chapter 3), which he implemented in 1907. Several of his physician colleagues were unwilling to give up their ledger books of medical notes for this new idea. In fact, some were able to hold out for a decade. They trusted that the ledger on their office shelf would always be there; and in truth, in the first seven or eight years of its use, the integrated medical record often arrived too late—after the patient had come and gone. The building where the physicians were practicing had no mechanical systems to assist in moving paper records.

The first mechanical conveyance systems dedicated to moving medical records were installed in the new 1914 Mayo Clinic building, which was the first structure in the United States specifically designed to accommodate an integrated group practice of medicine. The goal was to move the record to the next point on the patient's schedule by the time the caregiver was to see the patient. To move the single copy of each patient's record through this building, Dr. Plummer and Minneapolis architect Franklin Ellerbe devised overhead carriages on cables. The system was not totally adequate, however, since this provided transport only on each of the four stories of the building, not between floors. They collaborated again on the 14-story Plummer Building, which opened in 1928, where they had to contend with the more challenging vertical movement of the records. So they had lifts and chutes installed; the lifts raised the medical-record packets up to a central distribution center where staff members sorted them and then placed them in chutes destined for each floor. Some were then placed on horizontal conveyors that carried them to desks serving each physician. The system of lifts and chutes on a somewhat grander scale was used in the 20-story Mayo Building constructed in two 10-story projects in 1950 and 1964. However, the mechanical systems that moved the records for nearly a century have now been rendered obsolete by the EMR.

In the 1990s, Mayo Clinic began migrating from paper to electronics. This transition is the most complex and costly systems engineering project Mayo has undertaken to date. The practices in Jacksonville and Arizona took the lead with Rochester following. The medical record must arrive before the physician can see the patient. In the era of the paper record, even considering the lifts and chutes, patient appointment itineraries had to allow up to four hours—a half day—between physician appointments to ensure that the paper record would be available. The EMR is instantly available throughout Mayo once information is posted. Thus, today, physician appointments must be spaced by only the amount of time required to move a patient in a wheelchair from one appointment to the next. Equipped with a stopwatch, the Clinic's industrial engineers have literally wheeled a "patient" between buildings and floors to establish time intervals between hundreds of different appointment locations and then entered that data into the rules applied by the computer that creates patient appointment itineraries.

The EMR also makes it faster and easier for a physician to consult with a colleague. With the paper record, physicians needed to be in the same room. Now two or more physicians can be at their desks and simultaneously view exactly the same screens of the EMR report online while conducting a "team meeting" by phone. Patient care needs are now supported with timely information more effectively and efficiently than at any time in the past century.

What, When, and Where—Getting Schedules Right

Each working day, Mayo Clinic patients are scheduled for thousands of different appointments for laboratory testing, clinical procedures, and consultations with physicians. This is not like filling seats at a concert or on an airplane where a filled seat is a seat filled. Many healthcare appointments must occur in a specific sequence, some must be separated from the others by several hours, and many require specific preappointment procedures. Scheduling appointments is not a glamorous management function, but it is, perhaps, the most fundamental because this is where healthcare delivery starts.

The evolution of the centralization of appointments, which followed by over 40 years the integrated medical record, is our second example of applied systems engineering at Mayo Clinic. In creating appointment centralization, the Clinic also recommitted to a "systems" mindset that has permeated the institution since Dr. Henry Plummer joined the practice in 1901. The early and subsequent use of *industrial engineering* or, as it is known more recently, *systems engineering*, has built an infrastructure that enables the integration of Mayo's large, complex operations. The daily scheduling task is huge for the institution, but Mayo must act small as each appointment itinerary is created for each individual patient.

The scheduling system is the backbone of destination medicine implementation. At several stages during the last 60 years, new technology has been leveraged to improve the scheduling process, increase operational efficiency, and, most importantly, improve customer service. When the post-World War II surge of patients arrived at Mayo Clinic, the system in place for obtaining appointments no longer worked. Under that system, each doctor could manage his or her own calendar, so in terms of access he or she operated like a cottage industry within Mayo Clinic. This meant that when a Mayo physician recommended that his or her patient see a colleague or obtain a blood test or an X-ray, it was the patient's responsibility to go to the doctor's clinical department or a laboratory to schedule the appointment. Immediately following World War II, many Mayo physicians returned to the practice after serving in the military. Patient volumes grew correspondingly. To provide space for these doctors and patients, Mayo constructed several "annex" buildings around its campus in downtown Rochester. Patients were bewildered as they wandered about town trying to find the doctor's office so they could schedule an appointment. Mayo Clinic's leaders saw the frustration and created the coordinating committee that was charged with developing the central appointment desk (CAD), an organizational unit that assumed responsibility for scheduling the laboratory tests and physician consultations requested by any Mayo Clinic doctor. The CAD lifted the burden off patients.

The planning and implementation of the CAD fell to a new administrative group that became what is known today as "systems and procedures." This important administrative group currently comprises some 50 industrial engineers and business analysts on the three campuses. According to Richard Cleeremans, who was hired into systems and procedures in 1950 and was head of it for many years, Mayo initially adopted the scheduling system from the Pullman Company, which operated sleeper cars on the railways. The system was primitive, but it worked. For each Pullman car, the schedulers had a card with a line for each sleeper unit available. When a customer asked for a reservation, the traveler's name was entered on the line. In its application to Mayo Clinic, Cleeremans explains, "We knew, for instance, how many blood tests could be done in an hour, because we had done timings on that. So the appointment card for blood tests had a certain number of slots per hour. These were filled in at the CAD. Couriers carried the completed cards to the appropriate check-in desks." Dozens of different cards were required for the various appointments needed. Patients learned of the scheduled appointments when they returned after a few hours to the desk of their first appointment. There they were given an appointment packet containing small envelopes providing the "address"—time and location—on the front with preparation instructions tucked inside. Each appointment had a separate envelope. This highly manual system vastly improved service to patients.

With modifications as new technology came along, the CAD served the organization for more than 50 years; it was closed in 2005. In the 1960s, the CAD began using telephony rather than the card system. The CAD staff called the labs and departments which had their own appointment coordinators to ensure that the patient got the right appointment or physician. The system depended heavily on the knowledge of the appointment staff members on both ends of the phone. Mark Hayward, chair of the division of systems and procedures, describes the operations of the CAD during that era:

> *They were long-term employees who knew how Mayo operated—they had a lot of the rules in their head about what had to come before what and what things could be done at the same time. Looking at the requested appointments, they would determine from experience what might be available first and then what should be next. Mayo picked the best people in desk operations to be in that group, realizing how important that function was to a good experience for the patient.*

By the 1970s, computer technology was available to assist in scheduling. But no appointment system designed and marketed for healthcare could accommodate the complex rules that Mayo's schedulers had internalized. Hayward indicates that Mayo ultimately found help in software ideas used by Boeing and NASA. Both organizations had rules for managing production and maintenance cycles that had complexity similar to the rules for Mayo appointments. "Driving this endeavor from the beginning was a concern for people coming to Mayo Clinic from out of town—we wanted to get them through in the fewest days possible. We developed a very sophisticated, very high-level system—for the 1970s," concludes Hayward.

While this software—with occasional upgrades—served well for some 30 years, the system was difficult to use. It could be operated only by the CAD staff, and even then it required at least six months to learn. The replacement system implemented in 2005 creates an optimized schedule in a few minutes via a computing technique used in industry for production scheduling. Called *genetic algorithm,* this search technique looks for a potential sequence for the patient's itinerary that complies with the rules written into the system for more than 8,000 different types of Mayo appointments. Sharon Gabrielson, section head for administrative operations support in systems and procedures, explains the complexity: "It can handle a CT scan where many variables are considered. For instance, is the patient pediatric or adult, male or female, diabetic or not diabetic? Different combinations of these features assign patients to different machines, different rooms, or different technologists." The system, for the first time, includes travel time between appointments as well as realistic times for a procedure—getting into an exam gown, the procedure itself, recovery from sedation if applicable, and getting back into street clothes. These changes have significantly reduced the number of patients who show up late for appointments that had previously been scheduled too close together.

But more importantly, the new system is Web-based and intuitive for anyone who uses the Internet. It is so simple that all desk staff members can operate it with minimal training. As a result, the centralized CAD operation was rendered obsolete. Gabrielson notes, "We were able to give 44 employee positions back to the institution, as well as the 4,000 square feet of space that was being used by the centralized CAD. And at the same time we decreased the turnaround time that patients were waiting to receive their itinerary by more than 60 percent."

Perhaps the greatest service benefit of the new scheduling system is that it can accommodate patient scheduling preferences. The 1970s system just told patients when to show up, so, as Gabrielson observes, "We had to manually reschedule many of the 'optimized' schedules because they would not work for the patients." Rescheduling cost Mayo hundreds of thousands of dollars a year—an unnecessary expense once information technology became available to solve both the technical requirements of Mayo Clinic appointments and the service needs of patients.

Still, in spite of six decades of improvements, Mayo Clinic does not have the perfect appointment system, particularly for initial appointments. In fact, mystery shoppers hired by Mayo in recent studies were often turned down for appointments even though their medical scenarios should have always resulted in an appointment. In addition, not all doctors or even clinical divisions fully trust that the latest system will place patients appropriately on their calendars. Just as Dr. Plummer experienced a century ago, some physicians are not ready to buy into the new system. So these physicians block automatic access to some or all of their calendars. And, true to its history, the "Mayo way" is to try to win over skeptics by demonstrating that the system does work.

Improving Efficiency and Service

On any Sunday afternoon, the coming week's appointment calendar for many laboratories and specialist physicians and surgeons at Mayo Clinic will have large numbers of open appointment slots. This is not a cause for alarm; it is by design. For nearly six decades, Mayo Clinic has deliberately planned to accommodate the clinical tests and physician consultations that Mayo physicians would order beginning each Monday morning.

Mayo Clinic distinguishes between two primary appointment types: (1) external appointment requests from referring physicians or patients outside of Mayo Clinic and (2) internal appointment requests—also called "downstream" appointments—for patients after they have been examined by a physician. As noted in Chapter 2, Mayo Clinic cannot meet all external requests for appointments, although physician referrals do have high priority. However, once a Mayo Clinic physician sees a patient, the institution places high strategic priority on processing tests and consultations quickly, so the systems must move the patient through these steps as efficiently and smoothly as possible. Hence, the open slots in the appointment calendars.

The division of systems and procedures and its systems engineers have conducted studies for decades to help keep clinical capacity in balance, particularly with internal—"downstream"—demand, so that patients can experience the efficient service associated with Mayo Clinic. Before computers, much of the work simply amounted to counting. So the industrial engineers developed ratios which showed that, for every general exam started, the organization needed to expect a given number of chest X-rays, blood tests, orthopedic consultations, urology consultations, and so on. The calendars for all these downstream appointments held slots open for these referrals that the upstream physicians would order each day.

Today, of course, computers do the counting. The current appointment system not only optimizes appointments but also provides management with the best appointment analytics in the history of the Clinic. Heretofore, the appointment utilization reports were based on old data showing fill rates for appointments some 30 to 60 days earlier. There was not much that managers could do with that data. The current analytics identify prospective demand. With several years of data in the system, the systems and procedures analysts create models of future demand based on current information. John Osborn, systems and procedures analyst, explains:

> *As physician calendars must be in our system 12 weeks in advance, we can identify scheduled appointments in general internal medicine as well as other clinical areas typically making consultation requests. Knowing the patient appointments in those upstream areas during a*

*given week lets us, for instance, tell neurology what demand they can
expect in that future week. Neurology can then build its calendar for
physician availability to accommodate the internal consults expected for
that week. But the system can also help the neurology department know
that it needs to reserve certain appointment slots for external appointment requests for patients with a very specialized neurology need.*

As these models are used over time, they become more sensitive
and offer large dual benefits. First, patients benefit from the seamless service that is created. Second, the institution benefits because
the productivity of physicians, labs, and procedural areas is optimized
as well. This second point should not be lost, for the same infrastructure that benefits patient service simultaneously benefits the
financial operations of Mayo Clinic. This type of analysis is relatively
common in industry, but it is relatively uncommon in healthcare.

Recent history in the department of radiology in Rochester illustrates why these models are so important. In the mid-1990s, market
demand exceeded the capacity for growth at the Rochester campus.
In addition to the increasing numbers of patients to serve, the
department of radiology faced more demand per patient because the
new technical capabilities in diagnostic imaging itself created more
demand from the rest of the practice. The size of the department
was no longer synchronized with the internal and external market
demands, resulting in a huge bottleneck.

The department had a stellar reputation for the clinical quality of
its work. However, by 1998 when Dr. Stephen Swensen became
chair of the department, its service quality—particularly appointment access—was a source of considerable dissatisfaction for both
patients and Mayo's medical staff. "Appointments for routine MRIs
were out for weeks and occasionally months, and there were challenges in CT as well," Dr. Swensen recounts. Patients were not completing their diagnostic tests because they could not afford to stay in
hotels for two weeks awaiting an MRI or to return to Rochester in
two weeks. The destination medicine strategy suffered as a result.

Dr. Swensen initiated service system improvement projects with
one of the most important goals being access to *same-day or next-day*

appointments for every exam the department offered. "If we were patient-centered, we could not have patients waiting days to get a CT or MRI exam," he explains. So the department worked in teams that were charged with utilizing existing scanners more efficiently and effectively. Teams were cross-functional as they were composed of the appropriate technologists, nurses, desk staff, administrators, and radiologists for the specific project. The teams used process-improvement tools such as "Lean," developed by Toyota to elimi-nate waste from processes, and Six Sigma, initiated by Motorola as a data-driven approach to identify and eliminate defects in processes. The results are impressive and include the following:

- Net operating income increased over a three-year period by nearly 40 percent.
- Variation in the selection of imaging protocols or doses of contrast media by the radiologists was significantly reduced.
- A six-minute reduction in imaging time per MRI patient (via Six Sigma) yielded an extra appointment per day per scanner and a more than $4 million gain annually.
- Timely, 24/7 access to diagnostic studies in the hospitals led to earlier diagnosis and fewer days in the hospital.[3]
- Chest radiograph technicians reduced the amount of walking they did by 90 percent per male chest patient, and patient time in the department plummeted fivefold.
- Patient satisfaction for chest radiography service showed a signif-icant improvement.

These improvements in efficiency were, consistent with Mayo's values, the result of teamwork. "They were motivated to make patient care better. And at the end of the projects we gave one another a standing ovation for the success we found," reports Dr. Swensen.

But efficiency alone did not eliminate all the queues of patients seeking appointments. Additional appointments were made with extended hours including scheduling on weekends. Eventually, more CT and MRI scanners as well as additional radiologists were needed. In fact, the number of staff radiologists doubled from 75 to 150 during

Dr. Swensen's eight-year term as chair. Today, the department has same-day or next-day access for CT and MRI exams more than 99 percent of the time, and the annual number of studies has more than doubled from 500,000 in 1998 to more than 1.1 million now.

Mark Hayward hopes that this imbalance between demand and access will not happen again because the analytic capabilities of the recently installed appointment system can track demand growth trends. "If we have enough demand to fill 12 machines a week and we only have 10, we could again face in radiology or some other department a situation like Dr. Swensen confronted in 1998," Hayward says. So the division of systems and procedures also assists in right-sizing operations into the future. As Hayward observes, "You can't add an MRI overnight" because MRIs, like much major medical equipment, require specially prepared space before installation.

Getting the overall institutional size right as well as the relative size of internal components is a difficult challenge but essential for delivering both excellent service and strong financial performance. Today organizations have access to electronic technology that, in many ways, makes rational growth possible. Mayo Clinic has been an early adopter of many of these tools. "Electronics is obviously the reason our growth has been possible," says Craig Smoldt, chair of the department of facilities and support services. "With what we had when I came to work here in the 1970s, there is no way that we could have grown to this size. Everything was typed out because we had no e-mail, the billing process had many manual operations, and medical records were all in paper form. The volume of patients and employees today could not be supported except by the electronic systems in place today." By adopting technology as it came along, Mayo Clinic has been able to do things that were unthinkable a decade or two earlier. The appointment system is a good example. Smoldt says, "I don't put a limit on the size of the practice in one location today, as I don't think we know what technology will bring."

Patients benefit from Mayo Clinic's commitment to provide care as quickly and efficiently as possible. All three campuses track in some way the length of time required for national and international patients to complete their appointment itineraries, and all campuses are a bit short of meeting their goal. Rochester, for instance, tracks a subset of these patients with the goal being that patients will begin and end their clinical appointments within a calendar week 95 percent of the time. The operation has about a 10 percent gap to close, but still approximately 80 to 85 of every hundred patients sampled do complete their clinic itineraries by 5:00 p.m. on the Friday ending their appointment week. A 100 percent success rate cannot be achieved because some patients' requirements are unexpectedly complex; for instance, doctors may discover a major cancer on day three of their tests and examinations. And patients whose first appointment is on Thursday or Friday will likely need to stay over the weekend. Still, this is another example of how Mayo fine-tunes its operations to offer patient-centric service that expedites diagnosis and treatment for virtually all patients. This effort has helped Mayo Clinic attract patients who feel they must seek clinical care beyond their more convenient local and regional providers—and patients who live close by benefit as well.

Without Delay

Although integrated medical records and the optimized appointment schedules are the visible signs of Mayo Clinic's efficient delivery system, behind the scenes there are literally thousands of technologists, technicians, transcriptionists, and physicians who apply their expertise to hundreds of different scans, clinical tests, diagnostic procedures, and reports. In many ways, these employees function as the most remarkable part of the Clinic as they quickly turn out complex reports and post results promptly to the EMR.

For example, in the echocardiography laboratory, the standard Mayo Clinic procedure is for the cardiologist to review the study performed by a sonographer before the patient is discharged from the test. Once the study is accepted by the cardiologist, the report is generated. Narrative portions of the report are written largely by selecting standard language from pull-down boxes in the electronic report tool. Within about five minutes of the patient's discharge, the results are available in the EMR. In contrast, most echocardiogra-phy laboratories collect studies for a cardiologist to read at the end of the day. At Mayo, other cardiac studies such as the ECG and stress tests also are read throughout the day by the on-duty cardiologists. Those results are typically posted to the EMR within one hour and rarely are posted more than two hours after the patient leaves the appointment.

In the clinical laboratory, results are available on the EMR in an average of 96 minutes after blood is drawn. Pathologists are avail-able near surgery suites, and they provide rapid analyses of "frozen section" slides from tissue removed during surgery. The frozen sec-tion report goes to the surgeon about 10 minutes after the tissue arrives in the lab. Permanent sections of the tissue are then prepared, and the confirming report is completed the next day.

Radiology also provides rapid turnaround. Today virtually all images are collected digitally. Both conventional dictation/transcription and voice-recognition capability in computers are used to obtain rapid report turnaround. When using voice recognition, the radiologist can see the report generated on the computer as it is dictated. After manual editing, the images and the reports are released in urgent situations within 15 minutes for the requesting physician to view. The live dictation/transcription systems perfected over 80 years in Mayo achieve even faster turnaround in urgent cases for reports on conventional, "flat" images. The typical turnaround in nonurgent situations ranges from 30 to 90 minutes, according to Dr. John M. Knudsen, practice chair for the department of radi-ology in Rochester. The time frame is longer for scans requiring 3-D imagery because the "exam" is not complete when the patient leaves the scanner. An hour or more of processing time is required. So, the reports for the more complex CTs and MRIs are posted two to three hours after the exam.

The above examples support the "well-oiled machine" metaphor that patients frequently use to describe the Clinic's operations. Many patients, particularly those coming for return visits, have various medical tests performed before seeing their doctor. "These patients often express amazement when I already have those results an hour or two later when they return to me for the consultation," observes Dr. Carl Lundstrom, a consultant in the division of general internal medicine. This operational element of Mayo Clinic exceeds the expectations of patients and influences the overall high satisfaction ratings patients give their care at Mayo.

Lessons for Managers

Mayo Clinic works diligently with a "systems" mindset to maintain its edge in expeditious and efficient clinical care that enables it to practice destination medicine. The fact that Mayo Clinic is a well-integrated operation under one umbrella rather than a constellation of business silos facilitates the destination medicine strategy. But less integrated and perhaps even "cottage industry" operations both inside and outside of healthcare can learn from Mayo Clinic's experience.

Lesson 1: Solve the customer's total problem.   Mayo Clinic is a "systems seller" competing with a connected, coordinated service. Systems sellers market coordinated solutions to the totality of their customers' problems; they offer whole solutions instead of partial solutions. In systems selling, the marketer puts together all the services needed by customers rather than requiring customers to do it themselves. The Clinic uses systems thinking to execute systems selling that pleasantly surprises patients (and families) and exceeds their expectations.

The scheduling and service production systems at Mayo Clinic have created a differentiated product—destination medicine—that few competitors can approach. So even if patients feel that the doctors and hospitals at home are fine, they still place a high value on a service system that can deliver a product in days rather than in weeks or months. The Clinic's record is not without blemish on this score, as the radiology example presented in this chapter illustrates. The Clinic in Rochester allowed radiology to become a serious bottleneck in the practice for too long. Still, when a new department leader defined a new service vision, the organization quickly accommodated, as the approach was based on rational systems thinking.

Patients not only require competent care but also coordinated and efficient care. Mayo excels in both areas. In a small Midwestern town, it created a medical city offering "systems solutions" that encourage favorable word of mouth and sustain brand strength, and then it exported the model to new campuses in Arizona and Florida.

Lesson 2: Use technology to support values and strategy. Technology is a tool to help an organization be what it wishes to be. Its purpose is to benefit its users, to enable their success, to make life better. Technology investments that do not benefit users, that thwart their success, or that make life worse are destined to cost the investing organization dearly. Technology designed strictly to save money usually results in an excessive waste of money and a mountain of heartache. All technology should solve real problems in the context of an organization's core values and strategy.

Mayo Clinic has benefited enormously and durably from major technological investments. These investments have in common their direct link to the Clinic's core values and strategies. The integrated medical record for each patient; the cables, lifts, and chutes; the CAD; the computerized algorithms for forecasting downstream appointments—the purpose of all adopted technology is to improve capability for practicing team and destination medicine for the benefit of patients. Saving money through technology has frequently been the result, but rarely, if ever, the goal. One does not need to work in healthcare to learn from Mayo's approach to technology.

Lesson 3: Innovation is a work in progress.   Mayo Clinic plans for the coming three to five years, but intends to continue in perpetuity. Mayo's buildings are built to last a hundred years—or perhaps forever. Dr. Will tolerated for a decade a few physicians who were very slow adopters of Dr. Plummer's integrated medical record. In Rochester, the physicians migrated from paper to the EMR over

10 years of gradual, piece by piece rollout. But, of course, eventually time ran out for the paper medical record; in March 2005 the EMR became the only record for current medical activity. Voice-recognition technology to "transcribe" medical dictation is currently used primarily by "early adopters" even though experience elsewhere shows that it pays back good returns in many situations. Mayo is reluctant to compel behaviors, particularly from physicians who are the central producers of medical care. So, rather than compel, Mayo demonstrates—it persuades with data.

Systems engineering is incremental, consistent improvement as technology and the market demand. The CAD was a dazzling innovation in about 1950. In increments, it was updated over the decades as computer technology matured, and it was ultimately rendered obsolete when new scheduling software delivered better service at a fraction of the cost. The paper chart was similarly treated as a work in progress throughout its history, and the EMR will be the same. No one at Mayo Clinic believes that its EMR is as good as it could and should be today. Like good companies everywhere, Mayo Clinic never feels that it is quite as good as it needs to be.

Summary

Mayo Clinic is a "destination of choice" for thousands of people seeking efficient, effective medical care, even in a competitive market. But the "Mayo mystique" has evolved from more than the stories. The Clinic's professionalism at all levels and the authentic living out of core values and strategies create the dramatic stories patients love to share.

Mayo Clinic delivers efficient care—the cornerstone of practicing destination medicine—because it functions as an integrated physician-led organization. Systems thinking and technological innovation have facilitated efficiency in medical recordkeeping and accessibility, in scheduling appointments, and in synchronizing procedures. The resulting overall efficiency minimizes inconvenience to the patient and optimizes access to information for care providers.

This support system allows Mayo Clinic to fulfill its commitment to most patients who enter its doors.

Solving the customer's total problem, using technology to support values and strategy, and innovating with systems engineering—these basic precepts chart the way for other enterprises to become a destination or supplier of choice.

NOTES

1. Helen Clapesattle, *The Doctors Mayo* [abridged] (Rochester, MN: Mayo Foundation for Medical Education and Research, 1969), p. 209.
2. Proctor P. Reid, W. Dale Compton, Jerome H. Grossman, and Gary Fanjiang, eds., *Building a Better Delivery System: A New Engineering/Health Care Partnership* (Washington, DC: The National Academies Press, 2005), p. 13.
3. Lawrence H. Lee, Stephen J. Swensen, Colum A. Gorman, Robin R. Moore, and Douglas L. Wood, "Optimizing Weekend Availability for Sophisticated Tests and Procedures in a Large Hospital," *The American Journal of Managed Care*, vol. 11, no. 9, September 2005, pp. 553–558.

CHAPTER 5

PARTNERING FOR LEADERSHIP

"I knew within the first 10 days that I'd made a mistake," admits Jonathan Curtright, who is once again a Mayo Clinic administrator. Curtright was speaking of his experience in 2000 when he left for what seemed like his dream job. The newly appointed dean of the medical school at Curtright's alma mater was a Mayo Clinic physician who was aware of Curtright's administrative skills. He had offered Curtright a position as assistant dean for management in the university's medical school. For Curtright and his family, this was like going home. His parents live in the city, and only a couple hours away is the farm that has been in his family since 1826. He and his wife met at the university as undergraduates. He holds two graduate degrees—a master's degree in healthcare administration (MHA) and a master's degree in business administration (MBA)— from there as well. "That's where I'll probably retire," Curtright observes.

But in 10 months he was back at Mayo Clinic. Curtright explains, "The teamwork, partnerships, and integration that I took for granted, the air we breathe around here, the culture of Mayo Clinic that permeates this place is incredibly unique." Curtright details what brought him back: "Teamwork and partnerships. Everyone at Mayo—physicians, allied health staff, researchers, educators, administrators—believes in teamwork. And they work together with humility. And don't get me wrong. It's not utopia here, but I think there is a certain amount of cultural humility that enables people to work together as team members, as partners. That wasn't there— it wasn't there."

"I feel like somebody that had a kind of a near-death experience, if you will. I'm back for a second opportunity," Curtright concludes. He expects to remain at Mayo Clinic for the rest of his career.

Teamwork in clinical care helps Mayo Clinic translate the patient-first value into the patient experience. While Dr. Will had publicly recognized the importance of teamwork in patient care by 1910, he had not yet applied teamwork—except with his brother—in matters of management and governance of the clinical practice that was steadily growing. A decade later, however, the time had come to plan a long future for Mayo Clinic, and teamwork in leadership and management became another enduring hallmark.

Cooperation and collaboration came naturally to the brothers, particularly in patient care. The brothers differed in personality and professional style, and these differences led to some natural divisions of labor. The brothers realized from the outset of their practice that Dr. Will needed to occupy the leadership position. Dr. Charlie's son, Dr. Charles W. Mayo, expressed it this way: "Father didn't care for the executive end of things.... Uncle Will was the executive, the man with the drive, the man who put the ideas through, though they sometimes came from Father."[1] Harry Harwick knew them both well; he worked closely with them for nearly three decades as the first administrator for Mayo Clinic. Harwick explains them this way:

> *The two men complemented each other perfectly. Doctor Will, a natural leader, was rather reserved, analytical, dominating (though without arrogance), relentless in demanding perfection of himself and others, with an uncanny ability to foresee the future. Doctor Charlie was warm, understanding, and wonderfully humorous, possessing "the common touch" ... Often, the younger brother would influence Doctor Will toward a less stern approach to a problem. Often, in his turn, the elder brother would influence Doctor Charlie to temper impulsiveness with caution.*[2]

In this chapter, we examine how the founding brothers and Harry Harwick created a "succession plan" that enabled the Clinic to transition from the nearly 40-year tenure of a demanding leader, Dr. William J. Mayo—collaborating with a team of two (Dr. Charlie and Harwick) —to leadership built on a wide base of partnerships and collaboration. We discuss the physician-led culture as it exists in the early twenty-first century, and finally we identify systems and policies that support the governance and operations of this organization that functions in a way that breeds loyalty and attracts back a Jonathan Curtright. Our focus here is on how the spirit of partnership and collaboration pervades management and governance at Mayo Clinic today.

From Command and Control to Partnership Management

On December 31, 1932, Drs. Will and Charlie Mayo stepped down from their seats on the board of governors and away from formal involvement with the Clinic. Dr. Will had retired from surgery on July 1, 1928, at age 67, and Dr. Charlie had retired on January 2, 1930, at age 65 after suffering a retinal hemorrhage while performing surgery. The succession plan that was in place in 1932 enabled the organization to survive its founders who were arguably the two most celebrated surgeons of their day. The succession plan had been in the making for more than three decades as the brothers on four different occasions took bold steps that enabled a long-term future for Mayo Clinic. These steps affirm that, rather than "succession plan," it would be better to call this "succession planning," because it was an evolutionary process with the first stage involving decisions that were made near the end of the nineteenth century.

Step 1: A Partnership in Income Only

In the late 1890s, Drs. Will and Charlie, along with their father, were in a five-person "partnership" with Dr. Charlie's brother-in-law, Dr. Christopher Graham, who joined the group in 1894, and Dr. Augustus Stinchfield, who had joined in 1892. Drs. Graham and

Stinchfield had joined the informal partnership with only oral commitments. Dr. W. W. Mayo, then in his late 70s, suffered a serious
illness, and this precipitated questions about the survival of the partnership that would be affected by death. Will and Charlie learned
that a probate judge could rule that the partnership be dissolved into
five shares for purposes of settling the estate of any one of the partners. Though no historical documentation exists, the brothers probably recognized that the reputation of the practice was largely based
on the surgical outcomes enjoyed by their own patients. Thus,
Dr. Graham and Dr. Stinchfield, who had not invested in the partnership, had not contributed significantly to the equity represented
by the practice itself.

Knowing then that a death of any one of the five partners could
disrupt clinic operations and patient care, the brothers devised an
alternative. Drs. Will and Charlie proposed a partnership limited to
participation in income—the practice itself and all capital assets and
securities were conspicuously separated from the partnership agreement. At retirement or death, the partner or heirs would receive "a
sum equal to the amount of his income in the year preceding his retirement or death."[3] Will and Charlie signed the contract and presented
it to the others to sign. Drs. Graham and Stinchfield refused to sign
for two years, as their understanding of the partnership included a
share of all the assets. Then, as historian Helen Clapesattle notes,
"The steel in Dr. Will came out."[4] The holdouts signed after being
told that if they did not sign, the partnership would be dissolved.

At this point, neither Will nor Charlie could have imagined what
Mayo Clinic could become, in even their own lifetimes. This was
still a small practice and was not officially known as "Mayo Clinic"
for more than another decade. They worked in the rented space of
a recently constructed Masonic temple. Outside, the streets were still
unpaved. Horses, some with saddles and others attached to carriages,
waited at hitching rails in front of the offices. But by creating a partnership in income only, Will and Charlie had, perhaps unwittingly,
laid the organizational cornerstone for what was to come. All the
physical and financial assets of the organization were protected by
this arrangement and were in the ownership and control of the

brothers who, in turn, became the employers of salaried physicians. No evidence suggests that they made this move with a vision beyond ensuring that the care of their patients could proceed uninterrupted by the retirement or death of a partner.

Although the Mayo brothers had learned to value their colleagues as collaborators and partners in clinical care, they had not yet created the collaboration in management and operations of their medical practice that has become so much of their legacy.

Step 2: Mayo Properties Association

In 1908, Dr. Will offered a bookkeeping position to a local bank clerk, a 21-year-old high school graduate, Harry J. Harwick. Over his 44-year career at Mayo Clinic, Harwick rose to the position of chair of administration and played an important role in helping the Mayo brothers plan for long-term success. Together, Dr. Will and Harwick developed the basic management and governance structures that are still in place today at Mayo Clinic. In Harwick's own account of these events, he notes that this was made possible because "the Mayos believed that, beyond decent financial security for themselves and their partners, surplus money should be returned to the public in the form of better medicine."[5] This firmly held ethic complemented a similar ethic lived every day at Saint Marys Hospital by the sisters of Saint Francis of Assisi whose vows included poverty. They worked, without pay, 12 to 18 hours per day for six or seven days a week serving patients and supporting the Mayo Clinic doctors. The impact of this altruistic ethic held high by both the Mayo brothers and the Franciscan sisters has significantly contributed to the long-term success of Mayo Clinic.

Meanwhile, the practice dubbed by visiting doctors as the "Mayo's Clinic"[6] was growing. Additional physicians were hired, and the Clinic outgrew its rented space in the Masonic temple. Because the brothers personally retained the earnings of the clinical operations, they were in the financial position to construct a large outpatient building, which was opened in 1914. Harwick notes with some irony that this building was designed to meet the needs of the Clinic "for all time" but soon was inadequate because patient volume had increased dramatically—by about 300 percent—by 1917.

By 1918, Drs. Will and Charlie realized that their clinical operation was unique and had the potential to survive them. With the opening of the 1914 building, the organization had become known as Mayo Clinic. They knew in general that they wanted to form some kind of organization that would hold Mayo Clinic in trust in order to sustain the clinical operation as well as the medical research and education programs. They initiated a plan, as Harwick notes, at this time when both were "of middle age, vigorously healthy, at the height of their brilliant careers, with every reasonable expectation of remaining professionally active for many years to come."[7]

After about a year of intense study, they created Mayo Properties Association in 1919. In signing the deed of gift, the brothers transformed Mayo Clinic from a for-profit to a not-for-profit organization. The brothers turned over all the present and future earnings of the Clinic in addition to all buildings and equipment, all cash and securities, to this new charitable organization. They acted according to their altruistic values by contributing most of their personal wealth with this transaction. This gift today would exceed $50 million, according to John Herrell, retired chief administrative officer of Mayo Clinic. The legal structure they created and pressed Drs. Graham and Stinchfield to accept about two decades earlier seems fortuitous. Without that painful episode, Mayo Clinic likely would not exist in the twenty-first century.

The Mayo Properties Association was directed by the agreement to use its financial assets to promote medical education and research. Harwick writes, "The Association was to be directed by a self-perpetuating board of members serving without compensation. The document spelled out that 'no part of the net income of this corporation or of its property or assets upon dissolution or liquidation shall ever inure to the benefit of any of its members, or of any private individual.'"[8] This emphatic stipulation underscores a basic value of the Mayo brothers, which held that net revenues from clinical operations must benefit patients and the community rather than provide excessive income to healthcare providers.

Step 3: Transition to Board of Governors

Clinical medicine as a "cooperative science" at Mayo Clinic had been very well developed by the 1920s. Dr. Henry Plummer's creation in 1907 of the common medical record that all doctors and nurses used in the care of both inpatients and outpatients was the most significant single factor that enabled partnerships in patient care. Dr. Plummer also guided the design of the 1914 building so that it would accommodate the Clinic's team-based medical practice. But management and governance of Mayo Clinic had lagged. The hiring of Harry Harwick for financial and administrative operations, however, would ultimately have an impact comparable to Dr. Plummer's innovative clinical operations. When Harwick started in 1908, the 12 staff physicians "had been in the habit of setting their own fees, collecting them when and where possible, and carrying the money casually in their pockets for days and weeks at a time."[9] They kept no records to document most of the charges or collections for clinical services. Expenses were not tracked either; doctors and their staff just ordered what they thought they needed. Harwick initially faced opposition when he began to create basic accounting processes and procedures.

Until the early 1920s, the governance of Mayo Clinic had been simple; Dr. Will in consultation with Dr. Charlie made the decisions. But the brothers, fully aware of their mortality, realized that this model could not sustain Mayo Clinic for the long term. They still needed to create the administrative complement to clinical collaboration. By passing most of their personal wealth into Mayo Properties Association, they had already communicated clearly that Mayo Clinic was no longer a family business; Mayo Clinic was much more than just the brothers Mayo.

The sustainable model for management and governance they created with the help of Harry Harwick was the board of governors for Mayo Clinic, which they implemented in the early 1920s. The board initially was responsible for the administration and operations of the Clinic. But as it matured, it also dealt with policies. Through the creation of this group, composed of seven physicians and Harwick, Dr. William J. Mayo was signaling that he would end the dominant control of the Clinic affairs that he had shared with his brother for more than three decades. Harwick notes that some in the organization "scoffed at this 'governing' group," because the move initially seemed meaningless since Dr. Will served as the chair of the board of governors until his resignation at the end of 1932. While initially "the prestige of the Mayos was the deciding factor in any controversial situation," Harwick reports that that changed over time.[10]

Dr. Will approached the transition with the same measured discipline that had served him well as a pioneering surgeon. He began to change management and governance into a "cooperative science," a partnership of peers across the organization. Harwick notes that gradually over the next few years Dr. Will passed along tasks to other members of the board of governors. When the brothers officially resigned from even the administrative affairs of the Clinic in 1932, the transition to the next generation of leaders was seamless. As their health permitted, however, they continued to come to their offices when they were in Rochester, and they were available as senior counselors when such service was requested. Away for the winter in Tucson, they received their first report from the Clinic. Helen Clapesattle reports that Charlie read it and then smiled at his brother, saying, "Well, well, this is quite a comedown for us, Will. They're doing better now we're away than they did when we were there."[11] Dr. Will, the dominant leader, effectively stepped away, first from surgery itself, then from his professional associations, and then from management of the Clinic with remarkable and exemplary grace. In each case, his comments reflect respect for the next generation of leaders. His example still stands as a model to each generation of clinical and administrative leaders approaching the end of their Mayo Clinic careers.

Step 4: Participative Governance through Committees

To complement the board of governors, Dr. Will in 1923–1924 instituted a number of committees (clinical practice, education, research, personnel, finance, and several others) that would look after many aspects of the management of the Clinic. Harry Harwick admitted that this move was made against his objections. Looking back on the decision a couple of decades later, Harwick conceded that Dr. Will was right. The committees served as a training ground for future leaders at the level of the board of governors and leaders of clinical departments and divisions. This participative management system also functioned as a good way to extend an understanding of management and the business dimension of medicine to the medical staff.

Succeeding generations of leaders—both administrative and clinical—have continued the essence of each of the four steps that the brothers initiated. Since the time Drs. Graham and Stinchfield agreed to work for salaries only, all physicians at Mayo Clinic have been salaried—even Drs. Will and Charlie accepted salaries after 1923 when they officially dissolved the partnership and the physicians became members of a voluntary association known as Mayo Clinic. Mayo Properties Association evolved into Mayo Foundation, which is the umbrella organization for all Mayo Clinic operations and assets today. The public trustees of Mayo Clinic still serve without remuneration. Both the board of governors and the committee system have survived the test of time without major changes—just a few adjustments over the years.

Twenty-First Century Partners in Leadership

In 1908, 12 physicians, including Drs. Will and Charlie, made up the medical staff of "Mayo's Clinic"; about 2,500 staff physicians now serve on the three campuses. In spite of that growth, Mayo Clinic remains a *group practice of medicine*. This characteristic, according to Shirley Weis, who began her tenure as chief administrative officer of Mayo in February 2007, is fundamental to understanding the organization. Harry Harwick called it a "voluntary association of physicians" and "a group of individuals who have certain aims and objectives."[12] Weis observes, "What makes Mayo Clinic work today is the fact that physicians here understand it is *their* practice." Robert Smoldt, predecessor of Shirley Weis as chief administrative officer, agrees that the group practice image is accurate, but he adds that the major commitments to medical research and education distinguish Mayo from most other group practices.

In his analysis of the physician-administrator partnership, John Herrell, chief administrative officer from 1993–2001, writes:

> *Physician leadership does not necessarily mean physician management of everything, but physician leadership is an essential element in the direction of everything. ... What differentiates Mayo Clinic is the structure that makes the physician accountable for what happens throughout the institution. If the institution fails, the physicians have only themselves to blame. This fact affects physician behavior at Mayo Clinic in a positive way. They must keep the institution's interests in mind because those interests are aligned with their own.*[13]

Physicians have shaped the practice of medicine at Mayo Clinic into a system of care that not only satisfies patients but also physicians. One indication of the physicians' satisfaction is a voluntary turnover rate of less than 2.5 percent across the three campuses. Dr. Kirk Rodysill, an internist, informally surveyed his former medical resident colleagues from the University of Minnesota about 10 years into his career, and he learned that, "The happiest of the physicians surveyed worked at Mayo with most of the other physicians unhappy in their practice." So he joined Mayo Clinic himself.

Mayo Clinic always has been physician-led. Dr. Robert Waller, who retired as president and CEO in 1999, is frequently quoted for his self-deprecating quip, "Mayo has a president, but it also has 1,500 vice presidents." He was simply acknowledging that he was leading an organization made up of highly educated physicians. Dr. Hugh Smith, who retired as CEO of the Rochester campus in 2005, explains, "Most physicians don't take well a 'no' from nonspecialists outside their medical field. And they take it even less well from administrators." At Mayo Clinic, the wishes of each individual physician are not necessarily honored, but it helps that the decision makers are fellow physicians. Physician leaders create a peer-to-peer relationship in managing the needs, hopes, and frustrations of the highly educated, professional physicians who comprise the group practice of medicine at Mayo Clinic.

Teamwork in Leadership: Physician-Administrator Partners

The relationship between Harry Harwick and Dr. William J. Mayo is the prototype for hundreds of management relationships at Mayo Clinic today. Dr. Will was clearly in charge, but his relationship with Harwick was based on their respect for each other as peers. They engaged in serious give-and-take conversations during the development of the current management model.

The model continues nearly a century later at most levels of the organization. These partnerships, however, exist today not in homage to a 100-year-old teamwork aphorism from a founder, but because they enable a continuous focus on the needs of the patient even in the face of fiscal and operational challenges. James Anderson, chief administrative officer of the Arizona operation, identifies why the physician-administrator model is successful: "... high-quality management decisions emerge from the healthy tension between the patient-first advocacy of the physician leader and advocacy for fiscal responsibility from the administrator." Trustees expect a bottom line of net revenue every year to sustain operations. Sustaining the mission over the long term requires intense cooperation and attention to service delivery and financial matters by all physician and administrative partnerships. John Herrell adds, "The physicians have as much at stake as administrators do to ensure that the institution prospers financially. Administrators have as much at stake as the physicians do to ensure that the patients are well cared for...."[14]

We illustrate the nature of these partnerships by describing the division of cardiology in the department of medicine, although the model applies to every clinical discipline. The chair of cardiology, a cardiologist, is paired with an operations administrator. The chair is responsible, most importantly, for the vision and strategic direction of the practice as well as the clinical activities staffed by cardiologists: the outpatient (office) practice, the cardiac diagnostic laboratories such as echocardiography and cardiac catheterization, and the hospital practice. The chair is also responsible for the individual cardiologists—their career development, their research, their practice, and performance reviews.

The operations administrator is responsible for day-to-day operational administration of the cardiology practice. This includes oversight of all the allied health staff (nonphysicians) required to operate the clinics and the clinical laboratories for the practice. The administrator has managers or supervisors as direct reports. Managers and supervisors typically are experts in the clinical or technical function they supervise, be it desk operations or a cardiac catheterization laboratory. The operations administrator also works directly with physicians, for instance, in developing a proposal for a new clinical initiative championed by a physician in the division. The administrator would help shape the proposal and the presentation and prepare them for the internal review and decision processes.

Another way to look at the administrator's role is described by James Anderson:

Physicians are educated to act creatively and independently with a focus on best serving the individual patient. The administrators are trained to apply concepts of managerial and organization theory, to foster group performance, and to provide systems and procedures that enable patient satisfaction, quality, and financial success. Effective administration will aggregate information and will help doctors look at the bigger picture—groups of patients or department operational statistics rather than lab values for the individual patient.

The physician chair is the face of the division. The administrator is less visible. Jeffery Korsmo, chief administrative officer in Rochester, uses the stage metaphor to describe the relationship: "Administrators enable the work of those who put their hands on patients. We are the backstage activity so the activity on the front stage can happen. The audience is the patients and their family." Dave Leonard, a retired operations administrator, echoes this theme: "Administrators provide the glue to hold things together and the lubricant to keep them running smoothly." It's the administrator's responsibility to ease the physician's administrative burdens as much as possible.

Although physicians bring to leadership a broad and deep clinical knowledge, the administrators bring a comparable knowledge of management and of the way Mayo works. Chief administrative officer Shirley Weis emphasizes, "In order to make the partnership work, administrators have to bring a lot of value. We are expected to make contributions based on our unique experiences and expertise." One physician leader acknowledged that, as a young chair, he sensed that he needed to engage with his staff for a planning exercise. As he attempted to describe what he wanted, his administrator responded, "You need a SWOT analysis." Although this tool used to identify "strengths, weaknesses, opportunities and threats" is an elementary concept among administrators, it is not a topic in the medical school curriculum. But, in turn, good physician leaders will guide administrators, for example, away from "efficiencies" that might compromise the best interests of the patient. Mayo Clinic physician leaders and their administrators learn from one another. They typically perform better as partners than they could alone; the leaders at Mayo Clinic all have a sounding board provided by the structural design of the organization.

But this arrangement works well only when the administrator and the physician respect each other as peers with complementary responsibilities. Dr. Douglas Wood, vice chair of the department of internal medicine in Rochester, describes the relationship that existed for over eight years between him, Dr. Nicholas LaRusso, department chair, and Barbara Spurrier, operations administrator: "When Dr. LaRusso said, 'This is the way it will be,' I could readily disagree. Barb could readily disagree, and then we would hash things out. When we did that, we came to much better decisions because that's a true partnership. It's not a partnership if the physician chair says this is what I think we should do, and the administrator just says 'okay, we'll do that.'" When internal medicine divisions had their quarterly reviews, both the physician chair and the administrator of these divisions met with Drs. LaRusso and Wood and Barbara Spurrier for a give-and-take discussion.

Physician leaders, of course, work with more than just their administrative partners. Physician partnerships are also vital. For the department chair of internal medicine, the physician chairs of its various divisions, such as gastroenterology, endocrinology, and allergic diseases, are significant partners. The clinical department chairs are some of the most important partners for a campus CEO. The CEO also depends on a strong partnership with the physician chairs of three major committees: the clinical practice committee, the education committee, and the research committee. Without an open, candid, mutually respectful, and trusting relationship between the CEO and these physician leaders, the Mayo Clinic management model will not work effectively.

Operations administrators are hired into the department of administration, chaired by the chief administrative officer, and are then assigned, usually for five- to seven-year terms, as an operations administrator for various administrative needs, most importantly those of clinical departments and divisions. Thus, the department of orthopedics does not hire its own administrator. Rather the administrator is assigned from the pool of administrative talent. Of course, the chair of orthopedics helps select the individual.

The physician-administrator partnership works for Mayo because Mayo works at making it successful. Part of the "art" of the physician-administrator relationship is the match between the two individuals. Every effort is made to pair the right people. Often a new, young physician chair will be matched with a seasoned administrator who knows the ropes of internal processes. A young operations administrator will typically first serve in clinical areas without known conflict and, hopefully, experience a good physician mentor who can convey how to work successfully with Mayo physicians. When a match does not work, as happens occasionally, the situation is analyzed without assuming that one party or the other is to blame. If separation is deemed the best option, then the administrator moves to a new position, as the generalist skills of administrators can be applied elsewhere. The administrator does not carry a stigma to the new assignment. If either the physician or the administrator repeats the scenario with different parties—suggesting a pattern—then physicians move out of leadership and administrators find a better fit inside or outside of Mayo.

Nothing is more important than finding the right individuals to lead, whether physicians or administrators. Dr. Hugh Smith notes that from the large pool of physicians at Mayo, potential leaders emerge. But he suggests that it is not enough to rely on the natural gifts of emerging leaders. "The nurturing of physician leaders is extremely important."

Physician Leadership: Grounded in Patient Care

The currency of respect at Mayo is clinical excellence. Mayo Clinic physicians must distinguish themselves in their specialties before assuming leadership roles. In addition, most leaders will have earned strong academic reputations as researchers and/or educators. Another dimension of the Mayo Clinic culture is the "reluctant leader." Leaders are typically invited into positions of leadership—they are asked by their peers to make a sacrifice for the good of the Clinic. Dr. George Bartley, CEO in Jacksonville, Florida, observes, "Almost nobody I know who is now a Mayo Clinic physician leader started off with that being their career goal. I was perfectly happy doing surgery and writing papers for a number of years, never giving management a second thought until I was asked to do my first administrative assignment."

Physician leaders inevitably sacrifice at least a part of the clinical and academic careers they have established, and most confess that they have a sense of loss as a result. If physicians appear conspicuously ambitious for high positions in leadership, their chance of rejection is high. Too strong an ambition for positions of leadership risks politicizing the organization too much. On the route to CEO positions, the physicians will usually have achieved the academic rank of professor. Some may have been a clinical department or division chair at some point in their career. Most will have provided leadership in a number of committee assignments. Additionally, evidence of leadership skills plus skills in communications and interpersonal relationships are basic expectations and requirements.

Absent from the list of required qualifications is formal training in business management. To date, no CEO-level leader at Mayo Clinic has held a graduate degree in business. The physician leader's primary role is as a visionary advocate for the patient's needs today and for the health systems of the future. In addition, the physician leader must be a trusted ear and voice for the medical staff and an inspirational, motivating leader of the organization. Mayo does provide some basic training in the business disciplines in its leadership development program; however, a physician leader must be first a physician, not an administrator. Becoming the CEO of Mayo Clinic does not spell the end of doctoring. Even those who retire from a high-level leadership position at age 65 or older often will work as part-time physicians for the first few years in "retirement."

To stay connected with patients and colleagues, physician leaders, with only a few exceptions, have continued to practice medicine for a certain amount of time each week. Dr. Hugh Smith emphasizes that the physician leaders ideally work with staff physicians in delivering patient care in order to remain relevant and credible to the physicians whom they lead. He relates the experience of approving in the board of governors the rollout of a new patient management tool in the electronic medical record. The implementation team assured the board that this was going to be a smooth, simple process. "So," Dr. Smith says, "I went down to the clinical unit, and tried to use it that afternoon. I was just hopelessly screwed up. The training program was designed by techies, and they knew it cold—they designed it. But to the typical busy clinician, this was another burden and another expectation for which they hadn't been prepared." With this firsthand experience, Dr. Smith was able to intervene with the implementation team before dozens of other physicians experienced similar frustrations. He concludes, "Relevance and credibility are essential for physician leaders. Without relevance and credibility there is no power."

Maintaining current clinical skills is also important because most physicians at the end of their leadership terms will return to the practice. For instance, Dr. Robert Hattery returned to the department of radiology to work in diagnostic radiology after he completed four years as the CEO of the Rochester campus. Three former chairs of the cardiology division now work as staff cardiologists. Virtually all leadership positions for physicians have "term limits." Some are hard and fast. For instance membership on the board of governors or the campus executive boards is limited to two four-year terms. Department and division chairs typically will hold a position for about eight years—though it might extend to ten or twelve. As department chairs often are appointed in their mid- to late 40s, they typically end their terms as chairs with more productive years ahead of them before retirement. Dr. Glenn Forbes, CEO of Mayo Clinic in Rochester, reflects on leadership terms at Mayo by citing King George III of England who reportedly said, "If George Washington voluntarily relinquishes power on a certain day and returns to the life of a common man after being president of the new colonies, he would be one of the greatest men of all time." Dr. Forbes continues, "You don't own any position of leadership indefinitely at Mayo. You're only there for a period of time to serve, and then you return to the practice or research or other administrative work."

Dr. George Bartley came to Mayo Clinic for a three-year residency in ophthalmology. He was asked to join the medical staff in 1986. His career since then follows a typical pattern for physician leaders. In 1992, while still in his mid-30s, he was appointed chair of the department of ophthalmology in Rochester. This appointment at a young age marked him as a potential physician leader outside his department. During his tenure as chair, Rochester's physician leadership appointed him to more than 20 different campuswide committees. These appointments gave Dr. Bartley an inside view of the issues and operations of many important administrative and management functions across the campus far outside the department of ophthalmology. But just as importantly, Rochester leaders were able to observe the quality of Dr. Bartley's contributions to the discussions, his work ethic and leadership skills in committee assignments, and his interpersonal interactions with a wide range of physicians and administrators from across the institution.

In 2001, Dr. Bartley was elected to one of the ten physician seats on the board of governors for Mayo Clinic in Rochester—more recently known as the executive board for Rochester. This appointment required that he step down from his role as chair of ophthalmology. Then in 2002, he was asked to become the CEO for the Jacksonville campus. His identity today is largely still built on his original professional goal—to be a surgeon, researcher, and educator. So it is not totally surprising that when he leaves his administrative office on Wednesday mornings for a half-day in the Clinic or the operating room, he assures colleagues that, "I am heading out for the best part of my week."

Given Mayo's tradition of rotational leadership, it is unlikely that he will remain as the CEO in Jacksonville until retirement. Perhaps another high-level leadership position in Mayo will be in his future. The opportunities are many, including some in the for-profit biotechnology activities emerging from Mayo's research programs. Or, of course, he might choose to bring his career full circle, back to his clinical and academic roots in ophthalmic plastic and orbital surgery.

Administrative Leadership: Grounded in Operations

Minnesota's Garrison Keillor claims ironically that in Lake Wobegon, "All the children are above average." Without irony, that phrase describes the physicians at Mayo Clinic. The intelligence, training, and professionalism of the physicians set a high standard for the administrators who will need to earn a peer-to-peer relationship in leadership. The administrators must be quick learners who thrive on new challenges and in ambiguous situations. The administrators must adapt to complement the styles, strengths, and interests of the several physician partners with whom they will work. Most importantly, they must be team players—individuals for whom savoring the accomplishments of the group is at least as meaningful as the taste of recognition for their personal contributions.

Although some readers might wonder why administrators would ever join Mayo knowing that the top positions all go to persons with a title of "MD," Shirley Weis emphasizes, "Administrators can have huge impact. Part of it comes from doing your homework, putting the material together, using data to give options, and helping guide colleagues and physician leaders. But the most important part is you have to be willing to do it without feeling like you are getting the credit for it."

Administrators, like physicians, join the staff originally in a probationary role. After three years, the physicians can move from senior associate consultant to consultant status. With that move they become members of the voting staff, which gives them a vote in the confirmation of the members of the executive board. Administrators have a similar promotion track. After at least five years of service with commendations and securing a significant administrative assignment, administrators also can be given voting staff privileges. These administrators are then identified as peers with the physicians.

Early in their careers, administrators are often rotated through a number of assignments in central functions so they come to understand "how Mayo works." They may work in departments such as human resources, finance, or research administration, receiving broad exposure to the culture and functions of the Clinic. Three primary training or experience routes lead to administrator positions: (1) directly from an MBA or MHA academic training program, (2) administrative experience in another clinic or hospital, and (3) outstanding administrative performance in a Mayo Clinic position such as physical therapy, the clinical laboratory, or nursing administration. Although those coming from any of these routes may have actually worked in a clinical discipline, they are not pigeonholed by that in their assignments. Rather, those who join the department of administration might work with any clinical department or many administrative departments in the organization. The career path of Marie Brown illustrates this point.

Brown joined the department of administration in 1993 after a 13-year career in the clinical laboratory where her leadership skills were noted and used in a variety of assignments. Her first assignment was as the administrator for three different internal medicine divisions, so she worked simultaneously with three different physician partners. Then in 1997, she was asked to serve as the secretary of the clinical practice committee (CPC), which is a major administrative assignment requiring nearly a full-time commitment. The committee oversees all the clinic and hospital operations, physician and allied health staffing, as well as clinical space and equipment budgets.

After completing a three-year term as CPC secretary, Brown spent two years as administrator for a surgical department. Following that she held another major committee secretary position, this time for the Mayo Clinic Rochester executive board, the highest level management group on the campus. There she reported directly to the chief administrative officer and was responsible as well for the budgets, planning, and operational tracking of the department of administration. In 2003, she was honored as the "distinguished Mayo administrator" in Rochester.

In 2007, she returned to her roots in the clinical laboratory, though not as a technologist: she is the administrative director of clinical operations paired with the physician chair of the department of laboratory medicine and pathology, a unit with about 2,500 employees. Mayo's administrative leadership program brings Brown to the laboratory leadership assignment with a rich perspective. She understands much more than just how the lab operates because she can see the laboratory from an outside perspective. She understands how the lab does and can interface with the entire campus. Her professional relationships extend to both the administrative and physician leaders across most of the institution.

Brown may not remain in this position until she retires. Possibly a new department chair might want her to provide a fresh set of administrative ideas. She might feel that she wants a new challenge, perhaps in Arizona or Florida. The chief administrative officer, as well, might be facing a demanding need that she could fill. A fundamental benefit of Mayo's administrative organization and culture is that Brown can be retained within Mayo Clinic management with each of these scenarios. Mayo's approach to professional administration enables the organization to retain gifted administrators by providing a career with many fresh challenges.

Subspecialists in Administration

Several physician leaders acknowledge that today physicians are less directly involved in the overall management of the Clinic than they were in times past. The role of the physicians in the core clinical activities is as important and pervasive as it has ever been, but as the administrative and management challenges in healthcare have become more complex, Mayo has turned increasingly to administrators with specialist expertise. As Dr. Douglas Wood observes, "Forty or fifty years ago, you didn't have to worry very much or at all about things like the antitrust law or labor law, compliance with laws and regulations for nonprofit organizations, or the details of Medicare and Medicaid regulation." Areas with little direct physician leadership are usually technically complex business disciplines or management of the technical infrastructure. As Dr. Hugh Smith notes, "Physician leadership works best in everything related to the patient."

Mayo Clinic employs hundreds of administrators in these various areas of business or technical specialization, and most often these administrators work without a visible, present physician partner except at the highest levels of the organization. Specialist knowledge is required to ensure that these functions work well. Many administrators, often with graduate degree expertise, will spend an entire career in areas such as information systems, materials management, accounting, investment management, planning, public affairs, communications, marketing, and facilities. But again, there is room for progressive advancement in at least the larger of the departments. These administrators can become members of the voting staff as well.

Physician involvement in these management functions does not have the same value as physician management of clinical activities. Nonetheless, by having physicians involved in the oversight committees, such as the marketing committee, the investments committee, or the facilities committee, the medical staff develops an appreciation for the complexity of healthcare management.

From Two to One: Integrating Clinic and Hospital

Although there are several hundred different physician group practices in the United States, Mayo Clinic differs from most. For instance, only 3 percent of physician groups have more than

50 physicians; Mayo has about 2,500. Most physician groups are single-specialty groups such as radiologists, surgeons, or pathologists; Mayo is a multispecialty group with depth in virtually all medical specialty and subspecialty disciplines. Mayo Clinic is further differentiated because it also operates its own hospitals.

Most group practices of physicians use hospitals—community hospitals and many academic medical centers—that operate separately from the physicians. Those hospitals have their own boards, and the fiduciary responsibilities of hospital administrators are not always aligned with the physicians groups that use the hospital. Often a hospital will depend on several physician groups that may, in turn, compete with one another. This situation leads to tensions as administrators and physicians jockey for positions of advantage. John Herrell writes, "Their relationship appears to be adversarial, and their interests are often not aligned."[15]

But at Mayo today the outpatient clinics and the inpatient services are integrated by budgets, patient services, clinical staff, and administrative leadership. This focus creates the singular alignment of mission, service, and outcomes that is so attractive to Jonathan Curtright whose story opens this chapter.

For nearly a century, Saint Marys Hospital in Rochester was operated by the sisters of Saint Francis of Assisi, but from its inception it was inseparably linked to the needs of Mayo doctors. The alignment of Saint Marys and Mayo Clinic was remarkably close for separate institutions. The Mayo father and his sons, for example, traveled around the United States to determine the best in contemporary hospital design in the 1880s, and the sisters built to their specifications. This cycle of physicians expressing needs and the hospital responding with state-of-the-art facilities continued throughout the years.

For instance, in the 1950s, Sister Amadeus Klein, head nurse on the neurosurgery unit, had a problem. Most of the six or seven surgeons requested that "their patient," fresh from surgery, be roomed next to the nursing station to facilitate easy observation. That was, of course, impossible; thus, the head nurse had to assign private duty nurses so the patients could be continuously monitored. Eventually, the head nurse, working with the surgeons, devised a better solution—a unit where all the patients could be observed from the nursing station. It was a major and expensive renovation, but the result was the first intensive care unit in the United States. Jane Campion, a retired administrator who spent much of her career with Saint Marys Hospital, notes: "In today's world, everybody is struggling for their piece of the pie.... Nobody struggled for the piece of the pie at Saint Marys; everybody struggled for that common vision. We're going to build and operate a building that will take care of patients. What a wonderful partnership." In 1986, the sisters of Saint Francis of Assisi formally signed documents that transferred ownership and management of Saint Marys Hospital to Mayo Clinic.

Today, Mayo Clinic operates four hospitals. In addition to Saint Marys Hospital, Mayo also operates Rochester Methodist Hospital, which dates from the mid-1950s, and is a closed-staff hospital where only Mayo Clinic physicians and surgeons care for patients. Ownership and operation of Rochester Methodist Hospital was transferred to Mayo Clinic in 1986. Mayo Clinic built its own hospitals in Phoenix and Jacksonville, which opened in 1998 and 2008, respectively. None of these four facilities has the traditional "hospital administration" found in most hospitals. Rather, Mayo hospitals operate largely through a physician-led hospital practice committee that is a subcommittee of the clinical practice committee on each campus. The key members of this committee—the physician chair, the nursing chair, and the designated hospital administrator—serve as a triumvirate for day-to-day operations decisions within the hospital.

But the walls of the hospital are mostly invisible in the overall operations of the Mayo Clinic enterprise. For instance, the chair of the department of nursing is responsible for all the nurses whether they work in the hospital or in the outpatient office practice. The clinical laboratory, the radiology department, safety and security, housekeeping, maintenance, and most other functions on each of the three campuses are integrated services meeting the needs of both hospital and clinic operations.

The integrated operations of the hospitals and the Clinic facilitate putting the focus on the needs of the individual patient. Because the budgets are deeply intertwined, financial considerations of either the hospitals or the Clinic are usually moot. But the most important benefit of the integrated operations is that tensions between the physicians and hospital administration simply do not exist because their interests are aligned. What is good for one is good for the other because they work for the same organizations and their salaries are paid from the same checking account.

Building Culture and Consensus by Committees

Committees are an integral feature of Mayo Clinic management and governance, and of all the elements of the organization, committees are perhaps the most controversial. The numbers alone might seem staggering: up to 80 committees deal with issues across each campus. In addition to these campuswide committees, departments and divisions have internal committees. The Mayo management model uses many thousands of hours of a precious and perishable resource—physician time—in its committee-based approach.

Much of the administrative work of the organization is accomplished through committees or task forces. Brown's curriculum vitae identifies 18 different committees on which she served in the department of laboratory medicine and pathology during her 13 years in the department. These committees ranged from dress and decorum, to hospital infection control, to the department library committee. Since joining the administration in 1993, Brown has been a member of more than 60 different committees. Many of these committees deal with the nitty-gritty details of department or division matters.

Rarely will a significant decision at Mayo Clinic be made by one or two individuals without counsel from colleagues. Dr. Hugh Smith explains his perspective on committees with a paraphrase of Winston Churchill's observation: "Democracy is the worst form of government except all the others that have been tried." Dr. Smith suggests that, "Committees are the worst kind of healthcare management and governance system except for all the others that have been tried." He then contends that while committees may slow decision making, implementation can be rapid once a decision is made because an organizational consensus has been reached.

Current CEO Dr. Denis Cortese notes that decision making at Mayo today does not come from the top as often as it did in the past: "I've been here 37 years. As we've gotten bigger, we've become more horizontal—less top down. There's no question in my mind that in the 1920s, if somebody wanted to do something and the Mayo brothers did not want them to do it, they didn't do it." Cortese then adds, "It has progressively gotten a little more difficult to get buy-in, more difficult to get a decision, and I think that's purely a function of how big we are." Committees comprise a large portion of Mayo Clinic's horizontal review.

Notwithstanding the sometimes cumbersome nature of Mayo's committees, Robert Smoldt, chief administrative officer of Mayo Clinic from 2001 to 2007, believes that committees work well as a form of participative management and governance in organizations where the primary workforce is made up of professionals such as doctors, professors, engineers, or lawyers who have academic credentials equivalent to those of the leadership. Leaders who remain connected to their peers retain their respect, but the leaders aren't held in awe. Professionals rarely respond well to commands from on high without an understanding of the rationale—after all, they are trained to ask "why?"

The committee system at Mayo Clinic provides a venue where the staff physicians can work to achieve consensus *before* a decision is made. For instance, in the 1990s Mayo Clinic in Rochester decided to develop relationships with physicians and hospitals in its region in order to develop a stronger regional presence and referral network. The first experiments came in early 1992 with two acquisitions. After a short time of reflection and analysis, the regional strategies committee and the board of governors agreed on an operational model for the network and its business strategy. Once these were in place, the committee acted very quickly to build Mayo Health System (MHS) as it was branded. By 1999, nearly 500 physicians were employed by MHS and served patients in 55 different communities.[16] The operations continue to grow; currently more than 800 physicians are employed, 16 hospitals are part of the system, and MHS generates more than $1.5 billion in annual revenues.

The committee system is at its worst when the same proposal is presented multiple times. In the recent past, the process could drag on for months. Some leaders observe, however, that when proposals languish in the committee system, it is usually because the proposal needs more work. However, it is also possible that the culture is too "polite" to state that the idea does not have enough merit for approval. When the committee system provides indirect, nuanced responses, it does not serve the organization or the proponents of the proposal well.

At its best, the committee review process identifies the impact of proposed activities—usually unintended—upon other parts of the operation. If a proposal is going to "gore another department's ox," the physicians on the committee usually will identify the problem. The committee typically will insist that the two groups need to work out a compromise agreement before the proposal can be approved.

Robert Smoldt, whose career spanned more than 35 years in Mayo Clinic administration, observes that the committee system "... works because the members of the committee are committed to Mayo Clinic and seeing the institution do well." Members of committees are drawn from many different departments, and in the discussion they would be expected to identify issues that might be created for their clinical home. At the time of the vote, however, members are expected to "wear their Mayo Clinic hat." Consequently, the partnerships created in committees are usually able to reach decisions that serve the common good.

Converging Governance

In 2006, Mayo Clinic initiated a major change in governance— a change designed to facilitate timely decisions. For about 20 years—beginning with the opening of clinics in Jacksonville and Scottsdale—the organization operated with three boards of governors. These boards had both governance and operational management powers. Above these boards was the executive committee composed of the Mayo Clinic leaders who were also on the board of trustees. The CEOs of all three campuses were members of the executive committee. Clearly this system had too much redundancy. For instance, when the department of public affairs proposed a major modification of the Mayo Clinic Web site, it first presented the proposal to the executive committee. But approval there was not sufficient to move forward because the proposal had to go on a "road show" to each of the three boards of governors who were responsible for the Internet positioning of their local practices. But in 2006, the Executive Committee became the single board of governors with governance decision power for all Mayo operations. The boards on the three campuses changed to executive boards with management and operations oversight of the campuses. Today a decision about the Mayo Clinic Web site could proceed following a single presentation to and approval from the board of governors. However, it still would be politically expedient to communicate with physician leaders on each campus so that they would not be surprised by a major shift in the Web presence of their practice.

Ultimate responsibility for major decisions rests with the Mayo Clinic board of trustees, which includes 17 public trustees and 14 internal trustees, most of whom are members of the board of governors. The late U.S. Supreme Court chief justice and Mayo Clinic trustee emeritus Warren Burger succinctly described the Mayo Clinic as ". . . a private foundation for public purposes,"[17] and it is those public purposes that the external trustees must protect. Public members elect and monitor the CEO, ensure the financial integrity and security of Mayo's operations, and assist Mayo Clinic's leadership in fulfilling the public purpose of this not-for-profit private organization. Bert Getz, Mayo Clinic trustee chair emeritus, indicates that the public trustees fulfill their duties with commitment unlike that he has observed on any other of the many not-for-profit or corporate boards on which he has served. He notes, "There is nearly 100 percent attendance at every meeting." Then he volunteers that the mission of the Mayo Clinic, its long history of success, and the quality of Mayo's leaders inspire the trustees to work on behalf of the Clinic. "I've never seen such selflessness and dedication as that demonstrated by Mayo Clinic's leaders," Getz concludes.

The Cultural Role of Salaries

Mayo Clinic's salary system is deeply rooted in the culture and the values that created this unique organization. The Mayo brothers were committed to paying all employees fairly and generously, though not lavishly. Dr. Hugh Butt, a retired physician who trained under Dr. William Mayo in 1936, suggests why Dr. Will believed that the salaried physician was a crucial element in the practice model he and Dr. Charlie had created: "Dr. Will said ... 'You know, they don't have to worry about anything. It doesn't matter whom they see, how long they spend, what they see, they just have to do the best they can for this patient here.'" The only incentive driving Mayo Clinic generations later is the best interest of the patient. Remuneration at Mayo Clinic for all clinical employees, including physicians and administrators, is based on a straight salary.

Some patients find comfort in knowing that Mayo Clinic doctors have no financial interest in any test or treatment that they recommend. Many patients have experienced having a Mayo doctor refer them to a colleague in the same medical specialty because of the unique expertise of the clinician. For instance, the brother of a Clinic employee arrived from Kansas with the diagnosis of a large adrenal tumor. The urologist who first consulted with the patient looked at the CT scan and said, "This is going to be a difficult surgery, and I have a colleague who has more experience with this type of tumor than I do." The needs of the patient were addressed, and neither surgeon's salary was affected. Dr. Robert Waller, retired CEO of Mayo Clinic, calls the salaried physician "a key principle of the Mayo culture" that keeps the focus of the practice on the needs of the patient.

All salaries at Mayo are established after considering commercially available salary surveys. Physician salaries are based on data from both other academic medical centers and the general physician market. The oversight of salary administration is an important function of a board of trustees committee that includes only public trustees. Mayo doctors typically earn salaries that are competitive with those of the marketplace.

Mayo's salary policies for physicians and surgeons also promote partnerships with a level salary system within groups of physicians who perform the same services. To be clear, the salaries of general surgeons and internists are not identical; their Mayo salaries reflect the difference in the marketplace. The same is true of interventional and noninterventional cardiologists who earn their respective market-based salaries. Pursuant to Mayo's policy, newly employed doctors earn a salary that will, with annual increases, max out in five years. Thus, a 38-year-old endocrinologist in her fifth year at Mayo would earn the same salary as a 62-year-old endocrinologist who had been practicing for 32 years, although the long-term employee would earn more vacation time. Mayo Clinic physicians also earn academic rank, moving from instructor, to assistant professor, to associate professor to full professor. But a higher academic rank, while providing significant prestige, does not move a physician to a different pay scale.

To a large extent, Mayo Clinic's culture self-regulates productivity. Mayo illustrates the perspective of Alfie Kohn, social critic of American workplace management: "If our goal is excellence, no artificial incentive can ever match the power of intrinsic motivation. People who do exceptional work may be glad to be paid and even more glad to be well paid, but they do not work to collect a paycheck. They work because they love what they do."[18] Indeed, Dr. George Bartley recalls the retirement note he received from his mentor, former boss, and colleague, Dr. Richard Brubaker: "Dr. Brubaker pointed out that he had never worked a day in his life. When he went to the office, and then to the Clinic, and then to the operating room in the hospital or to the laboratory, he went to work to play. So he looked at his 30 years at Mayo as being recreation and said he never worked a day in his life."

Mayo physicians have in most cases been top performers throughout their lives—in classrooms and medical training along with athletics, music, debate, or community service. Productivity, both clinical and academic, is measured and is part of regular performance reviews. Although the traditional "triple threat" physician—one who excels in practice, education, and research—is an increasing rarity because of time constraints, all physicians at Mayo Clinic are expected to excel in clinical care and at least one other endeavor: research, education, or service/administration. Financial incentives have not been necessary to motivate physicians who embrace Mayo Clinic's values and mission.

Recently, Dr. Bartley led a group in a thorough analysis of compensation systems. He and the group concluded that a productivity-based compensation system would not necessarily increase productivity significantly among physicians and, more importantly, could irreparably damage the Clinic's culture. This culture reflects, according to Dr. Bartley, an example of an organization like that described by Francis Fukuyama: "It is particularly easy for an individual to identify with the aims of an organization over his or her narrow self-interest if the purpose of the organization is not primarily economic."[19] To sustain high productivity, Dr. Bartley concludes that the major management objective is "to foster an environment of unity and trust."

When physicians assume leadership positions, such as becoming a division or a department chair, their salary increases as recognition of the additional responsibility. The increase, however, is not large—about 5 to 10 percent—but that salary increment stays with the individual throughout the rest of his or her career. Over the physician's lifetime, the salary differential becomes significant because a physician's pension benefit is based on the higher salary. This is important because chairs typically rotate every eight to ten years. Since it is not uncommon for individuals to become chairs in their 40s or early 50s, this salary policy removes any financial "penalty" for rotating out of a leadership position.

Dr. Hugh Smith observes that in most academic institutions salary goes down when a chair steps down. "So there is an economic self-interest for people to stay on in positions of authority. That gives you, if you are not careful, a gerontocracy. . . . And, it is not healthy!"

Mayo Clinic's salary policy reflects the institution's commitment to the perpetual refreshing of leadership.

Salary policies at Mayo Clinic are designed to complement the two main values—the patient-first focus and teamwork. Salary dissatisfaction plays a very small role in decisions of employees to leave Mayo Clinic.

Not Stars, but a Constellation

When asked about star physicians at Mayo, a retired campus CEO responded, "Mayo has a constellation in that I think that virtually everyone is a star. But there is no Big Dipper, there's no North Star, there's no star that really shines so that it puts the rest of us in dimness. When I say we don't have stars, I really mean that we don't have a star system where everybody worships the one or two stars."

Ask any leader about physician stars at Mayo Clinic, and you will be given a list of outstanding physicians whose distinguished careers include leadership positions in national and international professional organizations. Others mentioned may have edited major medical journals or authored the textbooks from which new clinicians learn. Some will have developed new medical technology or served as the principal investigator for a breakthrough study of a new drug. Distinguished educators are also identified not only for their impact on Mayo's own medical students or residents but also for their contributions to the organizations that accredit medical education. After identifying these outstanding individuals, the Mayo leader says something like this: "But none of them are treated like stars—they don't expect to be."

Robert Smoldt recalls one of Mayo Clinic's humble stars from his experience as an administrator for the department of orthopedic surgery in the late 1970s:

> *Dr. Mark Coventry was a star—he was one of the leaders who brought total joint replacements into the United States. Internationally, he was truly a star. But at the clinic he played by the rules that*

all his colleagues played by. We had orthopedic clinic where the surgeons would see consults that weren't really interesting orthopedic cases, but the patients needed to be seen. Dr. Coventry took that rotation just like everybody else. So I see Mayo's stars fitting themselves into the Mayo system of patient-focused care where they feel patients are better off with care by a team than by a star.

Outstanding Mayo physicians are frequently recruited by other institutions, but most remain at Mayo because they want to practice team medicine within the Mayo Clinic model of care. In the distant past, a few Mayo physicians successfully demanded, for instance, their own operating room set up to their liking, but today that does not happen. The request would need to be made to a committee of other physicians responsible for operating room access for all the surgeons of the Clinic. With a constellation of stars, the Mayo Clinic must rely on its overall systems to meet the needs of all physicians.

Robert Smoldt recalls what seemed like a crisis in the making when he learned that Dr. Coventry was retiring. At the time, he was the most well-known surgeon in the orthopedics department. His international reputation brought many patients to Mayo. As administrator, Smoldt anticipated that Dr. Coventry's departure would have a devastating impact on the department and its practice. But his retirement "didn't cause a ripple," Smoldt notes. The "bench strength" of Mayo teams is so strong that the retirements or vacations of well-known doctors have minimal impact on the quality of care or the "customer experience" of patients. The same applies when administrators leave the institution.

Lessons for Managers

Partnering in leadership came to Mayo Clinic later than teamwork in clinical care, but the model developed by the Mayo brothers and Harry Harwick has proved to be durable. This longevity suggests that the Mayo management model offers a paradigm worthy of study.

This does not mean that the management and governance structure of Mayo Clinic should necessarily be adopted by other service organizations. However, there is much to learn from Mayo Clinic's partnership-based leadership model.

Lesson 1: Align to succeed.   John Herrell explains why the shared management structure at Mayo Clinic works so well: "The physicians have as much at stake as administrators do to ensure that the institution prospers financially. Administrators have as much at stake as the physicians do to ensure that the patients are well cared for." This seems so simple and so obvious that one might think that this is how all healthcare must work. But that, of course, is not the case. Competing physician groups at a hospital spar on occasion. Doctors create physician-owned, single-specialty hospitals or outpatient services to capture dollars for physicians rather than to help a community hospital. In contrast, at Mayo Clinic every element of the care continuum is integrated into a single organization—the health of every cell of this organism depends on the health of the rest of the cells that maintain the vitality.

Other organizations should take notice. Mayo Clinic has created a very high degree of alignment with a workforce of more than 42,000 on three campuses in what is arguably the most complex and difficult-to-manage business in our economy. While much of Mayo's workforce is highly educated, that does not necessarily simplify the achievement of alignment.

Mayo Clinic's success is built around a humane idea—meeting the needs of patients. Well paid by a benevolent employer, employees at all levels are able to pursue a value higher than financial gain. Plumbers keep the water systems working so the clinical staff can care for patients. Custodians clean rooms so patients will be satisfied. A surgical fellow who had spent six years in a general surgery training program based in several different hospitals remarked 18 months into a two-year fellowship program at Mayo Clinic, "I've never heard Mayo doctors discuss money in the doctors' lounge at Mayo." This was a remarkable difference from the other hospitals he had known.

Lesson 2: Generosity begets generosity. Drs. William and Charles Mayo became models of selflessness by contributing most of their personal wealth to ensure that the institution that carried their name would survive them. Theirs was not an act of vanity; rather they were living by the conviction that beyond financial security for themselves and their partners, surplus money earned in healthcare should be returned to the public in the form of better medicine.

Mayo Clinic's story seems counterintuitive in an age of hyperinflated CEO reputations, salaries, and stock options in companies whose fortunes wax and wane. The Clinic's steady success has endured through years of depression and inflation, times of war and peace, changing demographics of the U.S. population, and generations of breathtaking innovations in medical technology. The core value, "the needs of the patient come first," is complemented by a culture and a management and governance structure that nurtures high discretionary effort, collaboration, and inclusiveness. Leaders who are perpetually refreshed by new challenges are committed to an idea much larger than themselves.

Though Drs. Will and Charlie were, in their lifetimes, viewed in the public arena as "bigger than life" stars, they refused to believe what the popular press said about them. Both knew that Mayo Clinic in their lifetimes was more than "my brother and I"; tens, then hundreds of colleagues, including physicians, nurses, technicians, administrators and others, worked as partners focused on the needs of patients to create and sustain Mayo Clinic. Mayo Clinic thrives because a benevolent employer fosters a generous, giving spirit in its workforce. Those who need to bask in the starlight of personal recognition or wealth thrive elsewhere.

Lesson 3: Participation fosters commitment. Most management decisions at Mayo Clinic are made by groups, not by an individual. The CEO of Mayo Clinic is the spokesperson for decisions of the board of governors. The same can be said for the CEOs of the individual campuses and department chairs for the affairs of a department. Rarely, if ever, is there a public statement without a consensus of colleagues in support. Without broad intellectual and emotional buy-in from the production staff—the doctors and other providers who touch the patient—genuinely humane healthcare services cannot be reliably delivered. The same, of course, could be said of all service organizations.

Good communication lies at the core of Mayo Clinic's consensus decision-making processes. After a committee decision, 10 to 20 well-informed individuals take their places alongside coworkers where they can often resolve fear or misunderstanding before it rages through the organization. The consensus process helps create a work environment conducive to focused work. Trust in the decisions of Mayo Clinic leadership means that the employees rarely need to fear for their jobs, arbitrary or capricious pronouncements are virtually unknown, and political intrigues are minimized. This work environment fosters the delivery of reliable, accurate, safe, and customized medical care for individual patients at Mayo Clinic.

Lesson 4: Build leadership bench strength.   After the Mayo brothers retired in 1932, the Clinic's future has never depended for a single day on the good health or survival of any one individual. Management and governance by consensus and committees have created ready successors who have been able to sustain the organization for more than seven decades. By engaging several hundred bright physicians and administrators in the management and governance processes, Mayo Clinic has continuously nurtured the next generation of leaders who believe in and live the values of the organization. The term limits associated with most leadership positions ensure the rotation of clinical department and division chairs, board of governors and executive board memberships, and even the campus CEOs. The administrative culture of Mayo offers frequent opportunities for lateral and upward career moves to give staff refreshing challenges at the individual level as well.

Summary

Mayo Clinic founders created a leadership model that continues to serve the institution well. For more than a century, the organization has charted a course along the high ridge of success. As in a trek along a mountain trail, there are ups and downs for any corporation as it lives through social, fiscal, and technological cycles. Mayo's model where leadership is rotated and revitalized as well as Mayo's consensus management and governance have, to date, identified the talent and the ideas that are able to surmount the challenges that arise along the trek. The partnerships and collaborations in management have served to create an internal environment that fosters the humane, sensitive, and personalized medical care that creates and sustains Mayo Clinic's reputation and brand.

Other organizations are successful with different models, but service companies, in particular, may find help for their challenges in the Mayo Clinic model of management.

NOTES

1. Judith Hartzell, *I Started All This: The Life of Dr. William Worrall Mayo* (Greenville, SC: Arvi Books, Inc., 2004), p. 138.
2. Harry J. Harwick, *Forty-Four Years with the Mayo Clinic: 1908–1952* (Rochester, MN: Mayo Clinic, 1957), p. 5.
3. Helen Clapesattle, *The Doctors Mayo* [abridged] (Rochester, MN: Mayo Foundation for Medical Education and Research, 1969), p. 227.
4. Clapesattle, p. 228.
5. Harwick, p. 11.
6. Clark W. Nelson, *Mayo Roots: Profiling the Origins of Mayo Clinic* (Rochester, MN: Mayo Foundation for Medical Education and Research, 1990), p. 120.
7. Harwick, p. 15.
8. Harwick, p. 17.
9. Harwick, p. 7.
10. Harwick, pp. 18–19.
11. Clapesattle, p. 417.
12. Harwick, p. 19.
13. John H. Herrell, "The Physician-Administrator Partnership at Mayo Clinic," *Mayo Clinic Proceedings*, January 2001, p. 108.
14. Herrell, p. 109.
15. Herrell, p. 108.

16. Kenneth E. Smith, "Mayo Health System: Development of an Integrated Delivery System in Southern Minnesota, Northern Iowa, and Western Wisconsin," in *Integrated Health Care: Lessons Learned*, J. William Appling, ed. (Englewood, CO: Medical Group Management Association, 1999), p. 308.
17. Mary Ellen Landwehr and Gregg Orwoll, "Warren Burger—Beyond the High Court," *Mayo Alumnus*, Fall 1986, p. 25.
18. Alfie Kohn, "Why Incentive Plans Cannot Work," *Harvard Business Review*, September–October 1993, p. 62.
19. Francis Fukuyama, *Trust: The Social Virtues and the Creation of Prosperity* (New York: The Free Press, 1995), p. 156.

The Drs. Mayo: the father, William Worrall Mayo (center) and his sons, Charles H. Mayo (left) and William J. Mayo (right)

Dr. Charles Horace Mayo

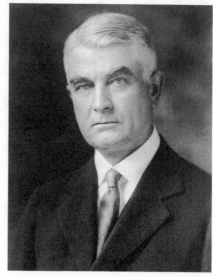

Dr. William James Mayo

Dr. William Worrall Mayo, nineteenth-century country doctor

Sister Mary Joseph served as administrator of Saint Marys Hospital for 47 years while also working much of that time as the surgical assistant to Dr. William J. Mayo.

Dr. Henry Plummer, inventor of the integrated medical record for each patient and designer of many of the early systems needed to support "destination medicine."

Harry Harwick, the first administrator of Mayo Clinic, worked with the Drs. Mayo to develop both the physician/administrator model for management and the Board of Governors for governance.

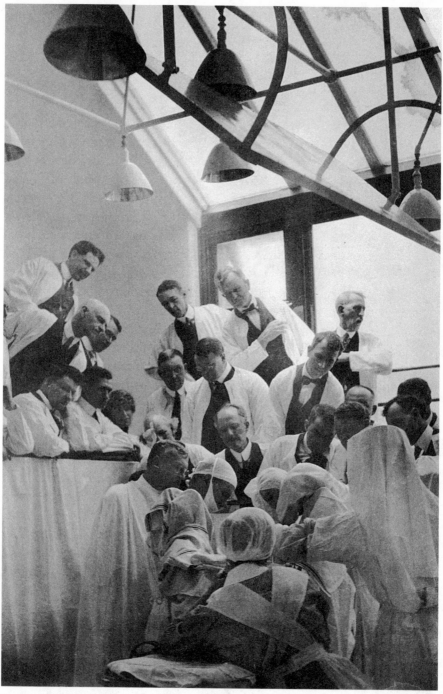

Dr. Charles H. Mayo operating with visiting physician observers in a Saint Marys Hospital operating "theater" with tiered risers and mirror mounted above the patient in about 1913.

1914 Mayo Clinic building, the first building ever designed to accommodate an integrated, multispecialty group practice of medicine.

1928 Mayo Clinic building known today as the Plummer Building in honor of Dr. Henry Plummer's role in its design.

Plummer Building's main floor elevator lobby richly ornamented in Romanesque style.

Lifts and chutes in the Mayo Building's medical record distribution center were rendered obsolete by the electronic medical record early in the twenty-first century.

Mayo Clinic Downtown Campus
Rochester, Minnesota

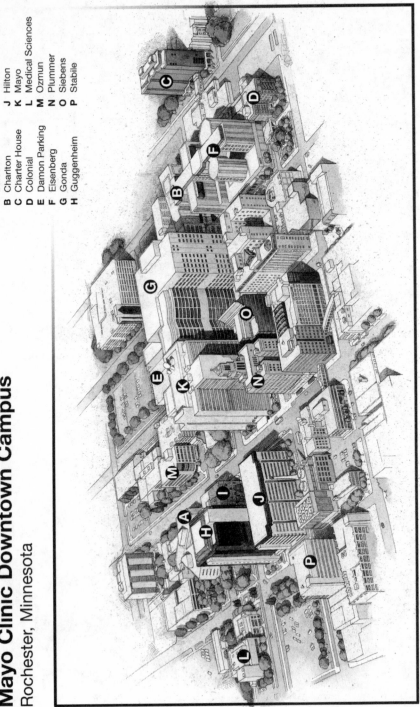

A Baldwin
B Charlton
C Charter House
D Colonial
E Damon Parking
F Eisenberg
G Gonda
H Guggenheim

I Harwick
J Hilton
K Mayo
L Medical Sciences
M Ozmun
N Plummer
O Siebens
P Stabile

Saint Marys Hospital Campus
Rochester, Minnesota

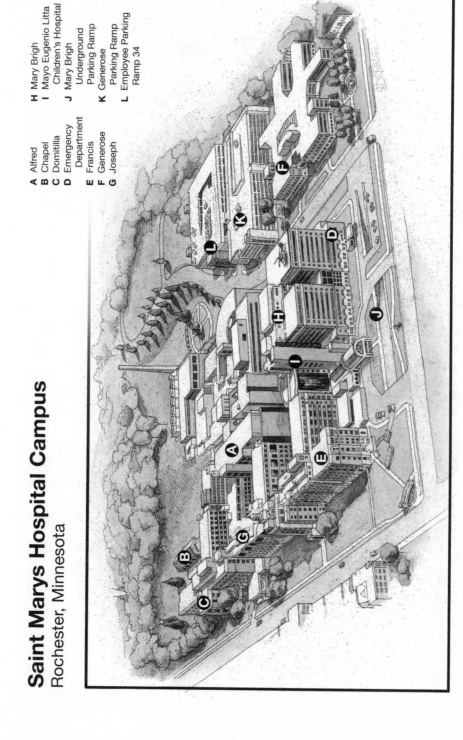

A Alfred
B Chapel
C Domitilla
D Emergency
 Department
E Francis
F Generose
G Joseph

H Mary Brigh
I Mayo Eugenio Litta
 Children's Hospital
J Mary Brigh
 Underground
 Parking Ramp
K Generose
 Parking Ramp
L Employee Parking
 Ramp 34

Gonda Building is Mayo Clinic's main entrance today. Opened in 2001, the 20-story building is linked with the Mayo Building and the Charlton Building of Rochester Methodist Hospital, forming the largest interconnected medical facility of its kind in the world, more than 3.5 million square feet.

Gonda Building's expansive lobby showing chandeliers (left) designed by famed glassblower Dale Chihuly and entrance to the Mayo Clinic Cancer Center (right).

Gonda Building's Landow Atrium with Man of Freedom sculpture at the far end

"I wanted to express the freedom, joy, hope, and love patients find at Mayo Clinic," this first-time patient explains. Moved by the music from a volunteer pianist, the dancer's extemporaneous expression brought tears to the eyes of many looking on.

Drs. Charles H. (left) and William J. Mayo, sitting on the steps of a family home.

Bronze sculpture of Drs. Charles H. (left) and William J. Mayo sitting on the "front steps" of Mayo Clinic in the Feith Family Statuary Park.

Mayo Clinic Building, a five-story outpatient facility located on the Scottsdale campus, has 240 exam rooms, outpatient surgery, endoscopy, laboratory, radiology, pharmacy, and multilevel underground parking.

The eight-story Davis Building on the Jacksonville campus supports the outpatient (office) practice as well as an adjacent 214-bed inpatient hospital that opened in 2008.

This wedding ceremony in the lobby of Mayo Clinic Hospital in Arizona was arranged by hospital staff on three-hours notice so a gravely ill mother in the bed directly behind the wedding party could attend her daughter's wedding.

After observing a surgery, coauthor Leonard Berry (left) joins Dr. Jonathan Leighton for a photo during Berry's sabbatical leave at Mayo Clinic.

Dr. Denis Cortese, president and chief executive officer of Mayo Clinic (left) and Shirley Weis, chief administrative officer

CHAPTER 6

HIRING FOR VALUES— AND TALENT

I came to the United States from South Africa in 1978 because I had been offered a job with a prominent academic medical center in the South. During the course of the three weeks I spent in the United States, I also looked at other academic medical posts. Though I was offered a number of positions, I told a physician friend that I'd like to take a look at the Mayo Clinic, which is very well known in South Africa. So my friend said, "That won't be a problem, I know Bob Brandenburg who is the chief of cardiology at Mayo." I got back a very nice letter where Bob said, "I have just stepped down as chief of cardiology, and I'm going to pass this letter on to Dr. Robert Frye, who is my successor."

One of the reasons that I nearly went to the medical center in the South was that it has a fantastic research faculty, including Nobel Prize winners. But, ironically that was also what concerned me, what made me hesitate. I really felt that clinical medicine was not what they were all about. In fact a leader there told me, "What we're about here is NIH [National Institutes of Health] grants. That's the currency of the realm. We are heavily endowed, and we are going to be the research center of the South—we will be the Harvard of the South." And I wanted to do both—academic medicine and clinical medicine.

I was competitive at that time for a number of positions—I was a Rhodes scholar from South Africa. I did my D. Phil. at Oxford, I'd written quite a few papers. So I came to Mayo for a day after I received an encouraging letter from Dr. Frye. By the end of that day I said to Dr. Frye, "If you offer *me a job, I'm going to take it." (I said this even though it was a miserable March day, slushy and snowing. And I'd left from Cape Town where it was late summer.) What differentiated Mayo Clinic for me right away were several things—the people, the camaraderie, the physical facility, which was excellent, the clear commitment to clinical excellence, plus the research opportunities. So I was attracted as a staff person to many of the core values. I loved the way people worked and was impressed by the quiet efficiency. But I was most of all struck by the fact that here was a place with great academic potential for me personally, because it suited my research interest, but clinical medicine and education were also taken seriously, and I wanted to do all three.*

Mayo Clinic competes best in the marketplace for its human resources by simply being Mayo Clinic. In his account, Dr. Bernard Gersh, currently professor of medicine, found that Mayo Clinic was the best fit for his values, his skills, and his interests as a clinician, educator, and researcher when he first came to the United States in 1978. He reached the same conclusion in 1998 when he was looking for a position after having left Mayo Clinic to serve for seven years as chair of the division of cardiology at another academic medical center. Again he had many options, and again he chose Mayo Clinic. But, he confesses, "It was not an easy decision." The reasons to return were somewhat different from those of two decades earlier. This time, he was struck with how "Mayo really was just powering on—it was stable—at a time when there was angst almost everywhere in academic medicine. Mayo's steady success really attracted me. Another thing that struck me was that people here look happy.... A year after I came back, I remember thinking, 'I'm really glad I came back—I'm really enjoying myself.'"

Dr. Gersh found himself drawn twice to Mayo Clinic in part by the people. He was not speaking of just his physician and scientist colleagues but also the staff employees who help create an environment where people work together in harmony. Robert C. Roesler, chief administrative officer emeritus of Mayo Clinic, titled his memoir *Principles and People: Key Elements of Mayo*. The spirit of the Clinic, he wrote, "... can live only through people, and it is the people of

Mayo ... who have been the most fundamental element of Mayo's success."[1] The reality of labor-intensive service organizations is that their people are their product. As stated in *On Great Service:*

> *Services are performances and people are the performers. From the customers' perspective, the people performing the service are the company.... A careless bank teller is a careless bank. An arrogant waiter is an arrogant restaurant. Service companies need the right people carrying the company's flag in front of customers.... They need to compete for talent market share as hard as they compete for customer market share.*[2]

Having the right people carrying the flag certainly applies to a healthcare organization whose customers—patients—arrive with high expectations. Healthcare services are highly personal and often intrusive. They are primarily delivered by persons of power—doctors, nurses, technicians—to patients at their most vulnerable—lying on exam tables or in hospital beds, wearing immodest "clothing" that depersonalizes them and veils any external signs of their station in society. Further, the patients are often in pain, fearful, or desperate. Finding and retaining the right employees for these ultrasensitive, customer-contact jobs is crucial. "Fortunately, we have been able to attract people who make that commitment to our values and principles and aspire to the mission of what we're doing," comments Dr. Glenn Forbes, CEO of Mayo Clinic Rochester.

Dr. Gersh's account contains themes heard again and again as managers and line employees reflect on their experiences in hiring and being hired at Mayo Clinic's three campuses. In this chapter, we examine how the institution assembles the human forces that compose Mayo Clinic and how that workforce is molded into A-team players who commonly deliver high-level service to people who may be at a low point in their life. The people of Mayo, to use Roesler's term, are the generations of employees whose personal values have harmonized with the values of the organization and whose talents are blended with those of others to serve humanity one patient at a time.

Values First

Carleton Rider, who was the first chief administrative officer in Jacksonville, relates that in the early 1980s the board of governors' "first and foremost" reservation about opening operations in new geographic regions was the prospect of hiring employees from outside the culture of the upper Midwest. He relates, "They couldn't imagine our replicating the quality of the allied health staff—the nonphysician employees—in Rochester." But they need not have worried. What is clear today is that employees' *personal values* must complement the salient values of Mayo Clinic. And these complementary values are not restricted to people living in the upper Midwest.

Hiring the right employees sounds simple when Dr. George Bartley, CEO in Jacksonville, starts to explain the ideal employee: "You identify the people whose core values resonate with our core value— the needs of the patient come first." Because Mayo is known for its values in the medical community, professionals who feel driven by patient care values sense that they are a good match and will often seek out employment at Mayo. "The professional environment for nursing career development is in place here in Rochester, and that word spreads across the country. Thus, we've found a steady flow of nurses who want to be here," says Theresa Elwood, RN, nursing placement coordinator. An employee in Arizona shared, "Actually, I chose Mayo Clinic for the way they feel about their patients. How they give their care, how they go that extra step. They put everything back into the organization so they can come up with more research to find better cures. That is really what drove me here." Dr. Bartley muses:

It is as if Mayo Clinic's values were seeded in the soil at the same time as the foundations of the buildings were laid. We can find those people—we don't have to transplant them from Minnesota. New sprouts come up in Florida. I encounter the Mayo spirit in individuals when I walk the hospital units, when I talk to employees in the hospital and in the Clinic. They've never been to Rochester. Still, Mayo Clinic's values are intuitive to them.

Research finds that high-performing service organizations practice *deliberate hiring*.[3] They take the time necessary to find just the right employees. One manager at Mayo Clinic, for instance, worked solo for nine months until he found the right replacement for an open position in a two-person work group. "Mayo is not an easy place to get hired," says Matthew McElrath, former chair of human resources (HR) for Mayo Clinic Arizona. "We go through so many steps, we have so many people involved in screening and interviewing, even at entry-level jobs, that the people who survive the drawn-out process really want to work here." What he is describing is not a tactic designed to test applicants, but the result of a deliberate and thorough process to hire people who will help sustain the Clinic's core values because these values are their own.

The Clinic's process works as follows: After screenings in HR and again in hiring units, three or four candidates come to campus for a 90-minute behavioral interview conducted by a panel of four to eight or more staff members from the hiring unit. Often, Mayo hires only one of the three or four candidates, and sometimes it hires none. Panel interviews are standard practice across the organization. Even Dr. Denis Cortese was selected as the CEO after members of the board of trustees conducted panel interviews with all the candidates under consideration. Because Dr. Cortese was the CEO in Jacksonville at the time, all the panel members, including the chair of the board of trustees, knew him well. Yet, the panel was not a mere formality. Rather panel members took the time to assess all of the candidates' responses to carefully selected questions. Likewise, Shirley Weis became chief administrative officer after she was one of several internal candidates interviewed by a panel made up of the CEO and several physicians from the board of governors.

In panel interviews, a standard set of behavioral questions is created based on the values one needs to be successful at Mayo Clinic and the specific skills one needs to be successful in the position. For example, a panel might use this question: "Tell me about a time when you had to disagree with your boss to keep a mistake from being made." In telling their story, candidates will inevitably need to portray their personal style of effective confrontation. Candidates may be asked to describe a past project that was particularly successful. Whether candidates use the word "I" or the word "we" is of interest to a Mayo interview panel. During the 90-minute interviews, panel members hear responses to eight to ten questions. Additionally, they are able to probe the candidates by asking for more detail. Candidates have the opportunity to ask questions that are sometimes revealing. For instance, a nurse candidate asked, "How much autonomy will I have in this position?" and thereby revealed that she had failed to recognize the teamwork focus of Mayo. The panel interviews as well as some one-on-one interviews allow team members to develop different perspectives regarding the candidates. At decision time, the panel members ask each other how well the candidates fit the organization and the role to be filled.

When hiring nurses, the behavioral interview in Rochester includes a case scenario. Case scenarios in this context are standardized clinical situations that a nurse might realistically experience at Mayo. The candidates need to think critically and describe how they would respond in the given situation. "We look at the steps they take in processing the scenario," observes Ruth Larsen, RN, nursing placement coordinator.

Physicians and research scientists are not all chosen by this process, but rather one that is equally, if not more, rigorous. Many new physicians are home-grown. As mentioned in Chapter 2, more than 60 percent of Mayo Clinic's physicians have had some of their training at Mayo Clinic. Although some might argue that academic programs risk becoming "inbred" when half of the faculty is trained where they are later employed, the corollary is that the culture that has produced a 100-year brand is sustained to a large extent by hiring physicians whose values fit with Mayo. "By hiring our own trainees, we can pick the best of the best. And they've seen us, and they're going to stay because they want to stay," states Dr. Victor Trastek, CEO of Mayo Clinic Arizona. Those trained in Mayo Clinic's medical school, residency, and/or fellowship programs have experienced "in-depth interviews" extending over a period of one to seven years or more. The training faculty focuses on finding the best matches for open positions in their area. The fit of the physicians clinically and culturally can be accurately ascertained in the training programs. Physicians outside of Mayo's training programs are most often invited to come to Mayo because someone at Mayo knows their work well and believes that they are a fit for the organization. As part of their interview, these candidates will typically present a lecture on their research or clinical interests.

Mayo Clinic's HR leaders are clear that the values match of candidates is the number one requirement for a successful Mayo Clinic employee:

- "Many will focus on skills first, but I say go to values first. Competency is irrelevant if we don't share common values."— Matthew McElrath, former chair of human resources in Arizona
- "It's more challenging and, perhaps, impossible to really modify someone's personal values. You can modify people's behaviors, but the underlying values remain intact."—Michael Estes, chair of human resources in Jacksonville
- "They come to us because of what we stand for, and they work here longer than others because of what they see and produce— our service. They are persons in line with our values and want to serve the patients—that is what makes the work rewarding. We look for the person who wants to be a member of a team, wants to collaborate with others, is open to discussion, and does not view himself or herself as smarter than the next person."—Kenneth Schneider, chair of human resources in Rochester

Mayo Clinic Arizona used a community hospital for its patients for the first 11 years of operation. As Mayo planned the opening of its new hospital in 1998, it faced the daunting task of hiring more than 1,200 new employees. To help the managers find the right candidates, Mayo leaders worked with a consulting firm to develop a screening tool that was based on the core values of Mayo Clinic. "We started by interviewing candidates whose values were matched most closely with the Mayo values that we intended to establish in this new workforce," states Debra Pendergast, RN, chair of the nursing division for Mayo Clinic Arizona. At the time the hospital opened, the Arizona market was experiencing a significant shortage of qualified healthcare workers. "We hired for some highly specialized technical positions where the applicant pool was limited and individuals did not have a good values match on the screening tool," she states. "In some instances we came to regret these exceptions." Overall, however, the hospital leadership team was pleased with its new workforce. Interestingly, compared to all other Mayo Clinic hospitals, the Arizona hospital has consistently earned the highest overall satisfaction scores from patients beginning with the first survey after it opened.

Fitting In or Opting Out

The following story told by Michael Estes illustrates an important attitude in successful employees in almost all organizations—a willingness to fit into an organization that they believe in.

> *A few years ago, we had a phenomenal find for a nursing position. Everyone who interviewed him said, "The competency is there, the attitude is there, this person is so alive, the values are there—it's just like he was born in Mayo, we've got to get him in here." But there was just one problem: he was in the Navy and had tattoos—lots of them. The solution was simple. Let's sit down and talk to him about why appearance is really important, that it's part of the professional demeanor. We had an easy answer—long-sleeved shirts. So, we counseled, "No matter that it is 97 degrees and 98 percent humidity. Please honor us, please honor the patients; wear a long-sleeved shirt." He responded, "That's a no-brainer; if that's what I have to do to become part of this institution, I'll wear gloves!" He has been with us more than five years now. He exceeded every expectation we had.*

Despite the need to fit in, the employees of Mayo Clinic are not clones of one another. The cornerstone values are not understood or applied identically by all of Mayo's more than 42,000 employees. But, in the end, those who stay for rewarding careers make peace with their employer and fellow employees. This sometimes over-looked dimension of developing the right workforce requires managers to recognize that hiring the right staff is just the first step and that employee orientation is just the second. These steps are not enough to mold an employee into a dependable long-term contributor to the organization. Each employee must feel that he or she fits, that he or she belongs comfortably in the organization. Enculturation during the first three to five years of Mayo Clinic employment creates the workforce that earns high satisfaction scores from Mayo patients and career-long employees.

Jane Campion, administrator emeritus with a 37-year career at Saint Marys Hospital and Mayo Clinic, states it well: "Mayo doesn't change for you, and there is some adaptation that you have to do." Dr. Trastek echoes her comment, "You can't buck the Mayo system. So you have to feel fine in playing by Mayo rules, so to speak, or you move on because you can't change the system." The Mayo culture is so strong, so well established, and so well subscribed to by the employees at all levels, that few individuals or groups will succeed as agents of cultural change. Most long-term employees will need to decide to fit in at Mayo. Although some high-level leaders have introduced conspicuous changes, after their leadership terms ended, the organization morphed back into the Mayo norms. The force of the leader's personality changed the appearance of the culture only in the presence of the personality. When Mayo's culture gradually changes, it is not an accommodation to style or preference; change comes only after a compelling, data-driven strategic case has persuaded the board of governors a change should take place.

Jane Campion suggests that many employees come into Mayo Clinic asking, "What can I do to help?" These are people poised to respond in positive ways to the organization. She also describes another group of employees who approach Mayo Clinic from a more neutral perspective—not hostile, but not gung ho. She has seen many of these employees "come and they catch it." All of a sudden they understand the spirit of Mayo Clinic, and they want to be a part of it.

Formal and informal mentoring programs exist throughout the organization. The most enduring is the informal "training" that comes by example or a brief comment like, "We do that this way at Mayo" from coworkers as they go about their work. Informal mentors will explain Mayo culture and various ways a new employee can fit in. Sometimes these communications come over a private lunch or in a hallway conversation where the significance of something the new employee just observed in a staff meeting is explained. Most employees will find a coworker or a supervisor who helps them learn "the Mayo way" in informal conversations during the early years of employment. But the informal programs are not always sufficient. Formal programs have been developed; for instance, in the department of internal medicine in Rochester all new physicians are matched with a mentor who will help explain the Mayo culture and the practice styles in the department. Formal mentorship programs also exist for many new administrators.

The goal of helping people fit in is not to develop a bland, vanilla organization where compliant employees blindly follow and agree. Within the Mayo culture there is room for what Dr. Nina Schwenk, vice chair of the board of governors, describes as "jarring individuals." These people, "Work within the boundary, but they just keep pushing at the boundary." Working in groups such as the clinical practice committee, or the executive board, or the board of governors, the challengers do help drive incremental change in the organization's culture. Dr. Schwenk explains, "For example, at Mayo, we've traditionally felt that one way to honor the professionalism of physicians was to give them a lot of independence in their clinical decision making. We were not inclined to tell highly trained physicians how to care for their patients." She clearly recalls the board of governors' retreat when a surgeon colleague challenged that tradition, which had become at least for some an untouchable part of Mayo's culture.

The surgeon, Dr. Bernard Morrey, past chair of the department of orthopedic surgery at Mayo Clinic and past president of the American Academy of Orthopaedic Surgeons, had been looking at the joint-replacement practice in his department. For hip or knee replacement for a given patient, one of a variety of different prosthetic joints could be implanted depending on the judgment of the surgeon; different surgeons had their personal favorites. He asked his colleagues if it made sense that any one of seven different choices would be in the best interests of the patient. With this question, he prompted both the department of orthopedics and the board of governors to think more rigorously about variation in care that seemed based on physician preference rather than on evidence-based best practice.

During her tenure on several high-level committees, Dr. Schwenk has seen individuals like Dr. Morrey at work: "They don't allow you to stay in your comfort zone. They, rather, make you bump up against your personal or organizational boundaries and challenge the assumptions that have created the boundaries." In jarring the organization, they bring great value. "This is what it takes to stretch thinking and vision and to move to transformational change and innovation. It requires that the person doing the 'jarring' is trusted and respected, so you allow yourself to be pushed to consider options that would otherwise be rejected offhand." Leaders at Mayo Clinic typically want some of these loyal rebels on strategic committees and work groups that offer a forum for their challenging minds. Success does not flourish in organizations where visionary employees say, "Yes, madam," while thinking, "Whatever you say." Yet, some of these jarring individuals do leave in frustration if they feel important change does not occur or does not occur fast enough.

To be sure, working at Mayo Clinic includes some irritants. Some of the physicians and scientists find the trip policy too confining as it offers all of them the same number of trip days per year (18), which they use for professional meeting attendance or presentation of a paper. Specifically, some personnel who are well known and in high demand as visiting professors and featured conference speakers sense that their work helps Mayo retain its reputation of leadership more than that of professionals who use the days primarily for attending meetings. Others are frustrated by the rules that restrict information on business cards. Others dislike the dress code. "You have to understand the institution, you have to understand the rules, and if you can, live by them. And if you can't, you're going to leave," Dr. Gersh comments. He adds, "And you have to get along with your fellow men or women—and not just physicians. Some people are very authoritarian, others yell and scream, and yet others want to do things only their way. They shouldn't stay."

In addition, Jane Campion notes, "There's the group of people who don't ever catch it and find Mayo very difficult. And most of the time they leave, which is fine—we sincerely wish them well. Most will find a place where they do fit." In spite of Mayo's best efforts at recruitment, screening, and interviewing, the values of new employees comfortably match up with the organization only about 80 percent of the time. "On a really good day, you get 90 percent," Michael Estes adds.

Most of the time, individuals uncomfortable with the values and the culture choose to leave the Clinic within the first few years. Clinic employees who stay for five years typically remain for the duration of their careers, unless family needs pull them away. In fact, about two-thirds of voluntary terminations indicate that they would like to work at Mayo again. For instance, an employee at Mayo's St. Luke's Hospital in Jacksonville wrote, "I did not want to leave without letting 'the higher-ups' know how much I regret having to leave and how much I have enjoyed my time here at St. Luke's. I count myself very, very lucky indeed to have been affiliated with the Mayo system." Matthew McElrath notes, "Only a third of the turnover is really dissatisfaction with working at Mayo. Two-thirds of the turnover are people who want to stay at Mayo but can't because a spouse is transferred or for some other similar reason out of their control."

A small number of the hires across all three campuses never align with the values, yet they don't leave. These individuals are usually—but not always—managed out of the organization. As one Mayo leader explains, "We must make sure that we clearly state what it is that we are about and then live up to that because ours are lofty aspirations and ideas. We have to be persistent and consistent—we have to walk the talk." Estes says, "We invite people to leave who are not aligned—those whose values conflict with those that we espouse. No matter how much good work and discipline on the front end, there are going to be mismatches, and if you don't manage those mismatches in a respectful yet disciplined way, then you will eventually dilute the culture and dilute the value set."

For the values to ring true, they must apply throughout the organization—to the allied health staff, nurses, lab techs, secretaries, accountants, physicians, and administrators. However, some leaders interviewed suggest that managers of the allied health staff have been the most committed in managing values alignment, particularly in addressing behaviors that violate a code of mutual respect. Since the early 1990s, Mayo Clinic has focused on matters of mutual respect as part of an initiative to hire and retain a diverse workforce. Dr. Morie Gertz, chair of the personnel committee in Rochester, emphasizes that all but a few physicians exhibit reliable, exemplary behavior to all the members of their team. However, he notes, some inappropriate physician behavior has been tolerated for many years. But for these few outliers, he suggests that several factors are creating a vigorous mandate for mutual respect, collegiality, and even-tempered behavior even in times of stress. First, allied health staff members are increasingly unwilling to accept behaviors they consider to be abusive. Second, it is increasingly clear to doctors that the eyes and ears and ideas and thoughts of every member of the team are needed to keep mistakes from happening. Third, Mayo's recently initiated biennial staff satisfaction surveys alert physician chairs of departments and divisions when the allied health staff and/or the physician staff feel that problem behaviors are not being addressed. It is hard to pretend there is not problem in the face of hard data.

The personnel committees on all three campuses have become more aggressive in addressing the issue of physicians who are not living the Mayo values or exhibiting respectful, collegial behavior to all team members. Some physicians have been suspended without pay or terminated. Shirley Weis, chief administrative officer of Mayo Clinic, hopes to increase accountability on the administrative team as well: "One of the things I will be working on with the team is to be able to look each other in the eye and provide constructive feedback. If something is not quite where it should be, we need to have frank, open conversations. I don't think that is a strength that we have uniformly in the organization."

As a sign of the change underway, a number of clinical departments and divisions in Rochester have voluntarily chosen to include 360-degree feedback in physician performance reviews; the 360-degree review is standard throughout the allied health staff. Input is solicited from the allied health staff—nurses, desk attendants, secretaries—as well as physician peers. All employees, including physicians, are evaluated on five principles derived from the Clinic's core values:

1. Continuously improves processes and services that support patient care, education, and research.
2. Fosters mutual respect and supports Mayo's commitment to diversity.
3. Fosters teamwork, personal responsibility, integrity, innovation, trust, and communication.
4. Adheres to high standards of personal and professional conduct.
5. Maintains and enhances professional/competency skills.

Most of the employees at Mayo Clinic find a comfortable fit with their employer. As noted in Chapter 5, the voluntary turnover rate among physicians is about 2.5 percent a year across the three campuses. In Rochester, the voluntary turnover rate among the non-physician employees is about 5 percent. In Jacksonville and Arizona, the annual turnover in allied health staff is about twice that of Rochester; however, this turnover needs to be understood in the context of the local markets. A 10 percent turnover rate for Mayo Clinic in Jacksonville is almost 300 percent better than that of the rest of the service industry in north Florida. Michael Estes comments, "So while we would love to leverage that number down even further, we know that what we are doing is largely working as we are three times better than the local organizations that look like us."

Hiring for Talent

Mayo Clinic needs both the right values and highly competent employees. High-performing organizations cannot tolerate employees who lack the talent for the positions they occupy. "First of all, they have to be excellent physicians—we have to know that clinically they will be superb. Excellent clinical care is the base on which Mayo Clinic exists," says Dr. Trastek. "They can be great researchers and educators, but if they aren't good doctors, then it isn't going to work. Or if surgeons aren't remarkably skillful, it isn't going to work. They've got to be excellent physicians and know how to care for people. Physicians must be smart on their diagnoses. That is all a given."

"We've been fortunate to have a strong applicant pool for our nursing positions in Rochester, so we've been able to screen for nurses who have been academically strong—graduated with high grade-point averages from good schools," says Ruth Larsen, RN, nursing placement coordinator. "Of course, we also are very interested in the values with special emphasis on compassion and teamwork—the values we assess in interviews." Doreen Frusti, RN, chair of the nursing department in Rochester, emphasizes that the standards for the nurses hired have been maintained even as nursing shortages have come and gone over the years. "We have very high expectations for nurses." She explains that nurses are hired and budgets allocated with the long-term view. "We invest our dollars in keeping enough staff and giving them the tools to take care of their patients as nurses are taught rather than using financial resources for sign-on bonuses to hire new nurses. We are fortunate to have the support of leaders to practice the profession of nursing with the ideals articulated in most academic training programs," she concludes. Ruth Larsen summarizes, "As nurses care for patients, the patients compliment staff and speak about it to their friends at home. These conversations then get to other nurses who decide they want to come to Mayo to work. It is a cycle that works."

Although panel interviews serve well in identifying the values of candidates, they also help identify competencies. Further, panel interviews can be learning experiences for the hiring team. Nan Sawyer, vice chair of administration in Rochester, emphasizes that "the panel process is unpredictable"—it is not a mere formality because the outcome has not been determined. She and her team were choosing from several internal candidates for an important leadership position. "Our final choice would not have been the leading candidate if we had just looked at the résumé. We identified one of the key competencies for a position as we were discussing what we had heard in several panel interviews. Colleagues helped crystallize what we needed out of the individual that you can't get out of the job description or résumé."

Any company that seeks long-term value from its employees must consider not only what each employee is at the time of hire but also what that employee can become. Although high competencies are expected of new employees at Mayo Clinic, these employees must also demonstrate the capacity to be good learners on the job. Nowhere is this more important than with physicians, given rapidly changing medical knowledge and the ongoing learning opportunity afforded Mayo clinicians as their notes, observations, diagnoses, and outcomes are reviewed by colleagues in the common medical record. Changes in medicine ripple through the organization, requiring most employees to master new skills over time.

"There's a sense in the employment market that you need to be a cut above to work at Mayo Clinic, and that's good in one sense—good candidates self-select. But it's bad in another sense because others that Mayo wants to hire self-select out of applying," comments Kenneth Schneider. The reputation for employees who are a cut above also fails to recognize the need for thousands of employees whose competence comes from narrow training or general knowledge and interpersonal skills. Like almost every other large organization, Mayo has thousands of jobs that don't require a college degree with honors, or even a college degree. The face of Mayo Clinic is, in part, the hundreds of staff at check-in and registration desks across the organization. A college degree is not required for most of these positions, but these individuals do need strong, values-based interpersonal and problem-solving skills. Most technicians in the testing laboratories will have at least an associate's or bachelor's degree and typically will become very proficient in a small number of procedures. These technicians must be trainable and reliable because they must precisely follow procedural protocols—lives depend on it.

For more than a century, Mayo Clinic has been training technical staff to meet the needs of the practice. Today much of the responsibility is carried by Mayo Clinic's School of Health Sciences with its programs that create the skills and proficiencies in many technical areas ranging from cytogenetic technologists and radiation therapists to nurse anesthetists. Overall, about 60 percent of the graduates of these programs sign on as Mayo Clinic employees. Dr. Nina Schwenk speaks of the role that this school plays for Mayo: "Here's where we grow our own, and then we pick the ones that not only do well but fit the culture. The ones who do well and don't fit the culture—they leave. The ones who are nice but don't do technically well—sometimes we actually hire those individuals and we train them some more. I think we have a harder time making people [be] nice than we do making people technically better."

Mayo Clinic also invests significantly in in-service training programs. Many are a single session with several hours of education; others might extend over a few days. These programs are run by HR as well as numerous other departments, such as nursing, finance, radiology, safety, information technology, and clinical laboratory. "These educational programs help develop and update the skilled workforce or reinforce the values needed to ensure Mayo Clinic's continued success," notes Patricia Handler Spratte, section head, human resources education and development in Rochester. The courses are aligned with the strategic and operational plans for the organization. Across the three campuses, thousands of courses are offered with more than 417,000 employee registrations in 2006—on average, around nine registrations per employee. A sampling shows general, clinical, and narrowly focused technical courses:

- Leading Change: Gaining Trust and Inspiring Confidence
- Skills for Handling Challenging Conversations
- Quality Academy: TEAMS Training and Lean Thinking
- Answering Tough Questions about Salary—The Manager's Role
- A Manager's Introduction to Business Law
- Mayo Tours—Glass Blower and Machine Shop
- Myths and Facts about Cancer Causing Agents

- Effective Use of Interpreters
- Goal Setting for Personal and Professional Growth
- HIPAA Privacy and Security Training
- Workplace Violence Module
- Mutual Respect/Sexual Harassment

The hundreds of courses offered through HR have two primary objectives: The first is to enhance the performance of individuals in their current positions be they administrators, managers, or line employees. Those in frontline positions can learn, for instance, how to listen empathetically to a patient. Managers can learn about managing performance, delegating, and skills for effective team leadership. The second objective is career development for existing employees who, for instance, might aspire to a management position, want to run more effective committees, or hope to find a new challenge outside of their current work unit. Thousands of employees enroll each year in programs to increase their efficiency with computer software, including Mayo's clinical systems.

Another important part of developing the talents and careers of employees is the professional development assistance program. By providing tuition support, Mayo Clinic encourages employees to take advantage of external educational opportunities that provide professional development for their current position or another position within Mayo. More than 3,500 employees participate in this program each year as they pursue certification or undergraduate and graduate degrees.

Niche Picking

In 2006, the 96-year-old Dr. Hugh Butt reflected on his three-month experience as the first-assistant to Dr. William J. Mayo in 1936. Dr. Butt took special care to communicate the spirit of paternalistic benevolence that Dr. Will expressed for the employees of Mayo Clinic. "'We are family,' Dr. Will said. 'We work as a family here, and doctors don't have to worry about nurses' salaries or their

salaries; they are satisfied to be here in this wonderful institution.'"
The family metaphor is still expressed in the twenty-first century.
Mayo Clinic culture views employees in human terms rather
than as an economic asset or a cog in a machine or an expense line
in the budget. This organization tries to find a position and an
environment—a niche—where unique individuals feel comfortable
and can genuinely contribute.

Dr. Robert Waller, retired CEO of Mayo Clinic, recalls "one of
the two worst days of my Mayo Clinic career." This, he recounts,
was the day when a Mayo Clinic leader called two long-term
employees into his office and told them they were fired. Further, he
had arranged for security officers to escort them to their offices to
retrieve personal items. And he ordered that they could not return
to campus again. This is the antithesis of the "Mayo family"
approach that has built a high performing and loyal base of thousands of employees. (And some months later the leader who insti-
gated the firings also moved on.)

Dr. Bernard Gersh says, "One of the strengths of the Clinic is that
there is a niche for almost everyone. I don't think there is such a
thing as a set of criteria that will determine if you're a successful
Mayo Clinic physician." His own contributions have been in several
areas: clinical care of cardiology patients, teaching and developing
the academic talents of junior faculty while publishing more than
700 papers, and creating international connections and visibility for
the Clinic. Dr. Gersh notes that his colleague, Dr. Gerald Gau, and
many others like him have contributed equally to the division of
cardiology as respected clinicians focused primarily on patient care.
Dr. Robert Frye's career has combined clinical care, research, academic
administration, and professional association leadership. He served as
chair of the division of cardiology in Rochester, then president of
the American College of Cardiology, and retired after a term as chair
of the department of medicine in Rochester. But his career did not
reach deeply into Clinic administration; for instance, he never served
on the board of governors. Similar to Dr. Frye, Dr. Hugh Smith
established a reputation as a scholar and a clinician before moving
into administrative positions. He followed Dr. Frye as chair of the

division of cardiology in Rochester, but then his career moved into enterprise strategy and administration. He retired as chair of the Rochester board of governors. All these individuals started from the same point—a staff cardiologist.

Although most employees find on their own where they fit in the organization, Mayo has some employees who, over time, become the proverbial "square peg" that does not fit in a round hole. Here's where compassionate management—the family touch—is evidenced, as the first impulse at the Clinic is for managers to help the employee find a square hole they can comfortably fit into. Several high-level administrators shared stories of valued employees who no longer fit the positions they occupied. Sometimes it was a case of burnout in persons with leadership or management positions. Other times, the demands of the job changed so much that an employee's skills no longer matched up with the need. In other cases, high-performing employees in a staff position were rewarded with a promotion into management only to learn that the demands of the position did not fit their skills or personality.

Because Mayo Clinic is a large organization, genuine opportunities—not make-work—can be found in many cases. "The Mayo way" expects administrative supervisors to look at the strengths of the individual rather than at the deficiencies. Several detail-oriented managers who no longer fit as generalist leaders of other managers have found rewarding careers focusing on management of complex projects where attention to detail is a virtue. Others without the interpersonal skills necessary to work as team leaders have found renewal in positions that capitalize on their keen analytical skills. Because internal transfers are so common throughout the Clinic even in positions of power such as the department chairs or members of the board of governors, these changes are typically handled in a business-as-usual manner rather than as a dramatic public event. In most cases, Mayo helps the employees who are failing or underperforming find a niche that better fits who they are and the capabilities they offer.

Other administrative examples of fitting tasks to the person include individuals who are doing excellent work on a large portion of their administrative tasks but have a potentially "fatal" weakness in one area. For instance, this might be a leader who is visionary, inspirational, and respected by those supervised but does not perform well in financial management or timely performance of detailed administrative tasks. In this case, the Clinic might assign an accountant or an associate administrator to this person, perhaps on a part-time basis to ensure optimal management. Furthermore, Mayo's leaders recognize that some management positions may, in fact, be too big for even an outstanding administrator. By supplementing or supporting what might be seen as a flaw or a weakness, Mayo is able to retain valued employees with significant talents.

Employees typically think of themselves as employees of Mayo Clinic rather than of a department, division, or work unit. In other healthcare institutions, employees might say, "I work for the cath lab" or radiology, human resources, or security. But when asked where they work, most Mayo employees will just say, "Mayo Clinic." True, this is a name brand that most Americans recognize, but the primary identification with the organization suggests that employees are attached to something larger than their current tasks. The unspoken contract is the expectation that employees will be treated fairly and responsibly by an organization in which they believe and in which they fit.

Circle of Loyalty

Mayo Clinic, the employer, is the important entity. Carol Hughes worked as a medical secretary in radiology for five years for Mayo Clinic Arizona before moving to southern California. In 2001 she decided to return to Phoenix, and she applied to return to Mayo Clinic. "I told myself that Mayo Clinic was the only place that I would apply. It's the only place that I would work in Phoenix," she recalls. She started work at Mayo just seven days after arriving back in town. Loyalty like this is earned by employers. It cannot be bought. Employees are loyal to an organization when they believe the organization is loyal to them. A short case study from Mayo Clinic in Jacksonville illustrates this "circle of loyalty."

A new Mayo Clinic hospital opened on the Jacksonville campus in April 2008. Previously, Mayo had owned and operated St. Luke's Hospital located nine miles away from its Clinic campus. St. Luke's was operated by Mayo as a community hospital for community physicians in addition to meeting the hospital needs of the Mayo Clinic practice. The new hospital on the campus is 100 beds smaller and available only to Mayo Clinic physicians and their patients. By translating 100 fewer beds into the full-time equivalent (FTE) employees needed to staff them, the Clinic determined that it would need between 350 and 400 fewer FTEs—approximately 500 fewer employees—to staff the new hospital.

Looking forward to the move date in April 2008, Mayo leaders needed to put a strategy in place that would allow the institution to simultaneously balance what might be perceived as competing or contradictory priorities: first, effectively execute a staff reduction initiative and achieve new targeted staffing levels and, second, sustain staff retention and commitment so that they had both the right number and mix of employees to staff the new hospital while maintaining Mayo's model of care and high patient care standards. Throughout the process, Mayo's leaders were also committed to helping ensure that St. Vincent's Hospital, the new owners of St. Luke's, also had sufficient staff to provide safe and effective care for all of the community patients remaining at St. Luke's.

In the summer of 2006, Mayo's leadership moved boldly. In all-employee Town Hall meetings, in the weekly employee newsletter, and on the Mayo Clinic intranet, leadership made a commitment that, "All St. Luke's current employees who wished to remain with Mayo, and who remained in good standing through the transition period, would have a comparable position on the new integrated clinic and hospital campus." This was a calculated risk, for 500 fewer employees would be needed. But in the eyes of Mayo leadership, the perceived downside risk of this strategy was far overshadowed by the upside benefit.

Following its promise to existing hospital employees in 2006 that they would be able to maintain their employment, Mayo made three strategic moves to help meet the goal of transitioning to the new hospital with significantly fewer employees while still being fully staffed on opening day and, most importantly, *without laying off a single employee*. First, a new employee category, St. Luke's Hospital 2008 (SLH08), was created; persons hired into these positions knew at the time of hire that when ownership changed in 2008 they would have a comparable position with St. Luke's Hospital, if they remained in good standing. This allowed Mayo to continue to hire employees it needed up through the transition date. The strategy also allowed employees in the SLH08 category to apply for internal transfers to Mayo when positions were open. Second, a category of limited tenure employees was created to cover the transition—these positions typically offered 24 to 36 months of employment and were designed to disappear between three and six months after the transition to the new hospital. Third, Mayo worked with a temporary staffing firm to supply some additional employees in nonclinical positions. This background work was completed in late 2005, and the strategy was ready for implementation.

In 2007, Mayo went through the first round of staffing positions in the Mayo Clinic Hospital. Of those employees who had been promised in the summer of 2006 that Mayo would guarantee them employment when the new hospital opened, more than 98 percent indicated that they wanted to remain with Mayo. According to Michael Estes, chair for the division of human resources, "A very small handful of employees—less than 50—said either 'I want to stay on the St. Luke's campus because it is closer to home,' or, 'I'm willing to take my chances on a different Mayo position versus the one that you have talked to me about.'"

Mayo needed all the employees who chose to stay on as Mayo staff, plus a few more, by the time the hospital opened. Both Estes and Jacksonville chief administrative officer Robert Brigham believe that this favorable result occurred because Mayo Clinic, in keeping with its values, made the first move to demonstrate loyalty to employees. They further point out that this should not be taken as an indictment of St. Vincent's as an employer—the SLH08 employees were in place to ensure the smooth transition. St. Vincent's and Mayo worked closely together for more than three years to plan the transition that has been a cordial win-win for both institutions.

Lessons for Managers

Mayo Clinic's values pervade its selection of employees, the assessment of their performance, and their positioning and development. Because high levels of technical proficiency are needed in every aspect of operations from clinical care to financial management to information systems to blood banking to building design to appointment scheduling, Mayo must also insist that all employees possess the technical skills that are required in their roles.

Lesson 1: Values first.   Mayo Clinic's long record as a high-performing clinical and business enterprise is a tribute to its employees. Healthcare organizations are among the most complex service operations in part because the service is so personal and customized. Patients are unique. And the employees who create these personalized and unique services—on the fly—have some of the most emotionally charged and intellectually challenging jobs in our economy. Healthcare is labor-intensive in the extreme. The essential element underlying the unique, personal services performed is the value set from which the spontaneous service flows; kindness and humanely sensitive acts come more reliably from underlying values than from training sessions. Values that individuals bring into adulthood usually change little over time—only major interventions will affect them. Mayo Clinic, like other high-performing service organizations, takes particular care in identifying people's values before they are hired. When hiring mistakes are made—as they sometimes are at Mayo Clinic—the organization must deal with values dissonance, for it is a poison in the culture.

Although other services are not as intimate as healthcare, most organizations would benefit from Mayo's values-first approach to employment. Kindness and humanely sensitive acts pay rich, brand-building dividends for other types of labor-intensive, interactive services: for example, helping a large-sized person find just the right apparel while preserving the customer's dignity; devoting extra effort to assisting a couple on a tight budget find an appealing, affordable home for their growing family; not giving up in helping a storm-stranded airline passenger book an alternative route home; patiently and personably answering an elderly caller's elementary questions to the call center line. Services are performances, and the personal values of the performers matter greatly—inside or outside of healthcare.

Lesson 2: Create a "cycle of success."   Mayo Clinic is slow to dispose of its employees. Mayo Clinic in Jacksonville went to extraordinary lengths to move from an existing hospital to a new, smaller facility that needed approximately 500 fewer employees without terminating even one employee who was in good standing. This is a statement about Mayo Clinic as an employer that will not be forgotten by the people affected.

Mayo is a relational employer. It hires people for careers, rather than for jobs. It works unusually hard to identify the right employees with the requisite values, talents, and potential for growth and then continues to work hard to effect a good fit between what the individual employee offers and what the Clinic needs. When a member of the allied health staff falls short in skills needed for a position, the typical impulse of a Mayo Clinic manager is to help the employee find a better match inside the organization. All employees represent an investment of thousands of dollars of recruiting and training costs. Employees who have found that they fit well in the Mayo culture are resources that can often be reinvested in other more promising positions in the organization. This helps explain Mayo's low employee turnover rates as well as the large number of employees who choose to make a career at Mayo Clinic.

Mayo is willing to invest significant time, talent, and money in selecting and developing employees, in part, because its leadership assumes that employees will stay throughout their careers. Of course some do not stay, but the assumption prevails and influences the overall approach to employee investment. The "career" assumption is critical—and unusual—and managers outside of Mayo should consider its applicability to their organizations. Many service organization managers consider high employee turnover as a given and try to minimize their upfront investment in people who will be soon departing—creating what Schlesinger and Heskett call the "cycle of failure."[4] Insufficient investment in employees leaves them unprepared to perform well in their work, and they then quit or are fired. The large percentage of employees leaving an organization discourages more investment. Because service quality and customer retention suffer as a result of the many inexperienced and poorly prepared employees, revenues decline, thus further reducing resources available to invest in employees' success.[5]

Mayo invests in a "cycle of success," as do other high-performance service organizations. The Clinic makes a substantial *upfront* investment to increase its chances of finding people who will fit its culture, be successful, and want to stay for a long time. The Clinic and its patients both benefit from the long-term, loyal staff members who know how to create the Mayo Clinic experience.[6]

Lesson 3: Cast a Broadway show.   The first rule of strategy execution in service organizations is to hire excellent people. Mayo's patience in seeking excellent people is instructive. Yes, it can be maddening inside the Clinic when there are openings to fill. And it can frustrate worthy candidates. Yet, in the end, the Clinic's time-consuming, collaborative hiring process is a cornerstone of its enduring success, for Mayo Clinic cannot be Mayo Clinic without superb people. Its core value/core strategy of team medicine becomes ineffective unless there are excellent people to form the team. The late Ron Zemke, a pioneering service quality writer and speaker, used to advise service company executives to think of hiring as something akin to casting a Broadway show. It needs to be done slowly.[7] Mayo Clinic is the poster child for "Broadway show" hiring. The interview panel process is equivalent to auditioning before a casting group. That successful candidates typically must pass muster through several screening phases is similar to the call-back system used in casting theatrical or other entertainment productions.

Organizations are often under pressure to lower hiring standards. Staff departures unexpectedly create openings to be filled. Customer demand exceeds forecasts resulting in an urgent need to add staff. Labor-pool shortages exist for certain types of positions. Declining profit margins focus attention on reining in salary and wage costs. Regardless of these forces, Mayo Clinic has generally been successfully stubborn in not lowering its hiring standards. In our research, for example, registered nurses expressed surprise at the rigorous interview process they underwent to be hired at Mayo, given the acute nursing shortage. As one registered nurse stated: "Mayo is very particular about whom they hire. With the nursing shortage, I figured with 17 years of experience, I would just walk in the door. There were three people throwing questions at me in the interview. Not everyone who applies for a nursing job here gets it, and that's incredible."[8]

Summary

An investment in employees is an investment in success for both the individual and the organization. In service companies, the service is a performance, and the employees are the performers. As the Mayo Clinic example shows, hiring the right people is the first rule; supporting and rewarding them is its corollary. Some basic criteria for evaluating potential employees include:

- Personal values complement the company's foundational values.
- Attitude is amenable—has willingness to fit into the organization as it is but has the courage to challenge status quo if necessary.
- Is talented in professional skills and in teamwork.
- Has potential to grow and develop expertise beyond present level.
- Is interested in a career, not just a job.
- Is loyal to employer.

Through deliberate hiring based on a rigorous screening process, interviewers find excellent people who will bring the production to life.

NOTES

1. Robert C. Roesler, *Principles and People: Key Elements of Mayo* (Rochester, MN: Mayo Foundation, 1984), p. 7.
2. Leonard Berry, *On Great Service: A Framework for Action* (New York: The Free Press, 1995), p. 167.
3. Leonard Berry, *Discovering the Soul of Service: Nine Drivers of Sustainable Business Success* (New York: The Free Press, 1999), p. 84.
4. Leonard A. Schlesinger and James L. Heskett, "Breaking the Cycle of Failure in Service," *Sloan Management Review*, Spring 1991, pp. 17–28; also see James L. Heskett, W. Earl Sasser, Jr., and Leonard A. Schlesinger, *The Service Profit Chain* (New York: The Free Press, 1997).
5. Berry, *Discovering the Soul of Service*, p. 133.
6. For an excellent discussion of how high-performance service firms invest in employee performance, see Sybil Stershic, *Taking Care of the People Who Matter Most: A Guide to Employee-Customer Care* (Rochester, NY: WME Books, 2007).
7. Ron Zemke, "World-Class Customer Service," *Boardroom Reports*, December 15, 1992, p. 1; also see Dan J. Sanders, *Built to Serve* (New York: McGraw-Hill, 2008), Chapter 4.
8. Leonard L. Berry, "The Collaborative Organization: Leadership Lessons from Mayo Clinic," *Organizational Dynamics*, No. 3, Fall 2004, p. 231.

CHAPTER 7

ORCHESTRATING THE CLUES OF QUALITY

*M*ary Ann Morris, who manages general services and Mayo Clinic volunteer programs at Mayo Rochester, likes to tell a story about her early days at the Clinic. She was working in a laboratory—a job that required her to wear a white uniform and white shoes. And after a frantic morning getting her two small children to school, she arrived at work to find her supervisor staring at her shoes. The supervisor had noticed that the laces were dirty where they threaded through the eyelets of the shoes and asked Morris to clean them. Offended, Morris said that she worked in a laboratory, not with patients, so why should it matter? Her supervisor replied that Morris had contact with patients in ways she didn't recognize— going out on the street wearing her Mayo name tag, for instance, or passing patients and their families as she walked through the halls—and that she couldn't represent Mayo Clinic with dirty shoelaces. "Though I was initially offended, I realized over time [that] everything I do, down to my shoelaces, represents my commitment to our patients and visitors.... I still use the dirty shoelace story to set the standard for the service level I aspire to for myself and my co-workers."[1]

A dirty shoelace hardly seems meaningful in the high-stakes context of caring for ill people. However, a shoelace is something a patient or anxious family member can see, a small but tangible piece of evidence about an organization and the intangible, technically complex medical services it offers. In effect, the shoelace plays a surrogate role, helping to tell a service organization's story. The shoelace is a clue about quality, one of many Mayo Clinic uses to tell its story cohesively, distinctively, and compellingly. The Clinic's clue management is exemplary, melding intuition and purposefulness in the quest to create a superior experience for patients. This chapter explains how Mayo orchestrates clues about quality—down to the shoelaces—based on the concept of managing clues to create the customers' service experience.

Customers Are Detectives

Customers always have some kind of experience when they interact with an organization. An experience is inherent; a positive experience is not. In interacting with organizations, customers consciously and unconsciously filter clues embedded in the experience and organize them into a set of impressions, some rational and others more emotional. Anything perceived or sensed—or conspicuous in its absence—is an experience clue. If customers can see, smell, hear, or taste it, it is a clue. A doctor who enters an exam room to meet a seated patient and remains standing while questioning the patient is likely to convey a different set of clues than a doctor who immediately sits down and interacts with the patient at eye level. Specific clues carry messages, and the clues and messages converge to create the customers' service experience that influences customers' feelings. What customers feel while the experience is occurring becomes part of that experience. For example, does a service experience make customers feel safe, confident, efficient, smart, respected, or worthy, or does it have the opposite effects? In the case of the standing doctor, patients are unlikely to feel especially confident, respected, or worthy. These negative feelings may be accentuated if the doctor remains close to the door, signaling even more directly the intention of making a quick exit.

In selecting and using services, customers see more and process more information than managers and service providers often realize. Customers act like "detectives" in the way they process and organize experience clues into a set of impressions that evoke feelings.

They process these clues when deciding whether or not to buy a service and in evaluating it while they are receiving it and afterwards. The more important, variable, complex, and personal the service, the more alert and clue-sensitive customers are likely to be. Consumption creates risk, and customers can be expected to do more detective work in conditions of elevated risk.[2]

Healthcare services are high risk, embodying importance, variability (resulting from labor and skill intensity of the services), complexity, and personalization. Patients' quality of life and life itself are at stake in healthcare, and the management of experience clues is particularly important to healthcare organizations. Yet, many other types of services also have elevated risk characteristics, thus extending the relevance of clue management principles across the service sector.

Three Types of Clues

Experience clues tell a service story in the most powerful way, and successful organizations noted for distinctive service tell their stories effectively through systematic clue management. Clues fall into three categories: functional clues, mechanic clues, and humanic clues. The phrases "mechanic clues" and "humanic clues" were coined by Lewis Carbone and Stephen Haeckel in a seminal article published in 1994. The "functional clues" terminology was added in later writings.[3]

Functional clues concern the technical quality of the service, that is, its reliability and functionality. Anything that influences customers' impressions of technical quality—by its presence or absence—is a functional clue. *Mechanic clues* come from inanimate objects and include sights, smells, sounds, tastes, and textures. Facilities, equipment, furniture, displays, lighting, and other sensory clues offer a visual presentation of the service, communicating without words. *Humanic clues* come from the behavior and appearance of service providers, for example, their verbal and body language, tone of voice, level of enthusiasm, and appropriateness of dress.[4]

While functional clues primarily concern the "what" of the service experience, mechanic and humanic clues primarily concern the "how." A service can be functional and still create negative feelings in customers because of how it is delivered. Consider this hypothetical situation of a patient going to a physician for a second opinion. The first physician diagnosed the patient's medical problem and concluded that surgery would be necessary. The second physician confirmed both the diagnosis and the recommended surgery. Both physicians provided a functionally correct service. However, they behaved quite differently. The first doctor seemed aloof and never referred to the patient by her name. In contrast, the second doctor was friendly, used the patient's name, and demonstrated compassion. The patient's perceptions (impressions) and feelings about the two experiences differed even though the functional clues were similar.

Clue Roles

Functional, mechanic, and humanic clues play specific roles in creating customers' service experiences. As Exhibit 7-1 indicates, functional clues primarily influence customers' rational perceptions of

Exhibit 7-1
Clue Influences on Customer Perceptions of the Experience

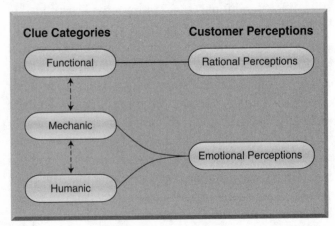

the experience, while mechanic and humanic clues influence emotional perceptions. Well-managed service organizations invest in excelling in all three clue categories, managing the emotional components of the service experience as rigorously as they do the functional components. The clue categories are viewed as synergistic rather than additive; the sum of the experience they create when presented cohesively is greater than the sum of the parts acting independently. The leaders of organizations effectively practicing clue management may not have heard of the concept of "managing clues" but they intuitively understand it—as Drs. Will and Charlie Mayo and Dr. Henry Plummer clearly did. It is a credit to Mayo Clinic's early leaders and many who followed that the Clinic has focused so much attention and investment in excelling in the "how" of service delivery and not just the "what."

Functional Clues: Instilling Confidence by Demonstrating Competence

Customers buy solutions to the problems that bring them to the market. They buy capability to communicate with others, not telephone service; capability to travel long distances, not an airline ticket. In healthcare, patients buy mobility and chronic pain relief, not knee surgery.

The solutions customers buy depend on functionality. In delivering quality service, nothing trumps performing the promised service correctly. Published research has consistently documented reliability as the single most important dimension for meeting customers' service expectations.[5] In an award-winning study on why customers changed from one service company to another, Susan M. Keaveney found that 44 percent of the customers surveyed switched (in part or solely) because of a core service failure, that is, a botched service performance. Core service failure was mentioned more than any other reason for switching to another provider.[6]

The primary role of functional clues is to strengthen a customer's (or prospective customer's) confidence in the reliability of service performance. Is this organization—or this service provider—competent?

Are the necessary skills and knowledge to perform the service well in place? Functional clues need to effectively address these questions. Because of their intangible nature, services are generally more difficult for customers to evaluate than goods. Many services, like healthcare, are technically complex, and customers naturally look for clues to help them assess functionality. Intangibility coupled with complexity encourage customers' "clue-alertness," which is further accentuated by the importance, variability, and intimacy of a service.

Mayo Clinic's core values and strategies of patient-first, collaborative, destination medicine have clearly contributed to its presentation of strong functional clues. The team-service model gives patients the sense that the Clinic is coordinating resources to provide the best possible care. The "union of forces" serves as a powerful functional clue. The systems and infrastructure investments required to provide the efficient, time-saving integrated medical care necessary to practice destination medicine also communicate the Clinic's functionality to patients and accompanying family members. Mayo's integrated, cumulative, electronic medical records reassure patients as this comment from a patient interview illustrates: "On my last visit, the doctor pulled up all my test scores from the past five years on a computer and showed me the trends and we discussed what to do. I thought that was excellent."[7]

Seriously ill patients are likely to be extra vigilant in sensing functional clues. The following story, provided by a Mayo Clinic cancer patient from a medium-sized city in the southeastern United States (we call him Don), reveals the crucial role of functional clues in customer experience management.

I had a strange discomfort in my throat for at least two years but was told that it was nothing to be concerned about. After about another year I was referred to a different physician who told me that I had a tumor on the base of my tongue. He also told me what kind of radical surgery he would have to perform on me. At that point I decided to go to the Mayo Clinic, and I was there two weeks later.

I was immensely impressed by Mayo's team approach to treatment. I had three doctors: Dr. Kerry Olsen, an ENT specialist; Dr. Robert

Foote, a radiation oncologist; and Dr. Julian Molina, a medical oncologist. What a difference from anything I had ever experienced before. I remember Dr. Olsen telling me that he would not operate on me because there were other modalities available for treatment. That one statement made a huge impression on me and boosted my confidence that I was going to receive the best possible care. The team prescribed a regimen of 35 radiation treatments and three chemotherapy treatments. My initial positive feelings about the team were such that I decided to stay at the Mayo Clinic for the treatments. My wife and I moved to a hotel in Rochester for over three months. The treatments were grueling—and that's putting it mildly—but I felt blessed to be at Mayo Clinic.

For two years after my treatments, we returned every three months to see the team for follow-up care. Now my follow-up visits are every six months.

Another thing I noticed very quickly was Mayo's operational efficiency. Uncertainty is a difficult feeling for most people. At Mayo, I never had to wait very long for the results of my tests and scans. Not only does this remove uncertainty for the patient, but it allows physicians to share information quickly. It enables the Mayo Clinic to be both effective and efficient, to do the right things and to do them very well.

During radiation treatments, I was bolted into a mask so I couldn't move my head. I remember after one of my last treatments I was feeling pretty rough. I recall saying to Jamie, the young woman who administered the majority of the treatments, "Jamie, I sure hope these treatments are going to do some good." She emphatically replied, "I don't hope *these treatments are going to do some good, I* know *they're going to do some good." She said exactly what I needed to hear at that moment. Physically, I felt awful, but my morale, attitude, and feelings of hope were soaring.*

During my three-month follow-up visits, I would always find Jamie and tell her, "I'm still here, you made a big difference in my life." When you are there every day for three months you come to rely on people like Jamie and Rose at the radiation oncology reception desk. For that period of your life they are a big part of the face of the Mayo Clinic.

Don's story demonstrates not only the salient role of functional clues but also the interactivity of the three clue categories (hence the two-headed vertical arrows in Exhibit 7-1). The same stimulus can offer more than one kind of clue. Jamie's emphatic assertion that she *knew* the treatments would help not only was a powerful functional clue but also a powerful humanic one. She provided a timely and much-needed dose of emotional support for Don. Kindness coupled with competence can go a long way.

Mechanic Clues: Influencing First Impressions, Expectations, and Value

Mechanic clues come from the tangibles that offer a physical representation of the intangible service. Typically, customers purchase a service before they actually experience it. A salient role for mechanic clues is making a good first impression. Customers commonly experience mechanic clues to some degree before experiencing functional and humanic clues. Mechanic clues frequently influence customers' selection of a service. Customers lacking prior experience with a particular service—for example, travelers visiting a new town who need to select a hotel or restaurant—often base their choice primarily on the appearance of the facilities. While the role of functional clues is to instill customers' confidence in the competence of the service during and after its delivery, one role of mechanic clues is to make the customer feel smart about buying the service in the beginning.

Mechanic clues influence customers' service expectations because they create first impressions. This is important because customers' perceptions of an organization's service quality come from their evaluation of the service they received in relation to their expectations for the service.[8] Mechanic clues make implicit service promises suggesting to customers what the service should be like. An elegant restaurant with table cloths and soft lighting promises a more distinctive experience and a higher level of personal service than a more conventional casual-dining establishment. Thus it is essential that the design of mechanic clues fits and supports an organization's intended market positioning, thereby signaling precisely the kind of experience that it seeks to deliver.

Because mechanic clues are part of customers' experience, they influence how customers feel about the experience and their perceptions of value. The influence of mechanic clues on perceived value typically increases as customers spend more time in a service facility.[9] Starbucks' remarkable success is the result not only of the consistent quality and innovative variety of its coffee products but also of its providing a relaxing space where customers enjoy the company of others or solitude with refreshment. Tables are spaced apart so customers can have private conversations or be alone with their thoughts (or their laptop or a book). Starbucks' tables are round because research indicates that a customer who is alone is more psychologically comfortable at a round table than a square one.[10]

No One Wants to Go to the Hospital

Mechanic clues are important in healthcare. Healthcare is an unusual service in many ways, including the stress it creates for customers. Being a patient is about the least amount of fun anyone can have as a consumer. Patients experience stress from their illnesses or injuries that may involve pain, reduced physical capabilities, anxiety about medical tests and scheduled procedures, and uncertainty about the future. They may also experience considerable stress from the facilities in which medical care is provided—especially hospitals, which can be intimidating, noisy, barren of emotional support, disconnected from nature, and imprisoning.[11]

Healthcare cannot be separated from the settings in which it is delivered,[12] and these settings offer myriad opportunities to help calm patients (and their loved ones), to uplift their spirits, and to create a sense of healing. As Table 7-1 illustrates, Mayo Clinic's facilities design philosophy centers on helping to relieve the stress of people using the buildings—patients, family and other visitors, and staff. It is difficult to imagine any other kind of building in which its users are under more stress than medical buildings. Accordingly, the goal for the Clinic architects and designers is to create physical spaces that help moderate the stress of occupants rather than heighten it.

The lobby of Mayo's Phoenix hospital offers a pleasing entrance to the facility with its atrium design, stonework, indoor waterfall,

Table 7-1
Mayo Clinic Facilities Design Philosophy

Mayo Clinic Buildings Should Help Relieve the Stress of Those Who Use Them by:

• Offering a place of refuge	• Symbolizing competence
• Connecting to nature	• Minimizing the impression of crowding
• Emphasizing natural light	• Facilitating way-finding
• Muting noise	• Accommodating families
• Creating positive distractions	• Pleasing employees
• Conveying caring and respect	• Enhancing practice integration

piano, colorful couches, and wall of windows that overlooks a mountain range. The outpatient clinic building features a large fountain and sculpture as well as a piano in its lobby. Both the hospital and clinic buildings display artwork loaned by local artists. Bryan McSweeney, retired chair of the division of facilities services at Mayo Clinic Arizona states, "Our buildings look imposing, so we try to counter this with a softness inside—the materials, the colors, the artwork. Patients are under stress, and we are trying to soften the feeling of the facility and create positive distractions to help relieve stress."

Another building that reflects Mayo's design philosophy is the Gonda Building, a 20-story structure that opened in 2001 as the new "front door" to the Rochester campus. The Gonda Building has a spectacular wide-open, two-level lobby that makes the space seem uncrowded, a marble stairwell and floor, large Chihuly chandeliers, a multistory wall of windows looking out to a garden, and pianos placed throughout the common areas. The marble and stone used in the building come from around the world— "just like the patients," as Craig Smoldt, chair of the department of facilities and systems support, puts it. Located in prime space in the corner of the upper lobby is the Slaggie Family Cancer Education Center. When asked why such a prized location was used for this purpose, Smoldt replied, "There isn't a disease that affects more people and families than cancer. The more visible the center, the more you remove the stigma of having cancer."

The Gonda Building presents a stream of clues orchestrated to lessen the burden of pain and illness. Without words, the building says to visitors, "Welcome to this place. Your comfort is our first priority." Dr. Kerry Olsen, the physician chair of the Clinic's facilities committee, comments: "We devoted a lot of attention not only to the overall design but to the materials we used and how we used them. What we tried to do was make sure that when patients came in the door, they knew they were in a place that was unique, that was special. We wanted to create a feeling of permanence, a feeling of expertise, and a feeling of caring and warmth."

Attending to Detail

Clues can converge to tell a cohesive story of the service, or they can clash and tell a disjointed one. Orchestrating clues of quality at Mayo Clinic requires managing the little clues with as much precision as the big clues. Thus, in the spacious lobby areas that present big clues, little clues are also important. For instance, a Mayo Clinic facilities team travels to the marble quarries to scrutinize the marble blocks for the slabs on the walls or floor to ensure that no potentially disquieting images of human forms or diseases are suggested by the natural designs in the stone. Mayo pays considerable attention to the effective management of clues throughout the patient experience. Making a good first impression in the public spaces of a medical facility is important; however, the scary part of a patient's experience occurs in private spaces, such as examination, hospital, and procedure rooms. Clue management needs to be at its best where patients spend the most time and are likely to be under the most stress. For instance, when the Mayo Arizona hospital was being built, an automobile was lifted into the building so that physical rehabilitation patients could practice getting in and out of a car in the privacy of the hospital.[13]

Few patients experience the levels of fear and stress that children do when they visit their healthcare providers. Mayo Clinic shows careful clue management in its Rochester facilities in efforts to calm and distract the fears of its pediatric patients. Throughout the

Rochester campus, pediatric facilities feature artwork by local school children that has been transformed into thousands of colorful ceramic wall tiles. The tiles provide visual interest disassociated from healthcare. In the pediatric section of the emergency department in Saint Marys Hospital, the resuscitation equipment in examination rooms is hidden by a large picture (which slides out of the way when the equipment is needed).

In 2007, the Mayo Clinic T. Denny Sanford Pediatric Center opened to serve the pediatric specialty practice. There the drinking water fountains come in three heights with the lowest at about 18 inches, perfect for toddlers. Rivers and animal tracks embedded in the carpet and tiles guide children to the examination rooms. The traditional Mayo Clinic exam room has been adapted to children. For instance, the desk for the physician has no 90-degree edges or corners; all have been rounded over in a large radius. When children lie on the tables of radiology imaging equipment, they see animal tracks embedded in acoustical ceiling tiles. The decorating theme is Minnesota flora and fauna, and much of the design is presented at children's eye level—for example, images are presented on the lowest 30 inches of the walls. The environment is designed to calm and subdue. Lighting is dimmed. Nothing in the area makes stimulating noise. Nothing flashes although electronic sensors in a back-lit wall of flora and fauna show subtle twinkles of fireflies when children walk by the wall.

Lighting design plays a prominent role in the Clinic's mechanic clue management. Perimeter lighting of rooms is considered to be essential to illuminate the walls. Robert Fontaine, who is director of campus planning and projects at Mayo Jacksonville and who has worked at all three campuses, explains: "I have never done a project for Mayo that hasn't used perimeter lighting, and the reason is that it washes the wall, makes the room feel bigger, makes it fresher and cleaner, and just creates a more pleasant kind of space. You can be in the room longer without it bothering you."

Mayo Clinic examination rooms are designed uniformly across the system to enable physicians to efficiently use any room. The rooms are bigger than a typical medical clinic room, 140 to 145 square feet versus 120 square feet. They also are quiet, thus reassuring patients about privacy. Extra heavy walls and ceilings are used in a "five-sided box" configuration, meaning that the ceiling is built like a wall (the fifth wall). Artwork decorates the room. Patients undress, hang their clothing, and dress within a curtained subspace. Two levels of lighting are available, background lighting and exam-level lighting. The examination table is engineered with drawers for linen, gloves, and equipment. The physician's desk is adjacent to a sofa where the patient and family members sit, an arrangement that removes the desk as a barrier. Robert Fontaine designed the one-armed sofa currently in use at Mayo: "The whole idea of the sofa is really critical and goes back to Dr. Plummer and his colleagues. They found that individual chairs weren't as flexible as a sofa. Perhaps the patient would arrive with a party of three or four people. Or, if the patients weren't feeling well, they could lie down. The one arm allows them to hang over the edge. The sofa is a statement of quality. Patients feel that it is different. Nobody else has sofas."

Quiet, Please

Noise in a hospital setting is a severe environmental stressor that produces harmful psychophysiologic effects, including elevated blood pressure, increased heart rate, and insomnia.[14] Hospital noise sources are numerous (pagers, alarms, hallway conversations), loud (nursing shift changes, use or movement of medical equipment), and distressing (a roommate crying out in pain).[15]

Most hospitals, including those at Mayo Clinic, can do much more to moderate the negative effects of noise. This opportunity was made clear through a continuous improvement project conducted by nurses in the surgical thoracic intermediate care area of Saint Marys Hospital. The nurses used noise dosimeters to obtain continuous recordings of decibel levels in the unit. The highest decibel levels were caused by the movement of equipment, shift change commotion, hallway phones, and bedside monitor alarms. Moving a portable X-ray machine past a patient room (recorded at 98 decibels) creates the same noise level as driving a motorcycle past the room.

Interventions in the unit in response to the study included moving the shift change location to a closed room, posting quiet zone signs near hallway doors and phones, and dimming lights in the unit at night to "signal" the need for quiet, halting middle-of-the night supply deliveries to the unit, modifying bedside cardiac monitor alarms to a lower level, performing routine chest X-rays earlier in the evening, and padding the bottom of metal chart holders outside of patient rooms.[16]

Cheryl A. Cmiel, RN, lead author on the original study, reports that the unit has sustained the interventions described in the article; however, the greatest challenge remains night noise created by conversations and unit activity. Doreen Frusti, RN and chair of the department of nursing in Rochester, challenged her RN leadership team to build on the gains achieved on the surgical thoracic intermediate care unit. All 57 nursing units in Rochester participated in noise perception surveys that were followed by at least one noise intervention selected by the individual units and a repeat of the noise perception surveys among both patients and staff members. In addition, noise dosimeters were placed on 31 of the nursing units. "The study shows that measurable noise reduction can be achieved when individual patient care unit teams seriously endeavor to decrease noise in hospital environments," notes Joyce Overman Dube, RN, nurse administrator of the postoperative surgical division, and lead investigator of the follow-up study.[17] For instance, gains have come when units worked with the engineering department to bolt down tray holders in food carts to reduce their noise and to install quieter wheels on some equipment. "Soft voice" signs by phones were also effective, as well as common sense interventions such as closing patient room doors and limiting overhead pages. Even with these interventions, however, "We still have noise levels too high too much of the time," indicates Frusti. "We still have work to do."

Humanic Clues: Exceeding Customers' Expectations

Human interaction in the service experience creates the opportunity to extend respect and esteem to customers and, in so doing, exceed their expectations, strengthen their trust, and deepen their loyalty.[18] Just as labor intensity can produce unwanted variability in a service, so can it produce desirable variability when a service provider performs with uncommon civility, thoughtfulness, commitment, or resourcefulness. Customer perception of a service provider's effort has been shown to have a particularly strong influence on satisfaction and loyalty.[19]

While functional clues are usually most important in *meeting* customers' expectations for services of all types (because functionality offers the core solution sought), humanic clues are usually most important in *exceeding* customers' expectations for labor-intensive, interactive services (because treatment of the customer is central to these experiences, and excellent treatment can create a pleasant surprise). The element of pleasant surprise is needed to exceed expectations, and the best opportunity for pleasant surprise is when customers interact with service providers.[20]

Many of the examples in this book illustrate the emotional impact of humanic clues. We include a favorite example here because it so beautifully captures the essence of strong humanic clues: extending respect and esteem to those one serves. The story concerns a Mayo Rochester emergency department physician, Dr. Luis Haro, and a Clinic employee's elderly mother whom he treated. It is told in a 2001 e-mail from the employee to Dr. Wyatt Decker, the head of the department. The e-mail is reprinted verbatim except for the sender's name.

Hello Dr. Decker,

I'm remiss in not sending you this e-mail earlier, but I wanted to recount an experience I had in the Emergency Room about three months ago with Dr. Luis Haro. I want to share firsthand with you what an extraordinary physician he is.

I live with my mother who is 91 and has fairly severe dementia. About three months ago, I came home to find her outside on the lawn. She had fallen, was unable to get up, and had a nasty bruise and scrape on her elbow. She is a tiny woman so I managed to get her up and we headed for the Emergency Room. Once there, we were seen quickly and everyone was very solicitous of her. She's also almost deaf so sometimes this is no easy task.

Dr. Haro introduced himself and was very patient and kind—and spoke with enough volume so she could hear him. As he examined her, he asked her to stand and take a few steps. As she began to do so, she bumped into him. My mother in her day was quite a wit and some of that has remained. She looked up at him after bumping against him and said, "Well, I suppose we could waltz." And he replied, "Yes, we could." He then proceeded to take her in his arms and waltz a few steps around the cubicle. My mother was absolutely enchanted as she loves to dance and I started to cry. The sight of this tiny fragile old woman being waltzed around the room by this most handsome young man was just too much. I don't think I've ever been prouder to be a Mayo employee than that night. To witness that interaction and know this is the caliber of doctor we have here, someone whose medical expertise is a given but whose compassion and kindness—and humanness—are extraordinary was very moving.

I know in the grand scheme of Emergency Medicine this scenario has little significance. My mother had a bad bruise and a scrape but really was just fine. Her physical symptoms healed in a day or two but the "healing" that occurred that evening with his interaction with her is really what sets Mayo apart and will last in my memory forever.

Writing as a patient's family member, I want to tell you that your department and Mayo are very, very lucky to have Dr. Haro as a member of staff.

Dressing for Success

One way Mayo orchestrates humanic clues is through its dress code. Patients do not encounter Mayo physicians in casual attire. Unless they are in surgical scrubs, Mayo physicians wear business attire at work. An excerpt from the Mayo Clinic model of care explains the policy: "The wearing of business attire rather than white coats is recognized by our patients as a unique dress code that projects an aura of expertise and respect for the patient accompanied by warmth and friendliness."[21] Although some may consider Mayo's formal dress code to be pretentious, it is, in fact, fundamental clue management. Just as airline passengers do not want to see their pilot in a golf shirt, neither do ill patients want to see their doctor in one.[22]

Traditionally, the nursing profession has been known for its white uniforms. More recently, nursing dress standards have relaxed in the United States, and nurses often wear colorful clothing. Mayo nurses in Arizona, however, do wear white because research shows that is what hospital patients prefer. Bridget Jablonski, a nurse team leader at the Arizona hospital, offers her perspective:

> *I've heard the rumor that nurses outside of Mayo don't want to work here because we have to wear white. I am proud to wear the traditional white uniform. I think that Mayo establishes a mode of professionalism with its dress code by not allowing every color pattern, and cut of a uniform. I think it helps to maintain a high level of professionalism, and it's actually what the patients want. It is my understanding that the administration surveyed the patients before we opened the hospital and found that the patients prefer to see the nurses in white. This traditional uniform makes nurses more easily identifiable, whereas in other organizations without such a dress code, patients don't know if the person coming in the room is the house-keeper, the nurse, or the physician. A lot of times it's dark, and you can't read the name tag or people don't introduce themselves.*

"We came to this dress code decision as we were opening the new Mayo Clinic Hospital in 1998," states Debra Pendergast, RN and chair of the nursing division for Mayo Clinic Arizona. "We knew that we needed a Mayo Clinic culture in place before the first patient arrived, and the all-white uniform was part of the message." Since almost all the 1,200 employees were new to Mayo Clinic employment, the dress codes for nurses and other employees were clues to employees and patients that the Mayo Clinic Hospital was not just another community hospital. "No other hospital we knew of in 1998 required 'all-white' dress for nurses," according to Pendergast.

Patient perceptions also helped shape the dress codes for the Mayo Clinic hospital in Jacksonville when it opened in 2008. Debra

Hernke, RN and chief nursing officer for Mayo Clinic Jacksonville, reports: "At Saint Luke's Hospital, the nurses wore print tops of any color they chose and coordinated solid-color pants. But to achieve a more professional appearance, nurses as well as other employee groups now wear solid-color uniforms. For instance, nurses dress in ceil blue." Clues from nurse's uniforms are also part of the culture at the hospitals in Rochester. "We require solid scrubs as well," notes Doreen Frusti, RN and chair of the department of nursing in Rochester. She further notes the teamwork value in the decision: "Each unit needs to come to a consensus for the color from a list of approved colors."

Ideal Physician Behaviors

A survey of Mayo Clinic patients reveals the importance of physician humanic clues and suggests how physicians can best present them.[23] The survey was administered over the telephone to a random sample of patients who had recently been served in one of 14 medical specializations providing a broad array of inpatient and outpatient services. A total of 192 patients split almost evenly by gender participated in the 20- to 50-minute interviews. The interviews focused on what patients liked most and least in their interactions with Mayo doctors.

Respondents ranged from long-time Mayo patients to first-time patients. They were encouraged to refer to any Mayo Clinic physician experience and were not restricted to their most recent visit. All 192 respondents could describe a "best" experience; only 89 could also describe a "worst" experience. The latter responses generally reflected mirror opposites of desired physician behaviors. As shown in Table 7-2, descriptors for seven ideal physician behaviors were identified in the study: confident, empathetic, humane, personal, forthright, respectful, and thorough. Definitions of these behaviors and representative patient comments from the survey also appear in Table 7-2.

The results of this study clearly show why Mayo Clinic (or any other medical institution) cannot rely exclusively on technical quality

Table 7-2
Ideal Physician Behaviors, Definitions, and Supporting Quotes

Descriptors for Ideal Physician Behaviors	Definitions	Representative Quotes*
Confident	The doctor's assured manner engenders trust. The doctor's confidence gives me confidence.	"You could tell from his attitude that he was very strong, very positive, very confident that he could help me. His confidence made me feel relaxed."
Empathetic	The doctor tries to understand what I am feeling and experiencing, physically and emotionally, and communicates that understanding to me.	"One doctor was so thoughtful and kind to my husband during his final days. He also waited to tell me personally when he found a polyp in me, because my husband died from small bowel cancer and he knew I would be scared."
Humane	The doctor is caring, compassionate, and kind.	"My rheumatologist will sit and explain everything, medication, procedures. I never feel rushed. He is very caring. If I call, he always makes sure they schedule me. He told me he knows when I call, it is important. I appreciate his trust."
Personal	The doctor is interested in me more than just as a patient, interacts with me, and remembers me as an individual.	"He tries to find out not only about the patient's health but about their activities and home life as well."
Forthright	The doctor tells me what I need to know in plain language and in a forthright manner.	"They tell it like it is in plain English. They don't give you any Mickey Mouse answers, and they don't beat around the bush."
Respectful	The doctor takes my input seriously and works with me.	"She checks on me. She also lets me participate in my care. She asks me when I want tests, what works best for my schedule. She listens to me. She is a wonderful doctor."

(Continued)

Table 7-2
Continued

Descriptors for Ideal Physician Behaviors	Definitions	Representative Quotes*
Thorough	The doctor is conscientious and persistent.	"My cardiac surgeon explained everything well. The explanation was very thorough. He was very concerned about my recovery after the surgery. I thought it was special how well he looked after me following the surgery. Not all surgeons do that. They are not interested in you after you are done with surgery."

*The quotes in this table are excerpts of longer quotes in the transcripts. Respondents commonly mentioned multiple attributes in describing their best physician experience. For example, the quote used to illustrate "humane" also incorporates "respectful" and "thorough" and was coded accordingly.

Source: Neeli M. Bendapudi, Leonard L. Berry, Keith A. Frey, Janet T. Parish, and William L. Rayburn, "Patients' Perspectives on Ideal Physician Behaviors," *Mayo Clinic Proceedings*, March 2006, p. 340.

to build a superior reputation. Technical quality is often difficult for patients to judge even after the medical service is performed. The open-ended invitation to, "Tell me about the best (worst) experience that you had with a doctor in the Mayo system" did not preclude respondents from mentioning the doctor's technical proficiency, but they rarely did. It is not that technical quality is unimportant because it clearly is important and a primary reason that patients choose to go to Mayo Clinic and other leading medical centers. However, how physicians interact with patients also is important and is considerably easier for patients to judge. Patients are adept detectives when it comes to humanic clues. They can sense that a physician (or other caregiver) is rushed, preoccupied, fatigued, aloof, disinterested, or alarmed, just as they can sense genuine interest, compassion, calmness, and confidence. With a service as anxiety-producing, complex, proximate, personal, and important as medical care, patients need compassionate behavior from their caregivers as well as technical competence. Humanic clues, not just functional ones, tell the real story.

Following a patient focus group interview at Mayo, a participating breast cancer patient sent a note to the researchers that eloquently conveys the role of humanics in the delivery of healthcare services:

> *We want doctors who can empathize and understand our needs as a whole person. We put doctors on a pedestal right next to God, yet we don't want them to act superior, belittle us, or intimidate us. We want to feel that our doctors have incredible knowledge in their field. But all doctors need to know how to apply their knowledge with wisdom and relate to us as plain folks who are capable of understanding our disease and treatment. It's probably difficult for doctors after many years and thousands of patients to stay optimistic, be realistic, and encourage us. We would like to think that we're not just a tumor, not just a breast, not just a victim. Surely, if they know us, they* [will] *love us.*[24]

Lessons for Managers

Services are performances. To obtain a service, customers interact with an organization—a telecommunications company, an airline, a bank, a package delivery service, a beauty shop, a hospital. Customers may interact with one or more human service providers as well as with the organization's facility, equipment, Web site, telephone system, and more.

The customer's interaction—or experience—with an organization is laden with clues that tell the service story. The issue for managers is not whether clues will tell customers (or prospective customers) a story of the service because they will; the issue is whether the clues will tell the *right* story. Managers need to orchestrate experience clues to tell the right story, and Mayo Clinic does this exceedingly well. Mayo's approach to clue management offers useful insights for managers in other service organizations.

Lesson 1: Know the story you want to tell. Every manager should ask this question: "If our organization were to suddenly disappear, would customers really miss us?" If the candid answer is something to the effect of "probably not" or "not so much," then the organization needs to be strategically and/or operationally overhauled to begin creating value for customers that currently is lacking. If the answer is yes, then the follow-up question to answer is: "What would they miss?" The answer to this question offers the basis for the story that the organization's clues should consistently and cohesively tell.

For more than 100 years, Mayo Clinic has known the story it wants to tell. It wants patients to understand that their needs come first, that the institution exists to serve them, and that it cares about each and every patient even though thousands enter its doors. It wants patients to know that if there is any way to help them with their medical problems, Mayo Clinic is up to the task and will find just the right expert or team of experts to provide assistance. It wants patients to know that Mayo is an efficient institution that doesn't dally around, that gets things done, and that does it in a coordinated way. It communicates these basic messages through specific clues.

Through a combination of values-driven intuition and purposeful policies, Mayo Clinic orchestrates an experience that creates feelings in many patients and their families that, more or less, include: "They really care," "They have their act together here; they know what they are doing," and "I've done everything possible by coming here; if they can't help me, no one else can either." For many patients who arrive on campus with complex or hard-to-diagnose or life-threatening illnesses, the Mayo experience inspires hope and instills self-esteem, a potent combination.

Managers seeking to improve their customers' experience should identify the primary feelings customers desire from the experience. What is it that customers want more than anything else? What drives customer preference? Managers can then articulate these desired feelings in a brief statement called an "experience motif" that can serve as the unifying framework for every experience clue. The motif can be the North Star that guides the orchestration of clues. All clues need to contribute to telling the right story.[25]

Lesson 2: Excel in each clue category.   Few organizations build world-class brands, and fewer still—far fewer—have been able to sustain them for a century. Central to Mayo Clinic's brand-building and sustaining achievement is its focused investment in the three clue categories: functional, mechanic, and humanic. Clinic leaders through the years have not used this specific terminology; however, they clearly understand the substance behind these terms. They understand that clinical quality is the foundation of excellent health-care service but not the whole of it. They understand that illness puts patients on an emotional roller coaster and that caregivers' kindness and empathy are a critical part of patients' experiences. They understand that doctors and nurses not only have to be proficient in their craft but also have to reveal their proficiency. They understand that buildings not only have to be functional but also distinctive, confidence-building, and stress-reducing.

Mayo Clinic teaches an important lesson by not relying solely on medical expertise to sustain its reputation, even though it was and is renowned for its medical expertise. To touch people emotionally, to establish a stronger connection with them, the Clinic seeks excellence in the nontechnical aspects of patients' (and families') experiences, too. The clue categories play different roles, and the Clinic has invested in them all, making competitive attack more difficult. As Lewis Carbone, founder of Minneapolis-based Experience Engineering, states: "Great experiences will generally have exceptional alignment of functional, mechanic, and humanic experience clues that evoke very rich emotional connections, consistently leading to strong preference and loyalty."

Lesson 3: Major in minors.   Mayo Clinic not only reaches across all the clue categories, but it devotes significant—and sometimes obsessive—attention to what some observers might consider minor clues. The "shoelace" story that opened this chapter is a vintage Mayo Clinic story that conveys the institution's focus on details. Mayo

Clinic is master of the little clues, not just the big ones. The exam room sofas with one arm, the doctor chairs on rollers enabling physicians to easily move right in front of their patients on the sofa, the hidden resuscitation equipment in the emergency department pediatric exam rooms, the curtained dressing spaces in exam rooms, the pianos and window walls and artwork and outdoor gardens—these "small" clues are quite powerful when they are experienced cumulatively as a reinforcing "clue stream." They create the feelings patients and their loved ones seek from a medical institution.

Dr. Breanndan Moore chaired the division of transfusion medicine at Mayo Rochester for many years. He tells about a time when his father, a nonphysician, visited and toured the Clinic. Dr. Moore picks up the story here:

> *As we were walking out of the building at the end of the day, I asked my father, "Dad, what was the most impressive thing you saw today at Mayo Clinic?" I was hoping he would say the blood bank. He thought for a moment, and then he said, "This back corridor in the lab here." He paused a moment and then added, "I bet no patients or important dignitaries ever walk along this corridor, right?" I said, "Yes, you are right." He then said, "Look at how clean it is. That tells me that the janitors have the right attitude. And if they have the right attitude, probably each layer above them in the organization also has the right attitude. Now that's impressive." I was initially disappointed at the sort of simplistic answer he gave me, but in fact it was very profound. I've always remembered it.*

Summary

A service may be intangible, but its essence is communicated to customers. Every aspect of an organization reveals the form and substance of its service. For this reason, from shoelaces to CT scans, nothing is left to chance at Mayo Clinic. By orchestrating a triad of clues—functional, mechanic, and humanic—this complex medical institution promises personalized, patient-first healthcare. And its customers testify that it delivers, which is a testimonial for the efficacy of orchestrating the clues of quality.

NOTES

1. Leonard L. Berry and Neeli Bendapudi, "Clueing in Customers," *Harvard Business Review*, February 2003, p. 106.
2. Leonard L. Berry, Eileen A. Wall, and Lewis P. Carbone, "Service Clues and Customer Assessment of the Service Experience: Lessons from Marketing," *Academy of Management Perspectives*, May 2006, pp. 43–57.
3. Lewis P. Carbone and Stephen Haeckel, "Engineering Customer Experiences," *Marketing Management*, Winter 1994, pp. 8–19; and Stephen H. Haeckel, Lewis P. Carbone, and Leonard L. Berry, "How to Lead the Customer Experience," *Marketing Management*, January–February 2003, pp. 18–23. Also see Lewis P. Carbone, *Clued In: How to Keep Customers Coming Back Again and Again* (Upper Saddle River, NJ: FT Prentice Hall, 2004).
4. Leonard L. Berry and Lewis P. Carbone, "Build Loyalty through Experience Management," *Quality Progress*, September 2007, pp. 26–32.
5. See Leonard L. Berry, A. Parasuraman, and Valarie A. Zeithaml, "Improving Service Quality in America: Lessons Learned," *Academy of Management Executive*, Spring 1994, pp. 32–44.
6. Susan M. Keaveney, "Customer Switching Behavior in Service Industries: An Exploratory Study," *Journal of Marketing*, April 1995, pp. 71–82.
7. Berry and Bendapudi, pp. 104–105.
8. Valarie A. Zeithaml, A. Parasuraman, and Leonard L. Berry, *Delivering Quality Service: Balancing Customer Perceptions and Expectations* (New York: The Free Press, 1990).
9. Berry, Wall, and Carbone, p. 49.
10. Michael C. Krauss, "Starbucks 'Architect' Explains Brand Design," *Marketing News*, May 1, 2005, pp. 19–20. To read more about Starbucks, see Joseph Michelli, *The Starbucks Experience* (New York: McGraw-Hill, 2006), and Howard Schultz, *Pour Your Heart into It* (New York: Hyperion, 1997).
11. Roger Ulrich, "Effects of Interior Design on Wellness: Theory and Recent Scientific Research," *Journal of Healthcare Design*, November 1991, pp. 97–109.
12. Jain Malkin, *Medical and Dental Space Planning*, 3rd ed. (New York: John Wiley & Sons, 2002).
13. Berry and Bendapudi, p. 106.
14. To read more about the effects of hospital noise and for a list of specific references, see Leonard L. Berry, Derek Parker, Russell C. Coile, Jr., D. Kirk Hamilton, David D. O'Neill, and Blair L. Sadler, "The Business Case for Better Buildings," *Frontiers of Health Services Management*, Fall 2004, pp. 5–24.
15. Berry, Parker, Coile, et al., p. 10.
16. Cheryl A. Cmiel, Dana M. Karr, Dawn M. Gasser, Lorretta M. Oliphant, and Amy Jo Neveau, "Noise Control: A Nursing Team's Approach to Sleep Promotion," *American Journal of Nursing*, February 2004, vol. 104, no. 2, pp. 40–49.
17. J. A. Overman Dube, M. M. Barth, C. A. Cmiel, S. M. Cutshall, S. M. Olson, S. J. Sulla, J. C. Nesbitt, S. C. Sobczak, D.E. Holland, "Environmental Noise

Sources and Interventions to Minimize Them: A Tale of Two Hospitals," *Journal of Nursing Care Quality*, July/September, 2008, vol. 23, no. 3, forthcoming.

18. This paragraph and the next are adapted from Berry, Wall, and Carbone, p. 49.
19. Lois A. Mohr and Mary Jo Bitner, "The Role of Employee Effort in Satisfaction with Service Transactions," *Journal of Business Research*, vol. 32, 1995, pp. 239–252.
20. See Leonard L. Berry, *On Great Service* (New York: The Free Press, 1995), pp. 89–94.
21. *Mayo Clinic Model of Care*, Mayo Press, 2000.
22. Berry and Bendapudi, p. 106.
23. See Neeli M. Bendapudi, Leonard L. Berry, Keith A. Frey, Janet T. Parish, and William Rayburn, "Patients' Perspectives on Ideal Physician Behaviors," *Mayo Clinic Proceedings*, March 2006, pp. 338–344.
24. This note was originally published in Bendapudi, Berry, Frey, et al., p. 343.
25. To read more about the experience motif, see Carbone 2004 (note 3) and Berry and Carbone 2007 (note 4).

CHAPTER 8

CREATING, EXTENDING, AND PROTECTING THE BRAND

I was called to the transfusion lab in the middle of night to look at a cross match before we could go ahead with a kidney transplant. As I left the lab, I noticed one of the techs was working. As it was then about 2:00 a.m., I decided that I'd talk to her later. The following morning I brought her into my office and asked, "What were you doing in the lab at two in the morning? You weren't working on the kidney. I know, because I was there." This young, blonde, blue-eyed, Minnesotan turned bright red, acutely embarrassed, and said to me, "Dr. Moore I was hoping you wouldn't see me." My heart sank when she said that. I thought, oh my God, what has she done? She continued, "I was doing the platelet antibody test during the day, and I accidentally used a solution of the wrong molarity and lost all the platelets. So by the end of the day when I read the tests on all the patients, it was a bust—and I knew it was a bust—I couldn't read it. So I was back doing the test again."

I replied, "That's really wonderful of you, but you probably could have done it today without having to come back last night in the middle of a January blizzard." She said, "Dr. Moore, I can't have the patients at Mayo Clinic waiting an extra day in the hospital because I fouled up a lab test." My jaw hit the floor at this point, so I said, "Well, that is very laudable. Make sure you put in for your overtime." She looked at me as if I had told her to rob the poor box in the church. She replied with a certain outrage, "Dr. Moore, I can't have Mayo paying me for my mistakes!"

I sat there thinking I don't believe I'm hearing this. This particular technologist was a hard-working young woman, a wonderful technologist, but in a way that was ordinary in our lab. Her attitude, her work ethic, her sense of ethics was such that this is just how she behaved. She was appalled that I would suggest that she be paid for her overtime at two in the morning. Employees like this are what make Mayo great.

As we have described throughout this book, Mayo Clinic's dedicated employees provide service quality that exceeds the ordinary again and again in the many service encounters patients and their families experience in an episode of complex medical care. This account of exemplary service told by Dr. Breanndan Moore, past chair of the division of transfusion medicine in Rochester, is particularly note-worthy because the service is so invisible. The employee wanted no one to know; she wanted no credit. Although this was in part because she had made an inadvertent error in a procedure, she labored every day invisible to the patients she was serving. She knew that there would be no bouquet of flowers or even a thank you for her efforts that cold night. No one would have faulted her for repeating the test during the next work day. But this employee, who had personal contact with patients only through tubes of their blood, still saw in her imagination the person whose blood she held. She was able to imagine that a patient—a person—might need to spend an extra day in a hospital bed because of her blunder. This task could not wait.

This story multiplied thousands of times each day is Mayo Clinic. The daily efforts of employees, some visible and others invisible to the patients, produce a healthcare experience unlike that most patients have ever experienced. For more than 100 years, daily accounts of these patient experiences, as told by more than 6 million patients, have established the Mayo Clinic brand of healthcare. In bits and pieces, the essence of Mayo Clinic seeps into the awareness of more than 80 percent of U.S. households as the story from the patient referred to as "Don" in the previous chapter illustrates:

I was in shock after hearing that I had cancer. However, after the surgeon described the radical surgery he would have to do, I was numb.

I remember getting into my car and calling my wife as I drove home. My exact words were "Honey, you are not going to believe this, I have cancer, and we are going to the Mayo Clinic." I never stopped to consider my insurance coverage because it didn't matter; I was going to the Mayo Clinic. Since then I have thought a great deal about what I had blurted out to my wife because it even surprised me a little given that Rochester, Minnesota, is over a thousand miles from where we live. I have often asked myself, "Why Mayo Clinic?"

Here is what I think. There are hospitals everywhere. To me the Mayo Clinic has always been a great deal more than a hospital. It is an enterprise of great minds, state-of-the-art medical research, the highest-quality medical care, and a dedicated staff of practitioners who choose to be there. It is also a place where all of my life I have heard and read that "medical miracles" occasionally occur. I did not have a broken leg or need heart bypass surgery. I had cancer, and based upon what I had been told would likely happen to me, I decided I needed more than a hospital. So all these factors led me to believe that the Mayo Clinic was where I wanted to be treated for my cancer and that just maybe one of those miracles might happen for me.

For several decades, Don had unconsciously built his understanding of the Mayo Clinic brand. In his version of the brand, Mayo Clinic stands apart from other healthcare providers, including the university medical center in his home town. It's as if he had created a mental file folder where he deposited a lifetime of references to Mayo Clinic from newspapers and news broadcasts, from comments in his social circles, and perhaps from references in movies, television shows, and novels. Over time, the file acquired a special label with a notation like, "Use for extreme medical needs," or, perhaps, as he suggests, "Use when you need a medical miracle." During the phone call with his wife, he spontaneously connected his stored brand knowledge with his desperate medical need, so he blurted out, "We are going to the Mayo Clinic."

Don's experience not only in deciding to go to Mayo but also in the clinical and service outcomes described in Chapter 7 differs only in the specific details from tens of thousands of patients who journey to Mayo Clinic each year. Not all are helped, and service lapses do occur. Most of the time, however, the Clinic's values and care system earn the confidence and praise of patients and their families, and Mayo Clinic has developed what is arguably the leading healthcare brand among U.S. consumers and one of the most powerful service brands in the world. In a 2007 national survey of primary healthcare decision makers in U.S. households, respondents were asked what healthcare institution they would choose for themselves or a family member if insurance or finances would permit them to go anywhere for a serious medical problem, such as cancer treatment, heart surgery, or neurosurgery. Responses were unaided. As shown in Exhibit 8-1, Mayo Clinic was mentioned by more than 16 percent of respondents. Preference for Mayo Clinic is nearly two-and-a-half times greater than that for the second-ranked institution.[1]

In earlier chapters, we describe how Mayo Clinic service is created and performed—partly it is the result of systems engineering as in the appointment system, but most significantly, it flows from the voluntary, discretionary efforts of employees who honor Mayo's

Exhibit 8-1
Medical Center Unaided Preference, Percent of U.S. Households

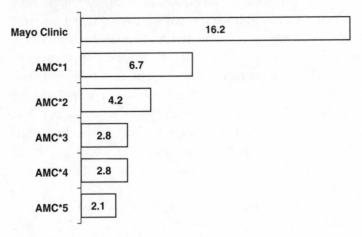

*AMC = Academic medical center
Source: Professional Research Corporation, sample size: 1,000

underlying values. We also examined the administrative and operational infrastructures that sustain its culture of service. Our purpose in this chapter is to distill the essential elements of the brand, describe how Mayo has both guarded this most valuable asset and leveraged and adapted it to the ever-evolving science and business of medicine.[2]

The Mayo Clinic brand was created by physicians and administrators and hundreds of support staff members dedicated to the humane delivery of clinical services. No marketing textbooks or marketing consultants guided the founding of the brand. Mayo had a one-person marketing staff from 1986 until 1992. To this day, it uses little media advertising to promote clinical care. Indeed, Mayo Clinic's brand story defies the commonly held assumption that great brands require great advertising.

In Exhibit 8-2, we present a generic service branding model that explains how a service organization can create a world-class brand by performing well for one customer at a time. Then we discuss how

Exhibit 8-2
A Service Branding Model

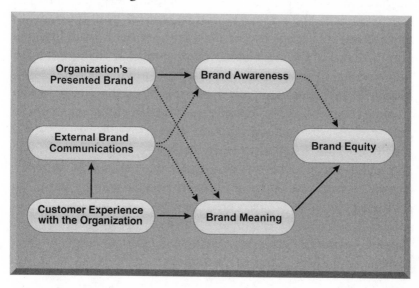

Mayo Clinic has applied this model in creating, extending, and protecting its brand.

Experiences Create the Brand

Branding plays a special role in service organizations because strong brands increase customers' trust of intangible performances.[3] The more consequential, complex, variable, and personal the service, the more customers need brand reassurance. Just as customers become more clue-sensitive when receiving services with some or all of these characteristics (Chapter 7), so do they become more brand-responsive. Customers of many kinds of services seek the assurance that they are making—or have made—a good choice. As Stan Richards, founder of Dallas-based advertising agency The Richards Group, stated in a presentation: "A strong brand is a safe place for customers."[4]

A service brand is essentially a promise of future satisfaction. It is a blend of what the organization says the brand is, what others say about it, and how well the organization actually performs the service—all from the customer's perspective. A brand is what the customer perceives it to be.[5] (Except where otherwise indicated, we use the term *customer* broadly to include those who have actually experienced the service and those who have not but could in the future.) Exhibit 8-2 is a visual representation of the relationship among the principal components of a service brand. The bold lines indicate primary influence, and the dotted lines secondary influence.

The *presented brand* is an organization's controlled communication of its identity and desired brand image through means such as the brand name, logo, advertising, Web sites, employee uniforms, and facilities design. The presented brand is the brand message the organization conceptualizes and disseminates; it is the organization's articulated brand. The presented brand directly influences *brand awareness*, which is a customer's ability to recognize and recall a brand. A customer's brand awareness affects brand meaning—how a customer perceives a brand.

External brand communications may be defined as information about the organization offered by independent sources but influenced by the organization. The two primary sources of external brand communications are word-of-mouth communications—often conveyed via the Internet—and publicity, including reports in the news media. These communications can affect both brand awareness and brand meaning but not necessarily in the desired direction given the independent sources of the information. Customers tend to be eager recipients of independent information about services because of the inherent difficulty in evaluating an intangible service prior to purchase. The greater the risk associated with a service, the more likely customers are to actively seek out unbiased information about it. Thus, customer-to-customer information sharing often occurs before a customer selects an attorney, automobile mechanic, college professor's course, doctor, or hospital.[6] Publicity also can be a factor in the development of a brand, and a major news story about an organization can transform the dotted-line influence portrayed in Exhibit 8-2 to bold-line influence.

Customer experience with the organization is the customer's cumulative experience in interacting with the organization. Those who have never interacted with the organization may form an impression from the presented brand and what others say. Experienced customers, however, rely on their actual experiences with the organization. These experiences are disproportionately influential in creating *brand meaning*—the customer's dominant perceptions of the brand. Brand meaning is a snapshot impression of the brand promise. It is the reputation or image that immediately comes to mind in reference to the organization.

Nothing trumps a customer's actual experience with an organization in shaping brand meaning. Organization-controlled communications such as advertising can play important roles in brand development, including generating awareness, encouraging customers to use the service, and providing language and imagery to frame the brand promise. What these communications cannot do is rescue a low-quality service. If customers' experience with the service conflicts with the advertising message, they believe the experience rather than the advertising. Smart executives understand that advertising effectiveness over time depends on advertised goods or services delivering what the organization promises.

For experienced customers, both brand awareness and brand meaning influence *brand equity* but not to the same degree. Brand meaning has the greater impact. A customer who is aware of a brand but doesn't like it will seek alternatives. Brand equity is the degree of marketing advantage (positive equity) or disadvantage (negative equity) a given brand has compared to an unnamed or fictitiously named competitor.[7]

Customers' actual experiences are salient in a goods-branding model just as they are in a service-branding model. However, for labor-intensive, interactive services these experiences are primarily with the people performing the service rather than with manufactured goods. A labor-intensive, interactive service brand can be only as strong as the people performing the service. Service providers' performances transform an organization's brand aspirations into brand reality.

Mayo Clinic leaders through the years have intuitively understood that the staff members performing the service are the "living brand." Staff members strengthen or weaken the institution's reputation with each service encounter. Accordingly, the Clinic has consistently invested in performing the service well rather than in advertising the service more, depending on positive patient and family experiences to create favorable perceptions of Mayo (brand meaning) and stimulate favorable word-of-mouth information (external brand communications). Mayo leaders have long understood that "... the brand deliverer ... walks around on two legs ..." as service researchers Leslie de Chernatony and Francesca Dall'Olmo Riley put it.[8]

The vertical arrow in Exhibit 8-2 from "customer experience with the organization" to "external brand communications" captures the essence of Mayo's marketing philosophy, which is to perform so well for patients that they and their families feel compelled to tell others about it. This is why the Clinic needed no marketing department for so long; the real marketers are those who perform the service and those who receive it.

A Big Brand from a Little Town

Rochester, Minnesota, is an unlikely place for an iconic healthcare brand to be founded. The story is now familiar: the brothers and their father earned their reputation for clinical outcomes, first, among the homesteading farmers and ranchers as well as among businessmen in the small communities throughout the upper Midwest. Hundreds, then thousands, of wives, husbands, children, and friends were alive and significantly improved through care delivered by the Drs. Mayo.

Recognition from the professional community came more slowly. In 1899, Dr. Will submitted an article to the *American Journal of the Medical Sciences*, one of the best monthly medical publications of the day. The article reported on more than 105 operations of the gallbladder and its ducts that Dr. Will had personally performed. The editor of the journal was incredulous about the number of surgeries mentioned in the article, so he began to investigate. Rochester had fewer than 6,000 residents. No surgeon in Philadelphia had performed this number of gallbladder surgeries. In a survey the year before, all the surgeons in Louisville together had performed only 106 such surgeries. The editor rejected the manuscript after concluding that the numbers were not credible.[9]

Dr. Charlie came to the notice of a well-known Chicago surgeon, Dr. Charles Beck, after Dr. Charlie observed him perform a surgery. As they visited, Dr. Charlie casually mentioned the number of these surgeries he had done—a number greater than Dr. Beck. Dr. Beck mentioned this to a colleague who indicated that he had just heard Dr. Will report at the American Medical Association meeting on case numbers and outcomes that many surgeons at the meeting did not believe. He suggested that Dr. Beck accept the invitation to go to Rochester to check on the tales being told by the Mayo brothers. Within a week Dr. Beck traveled there. "He watched the brothers do several operations, with a skill like he had seldom seen," and after looking at the hospital and the crowds of patients in the clinic, he was convinced that their reports and outcomes were credible.[10] This visit opened the leading medical journals to the brothers and generated a steady stream of visiting surgeons from around the world who traveled to out-of-the-way Rochester to observe their techniques.

Modern surgery was in its infancy when the brothers began their practice, so creative and innovative practitioners like the Drs. Mayo could have a broad impact on the profession. The recent advent of anesthesia had provided surgeons with the time they needed to complete complex surgery. But when the brothers came on the scene in the 1880s, most surgical patient mortality came from infections following "successful" surgery. Although the brothers were technically gifted surgeons, much of the Mayos' success can be attributed to their early adoption of sterile surgical techniques and the complementary "cleanliness is next to Godliness" ethic of the Franciscan sisters. The reputation that ultimately became the Mayo Clinic brand was based initially on both the outcomes enjoyed by the common, good folk who came for treatment, and later the approval of the profession based on clinical results published in the top medical journals.

By focusing on their patients' needs, more than 14 decades of Mayo Clinic physicians and leaders inadvertently built a strong healthcare brand. Even today, some Mayo leaders resist thinking of Mayo Clinic as a brand for fear that it will be one more reason to focus on the business of healthcare rather than patients' needs. It is fair to say that the Mayo Clinic brand is the fortunate by-product of an organization that recommits year after year to its central focus of service to patients. By investing in differentiated service, rather than in brand-building, Mayo Clinic has been rewarded with a brand—a reputation—that is more valuable than any endowment.

Delivering Care Worth Talking About

Mayo Clinic depends on spontaneous word-of-mouth communication. Mayo's market comprises an infinitesimal share of the U.S. and international patient population. Overall—including the patients it receives from the local markets around the three campuses—Mayo

Clinic's share of the total U.S. hospital admissions is tiny—about 0.37 percent. In states or metropolitan areas several hundred miles from a Clinic site, often only .01 percent of the population comes to Mayo Clinic in a year. So, for instance, a geographic area with a population of 10 million might generate only 1,000 patients. The economics of mass media advertising could not provide a positive return on investment even if the market share was doubled in these areas. Nevertheless, satisfied patients have reliably marketed Mayo Clinic for more than a century. Despite Mayo's tiny market share, the Clinic's brand research shows that about one-fourth of all household healthcare decision makers in the country personally know someone who has been a Mayo Clinic patient. This is because Mayo Clinic patients talk. The most recent study of patients' word of mouth finds that 91 percent indicate that they voluntarily say good things about Mayo to others. When asked to estimate the number of people they've spoken to, the average is 40 per patient. This is consistent with the responses for four iterations of the study over a decade. The survey also asks if these patients have recommended that someone else go to Mayo. About 85 percent say yes. Over the years, each of these patients has generated approximately five new patients.[11]

In addition to the favorable word of mouth these patients share with their friends and family, many express their loyalty through their charitable gifts to Mayo Clinic. For instance, in 2007 more than 97,000 benefactors—the vast majority of whom are grateful patients—provided gifts of more than $373 million in support of Mayo Clinic. In 2007, Mayo Clinic received a gift through an unusual twist on word of mouth. Sometime earlier, a wealthy international entrepreneur met with his attorney to draw up his last will and testament. To honor his parents, he indicated to the attorney that he wanted to leave his estate to a hospital. Through his attorney, he learned of Mayo Clinic and its preeminent status. Even though the benefactor was never a patient and never set foot on a Mayo Clinic campus, the story of the Mayo Clinic was compelling. The reach of the brand to that attorney and his client resulted in a $4 million gift.

Brands become assets for a company only when they have been internalized by those in the markets of interest. Before initiating formal brand management in 1996, Mayo Clinic had for decades focused intensely on protecting the reputation of the Clinic as if it were an abstract treasure that the organization owned and kept securely stored in a vault. It came as a revelation to many inside the organization that the value of the Mayo Clinic brand is based on the information, imagery, feelings, and beliefs that millions of consumers have stored in their minds as in Don's mental "Mayo Clinic folder." Brands are owned by the customers who make up the market. However, as our brand model suggests, organizations control as best they can the inputs that consumers use to create the brand concepts and brand meanings that influence their behavior in the market.

Mayo Clinic's brand research reveals how both patients and non-patients view the Clinic. A consumer from Des Moines who has never been on a Mayo campus describes Mayo Clinic in these words: "For people in horrible pain or dire health situations, Mayo Clinic provides a glimmer of hope. I know of several people who were in deep trouble and couldn't be helped by anyone until they got to Mayo, and they were saved there." A consumer from Dallas concurs, "You go to Mayo when you are really sick.... You only hear about Mayo when it's something specialized." Another individual from Texas states, "Mecca. Best of the best. Handles tougher or more difficult treatments and illnesses." A California consumer has little specific knowledge, "I just grew up with Mayo.... All I know is hearsay ... but it's a legend.... We need to believe it.... A symbol of hope." Mayo's brand monitor surveys, spanning over a decade, reveal that nearly three-fourths of U.S. household healthcare decision makers indicate that "They take comfort in knowing that Mayo Clinic exists." This kind of strong brand image and the others noted above provide both a place to start and a motivation to seek out Mayo Clinic in wrenching moments of medical need.

The patients who have experienced Mayo Clinic care reveal that their experience enables them to intuitively understand much about the Mayo Clinic model of care and values. For instance, a patient from California portrayed Mayo Clinic as a circle with four arrows pointing at a dot in the center. The patient explains, "The patient is the center." Another patient associated Mayo Clinic with a clock, commenting, "They spend real time with you, which is unique." Yet another patient explained Mayo Clinic in human terms, "Classy, sophisticated but humble. Not arrogant or egotistical ... quietly competent." Other patients provide a litany of descriptions of the Mayo Clinic brand:

- "[The physicians] belong to something greater than themselves ... history, tradition."
- "The business element is taken out of Mayo.... Their ethics are higher ... which gives me greater faith in their diagnosis."
- "These doctors are there for the love of medicine, not for the love of money."
- "Mayo is like a well-conducted symphony ... works harmoniously.... One person can't do it alone.... Teamwork, cooperation, compatibility."
- "What makes Mayo unique is that you see a team of doctors.... Doctors are questioned by their colleagues ... continually evolving, efficient, thorough, collaborative."

Mayo Clinic would never make some of these claims on its own behalf. The core of teamwork, patient focus, and altruism, however, is central to what Mayo Clinic strives to be; Mayo's leaders are gratified that patients intuitively understand the Clinic's intentions so well. Other comments may exaggerate reality, such as the comment about the removal of "business elements," but this attribute is related to the "salaried physicians," which, as discussed in Chapter 5, encourages the removal of economic self-interest from clinical recommendations. Patients notice many subtle clues while experiencing the Clinic, and they conduct the Clinic's advertising with enviable reach, frequency, and effectiveness. The high-stakes nature of healthcare service creates a prime opportunity for word-of-mouth communications. By delivering a patient-care experience worth talking about, the Clinic has capitalized on the opportunity.

Extending the Brand—Carefully

Until the mid-1980s, the only way to experience the Mayo Clinic brand was to travel to Rochester, Minnesota. However, in the mid-to-late 1970s, Clinic leadership began to consider creating a second base of operations. The board of governors actually heard a well-developed proposal for a second campus located in Jacksonville, Florida, but the board chose not to proceed at that time.[12] Yet leaders were uneasy about a future with only a single base of operations in Minnesota, which was the early testing ground for health maintenance organizations (HMOs). They feared that the very important regional market might be locked out of access to Mayo if patients were captured into a closed-panel HMO where patients were limited to physicians contracted by the HMO. Further, Medicare costs were becoming a political issue. Although the Medicare patients had been profitable, the move from "fee for service" to "case rates" in the mid-1980s would likely bring lower financial margins because the change was driven by a need to contain the rate of growth in Medicare payouts. And, Mayo's leaders felt that more convenient access to patients in the Sun Belt states would help secure the Clinic's long-term future.

Without knowledge of the yet-to-be-developed language of brand management, leaders intuitively realized that the Mayo Clinic name was an asset (brand equity) that provided leverage in new business operations they classified as diversifications. "The earlier proposal to expand to Jacksonville started from a patient benefactor and was championed by several Mayo leaders, but it was not part of a concerted planning effort," recalls Robert Smoldt, former chief administrative officer for Mayo Clinic. "In 1983, however, we went through a formal strategic planning process that extended over three or four months of meetings. And this time, the board of governors came up with ideas that stuck." This planning initiative led to the most significant changes at Mayo Clinic since the deaths of the founding brothers in 1939.

In this discussion, we focus on four brand extensions. The first three were approved almost simultaneously by the board of governors in 1983:

1. Extending geographically to Jacksonville, Florida, and Scottsdale, Arizona, which opened facilities in 1986 and 1987, respectively.
2. Transforming Mayo Medical Laboratories from a regional to a national and international service.
3. Publishing health information for the public.
4. Developing a network of community hospitals and clinics, known as Mayo Health System, which was initiated in 1992.

Viewed today from a strategic perspective, these four brand extensions are successful and have contributed positively to Mayo's brand equity through the services and goods that carry the Mayo name. However, all represented significant potential brand risk if they had been executed poorly.

Geographic Expansion

The geographic expansion of clinical operations presented a significant brand risk because it centered on the core brand of clinical care—the patient experience at Mayo Clinic. Replicating the essential character of Rochester's patient/customer experience on new campuses in Jacksonville and Scottsdale was the central challenge. This would require that many employees who did not know Mayo well would need to provide Mayo Clinic care almost flawlessly in new spaces, new communities, and new regional cultures. In retrospect, it seems audacious to try to replicate the experience of the century-old Rochester campus that was wrapped in the Mayo family legacy and staffed in 1983 by 810 physicians and 7,500 allied health employees. Each new site had one major building isolated on a 100-plus acre campus. And instead of some 800 physicians, each campus opened with around 40 physicians supported by about 250 clinical and allied health staff members.

Perhaps not surprising, the brand risk was mitigated successfully by careful planning and a deep understanding of the essentials of the patient's experience. To reduce the risk, management made two commitments: (1) replicate the patient experience as closely as possible in the new locations, and (2) transport the Mayo Clinic culture to Jacksonville and Scottsdale through experienced Mayo Clinic physicians and administrative leaders.

Building design was viewed as pivotal for sustaining the Mayo Clinic patient experience in a new location. Among other things, the patient examination rooms were virtual duplicates of those in Rochester in terms of size, layout, and equipment. Although the Clinic buildings in Jacksonville and Scottsdale were small in comparison to the 20-story Mayo Clinic building in Rochester, the architectural design and interior appointments reflected the same quality and ambiance as the structures on the original campus. Adopting and adapting the patient appointment, medical record, and patient correspondence systems from Rochester further replicated the experience. At each new facility, the clues reflecting Mayo Clinic quality were in place from the opening day. And, indeed, patient satisfaction studies conducted from the beginning of the Jacksonville and Scottsdale operations showed no statistically significant differences in satisfaction when compared to studies conducted in Rochester.

The Jacksonville and Scottsdale clinics opened with a solid core of experienced Mayo Clinic physicians and administrative leaders from Rochester. About 25 of the 40 physicians present when each clinic opened were transfers from Rochester. The entire administrative team and most of the operations leaders down to the level of supervisors also came from Rochester. As we discuss in Chapter 6, Mayo is able to hire support staff whose values fit the culture of Mayo Clinic. Furthermore, working for this brand-name organization seems to bring out the best in many employees. The employees are aware of the Clinic's reputation, and most do not want to be the person who fails to perform in accordance with this reputation. For instance, a young woman working as an admissions clerk in the Arizona clinic describes how she goes beyond the requirements of her job. If the patients seem confused or anxious, she might walk them to the location of their first appointment. She acknowledges that she is a "better employee at Mayo Clinic" than in any other job she has held because she doesn't want to "let Mayo Clinic down" by doing anything less than her best. By providing the tools and the time needed for staff to deliver high-quality care, Mayo makes it possible for the staff to deliver the Mayo Clinic experience.

Although the patient experience had been successfully re-created from the outset at the two new campuses, other parts of the strategic focus were unclear. The macrostrategy was in place, but, as Carleton Rider, the first chief administrative officer in Jacksonville, comments, "The microstrategic plan—the campus strategic plan—was missing. We started as a small multispecialty clinic, but there was no real plan of what was to come next." Dr. Robert Waller, who later became Mayo's CEO, chaired the diversification committee; he acknowledged the missing plan in a 1984 update that he gave to the board of governors: "We do not have all the details as to how this will be done." And then he immediately explained why: "If the details about the building, the systems and the practice needed to be complete before making a decision to build a new group practice in a new location, the chances would be unlikely that the facility would be built."[13]

Carleton Rider comments, "When you plant the Mayo Clinic seed in the ground, up come three shoots—clinical care, research, and education." Thus, within a few years, the new campuses embarked on plans to each become a full-fledged Mayo Clinic. This is what Mayo's leaders know how to do. Mayo moved incrementally forward in establishing two additional Mayo Clinics, when the board of governors had balked at just one a decade earlier. Few people today feel this was the wrong decision.

An unanticipated brand risk emerged, however. Without explicit instructions on how these campuses were to relate to Rochester, the relationships became a patchwork. One recent leader suggested in an interview that this ambiguity enabled the campuses to reflect "the personalities of their leaders." Some clinical areas, particularly the departments of neurology and neurosurgery, developed collaborative relationships from the outset. In other disciplines, the new leaders wanted to distance their programs from Rochester and viewed Rochester as a competitor rather than as a partner. Tensions developed.

In 2004, Mayo Clinic leadership stepped forward to remove the ambiguity surrounding the character of the three campuses; "One Mayo Clinic" became the mantra and strategic objective. This emphasis suggested that the campuses should work together strategically, administratively, and clinically to the extent feasible. Subsequently, substantive changes occurred. Governance is now centered in a single board of governors where there had previously been three. All campuses work from a single strategic plan. In 2006, the three campuses began simultaneously implementing the first common administrative software suite to manage functions such as financial and human resource services. The Mayo Clinic cancer center is recognized by the National Cancer Institute as the first multicampus "comprehensive cancer center," indicating that the campuses are working collaboratively in cancer research and cancer care. The Mayo Clinic transplant center is also working cooperatively across the campuses as are a number of other clinical areas in initiatives large and small. Administrative departments such as development, purchasing, planning, public affairs, human resources, finance, and information systems have largely removed the walls that once separated staff members by campus.

Mayo Clinic on three campuses is still evolving. Almost unnoticed is the fact that the Rochester operation itself was growing during the two decades in which the operations in Arizona and Florida were taking shape. For instance, the Rochester operation increased in its number of employees and newly constructed square feet of facilities about as much as the two southern campuses combined. But one thing is clear and central to the Mayo Clinic brand: the standard of care at any practice bearing the Mayo Clinic name must meet the same high level of excellence.

Reflecting on the experiences of the first 20 years, Carleton Rider observes that the Mayo brothers did not have a strategic plan for the Rochester campus. Their most significant partners—the Franciscan sisters—came because of a tornado, and the sisters built a hospital even though Dr. William Worrall Mayo was a reluctant supporter.

Dr. Trastek, CEO of Mayo Clinic Arizona, also makes the point that those who labor in Florida and Arizona were and are "truly pioneers," for they are creating the urban model—a successful Mayo Clinic in metropolitan markets. They are still "paving the way" for those who will succeed them in these new markets.

Mayo Medical Laboratories

With a staff of more than 800 individuals, Mayo Medical Laboratories (MML) is a clinical reference laboratory whose clients are typically large hospitals including many academic medical centers. The actual laboratory tests and analyses are performed within Mayo Clinic's department of laboratory medicine and pathology. MML's market is focused on esoteric tests that few other laboratories perform. To a large extent, the operation flies below the brand radar of consumers because it is exclusively in the business-to-business (B2B) category.

Mayo Clinic's department of laboratory medicine and pathology began to offer laboratory services for sophisticated, nonroutine clinical tests to physicians and hospitals around Rochester in the early 1970s. Initially, the services were a way to generate revenue from unused capacity in the laboratory. The strategy involved more than just providing testing data; the differentiating value in this service was Mayo-physician-to-community-physician consultation about results and their implications. Dr. Michael B. O'Sullivan, a pathologist and a retired CEO of Mayo Clinic Arizona, along with retired administrator Gerald Wollner were the founding leaders of this initiative. Dr. O'Sullivan emphasized from the outset that Mayo Clinic was not in competition for the local healthcare dollar. Rather, its goal was to help regional physicians offer a higher level of care to their patients. A small sales force and a courier service for the tissue samples supported the product line.

In the mid-1980s, MML moved from a regional market to national and international markets. The focus has remained on sophisticated, complex laboratory testing. Today, 25,000 to 30,000 specimens arrive by courier each day to be processed in Mayo Clinic laboratories. Reflecting on the beginning of this business endeavor, Dr. O'Sullivan states, "Even though 'branding' was not in vogue at the time, we were very much concerned not to harm the reputation of Mayo Clinic." Interestingly, his initial proposal for the program in 1971 also stated that, "While our program will be profit-oriented, profit *should not be* and *is not* our primary motivation." The board of governors saw in MML a source of revenue to continue to support medical research and education. Starting with the Mayo brothers, medical research and education had been funded out of clinical operations. However, with Medicare and other payers pressing providers for lower reimbursement, it seemed unlikely that net income from the practice of medicine could continue to adequately fund these missions.

The brand extension through MML has been successful because it leverages clinical knowledge into a solid business line. The extension did not require any significant investment of brand capital because the service was tightly linked to the high-quality everyday operations of Mayo's clinical laboratories. The risk was largely limited to the primary service elements—smoothly operating logistics that provide specimen pick-up and transportation, electronic communication of results, and verbal consultations when required. However, Mayo's leaders perceived risk in operating a large for-profit laboratory thinking that it might sully the purity of Mayo Clinic's position as a not-for-profit organization. The commercialization of Mayo Clinic along with the national sales force for the laboratory created some discomfort for the conservative organization.

Now, after several years of double-digit growth, MML has created challenges for the organization; these challenges have come from success. In 2000, seven laboratories competed in the United States for the majority of the reference laboratory business sector, and today MML is one of the four that remains. No longer is MML using excess capacity in the laboratories; instead it consumes nearly half of the testing volume in the department. Because the growth of MML has outpaced the growth of Mayo Clinic's core patient care operations, it comprises a larger share of the total operations. "These are good problems to have," says Dr. Franklin Cockerill, chair of the department of laboratory medicine and pathology. "Our growth reflects the market's desire for our differentiated service. We offer more than just a laboratory value on a report, for we still offer our clients the opportunity to communicate directly with some 150 expert consultants who help our client physicians use our findings optimally." MML has become a large and successful for-profit business and even a brand itself in the clinical laboratory business. The quality of the service provided to the client hospitals and physicians has not only created financial success but also ameliorated the risks associated with commercialization of a Mayo Clinic branded clinical service.

Health Information

In the early 1980s, Mayo Clinic's leadership approved an administrative division through which it would publish health information featuring first the *Mayo Clinic Health Letter* in 1983 followed by *Mayo Clinic Family Health Book* in 1990. This decision created the first brand extensions that leveraged the Mayo Clinic name in the consumer market. In using the Mayo Clinic brand to create revenue to support clinical research and education, several leaders had concerns that the altruistic reputation might be damaged. Today, Mayo Clinic has a robust consumer health information publishing organization working in both print and electronic media, and the organization has evolved into a multifaceted health management business.

Many healthcare organizations spend hundreds of thousands of dollars each year to mail newsletters to residents in their markets. Mayo Clinic has been able to leverage its brand to turn this model upside down with about 800,000 individuals paying an annual subscription fee for its two newsletters, *Mayo Clinic Health Letter* and *Mayo Clinic Women's HealthSource*. But there is one very important distinction: Mayo does not market its services in these publications. The newsletters provide useful, reliable, up-to-date health information to educate consumers and reinforce Mayo Clinic's reputation for medical expertise. The 1,448-page *Mayo Clinic Family Health Book*, with total sales of more than 1 million copies, is now in its third edition. Subsequently, other books ranging from cookbooks to a series on major diseases have been published. Together, this large library of health information reaches far more people than the Clinic reaches in person. The elasticity of the brand comfortably extends to health information that helps consumers manage their health. The current health information products meet this test according to market research.

The health management resources division recognized the importance of electronic media in the early 1990s and began producing CD-ROM titles, including the *Mayo Clinic Family Health Book*. The division launched a health information Web site, MayoHealthOasis.com, in 1996 as one of the earliest health information sites on the Internet. The name changed to MayoClinic.com in 2000 once the organization became more comfortable with the full "Mayo Clinic" branding of the site. This award-winning service now receives more than 13 million visits per month.

This Internet presence has stretched some boundaries for Mayo Clinic. The dot-com domain name raised a significant question about a brand that consumers believe is noncommercial. But market research in the 1990s revealed that few consumers were aware that the ".com" refers to a *commercial* domain category. Free to consumers, MayoClinic.com is financed by advertising and sponsorship revenue from companies providing health-related goods and services, as well as from syndication fees paid by other Web sites that license content from MayoClinic.com. Even today, internal critics question whether consumers might feel the integrity of Mayo Clinic is compromised when health information content is sponsored by, for instance, a pharmaceutical company whose products serve this disease category. After nearly a decade of this advertising, Mayo Clinic's reputation for integrity appears intact.

The greater issue facing the organization in recent times, however, has been the presence of two Web sites for consumers: MayoClinic.com, which focuses on consumer health information, and MayoClinic.org, which focuses on clinical services, appointment information, and electronic services for patients. Both sites show up on Web searches. Internally the editors can make clear distinctions between the Web sites, but consumers searching for either health information or appointment information can be frustrated if they happen to click first on the wrong site. A recent reorganization placed both consumer Web site teams under shared leadership to foster incremental integration so that patients and consumers are less confused and better served.

In the mid-to-late 1990s, the health management resources division expanded its library of print and electronic health information into a product line offered to major employers and insurers as a customized tool to help employees and members actively manage their own health. "Mayo Clinic Lifestyle Coaching" and the "Ask Mayo Clinic" nurse line are two of the telephone-based services marketed to employers and insurers. In Lifestyle Coaching, counselors work one-on-one with program participants, helping them to make changes beneficial to their health. In 2008, the coaching service was available for five lifestyle factors: healthy weight, exercise, nutrition, stress management, and tobacco cessation. The "Ask Mayo Clinic" nurse line is staffed by Mayo Clinic registered nurses who answer questions and offer health information to help people make more informed healthcare decisions and facilitate more appropriate use of healthcare resources. The Mayo Clinic Tobacco Quitline uses trained counselors to provide assistance to tobacco users who want to quit. Employers and some state tobacco cessation programs contract for this service developed by Mayo's own Nicotine Dependence Center.

In the view of some of Mayo current leaders, three brand risks remain: (1) eroding Mayo's reputation for integrity by the commercialization of the Mayo Clinic brand with what some believe are the unbecoming tools of direct mail used in marketing the print newsletters as well as by the department of development and advertising on MayoClinic.com, (2) inadvertently repositioning Mayo Clinic as a source of just health information rather than as a provider of choice for the most serious medical needs, and (3) frequent and diverse communications from a number of Mayo Clinic entities with worthy but parallel missions subordinate to the larger mission of clinical services addressing the needs of patients.

Regarding the first risk, Mayo Clinic is, in the view of some, tarnished by direct mail packages and practices that contrast so starkly with the clues of quality prominent on the campuses. However, both qualitative and quantitative market research have been unable to ascertain a negative brand impact of this marketing. Of course, market research could be missing something that is actually happening. John La Forgia, chair of the department of public affairs, likens established brands like Mayo Clinic to the light of stars, "What we see today is something that is old—experiences of grand-parents may bring Mayo to mind." So mistakes being made today might not show up in research for many years, when, of course, it would be too late to recover.

The second risk—positioning—is even more nebulous. It is clear that someone who reads health information in print or on the Web is having a brand experience very different from a patient's direct interaction with a doctor. Market research reveals that health infor-mation users do have a shallow view of the brand compared with patients, but Mayo's primary identity as the place to go for high-level clinical care is not lost on health information users. In fact, they have a richer understanding of Mayo Clinic than most other consumers who have only vague notions supporting Mayo's classic positioning as a "court of last resort."

The third risk—competing Mayo Clinic subordinate missions—reflects the complex interests of the organization. Not only does the health information group mail out millions of pieces of direct mail each year to solicit health information subscriptions and sales, but the department of development is sending out solicitations to poten-tial donors. Sales representatives are calling on companies to market health management resources. While all these activities are worthy and fully endorsed by the organization, none of them deals in any direct way with the multi-billion-dollar clinical enterprise that is the heart and soul of Mayo Clinic. This is the enterprise that provides care to over a half million patients per year. "These frequent and diverse communications complicate the task of communicating clear messages from Mayo Clinic," observes La Forgia.

Mayo Health System

The threats to unfettered patient access posed by HMOs in the 1980s became more pronounced in 1992 as President Bill Clinton was elected with a seeming mandate for healthcare reform. Many in healthcare management expected that this time U.S. healthcare would be formed into regional networks where HMOs and other insurers/payers would, along with physicians and hospitals, become part of a closed system that would be responsible for all the medical services of a defined population. Patients opting out of their network physicians and hospitals would face large out-of-pocket costs. Hospitals and physician groups around the country scrambled to find partners lest they be isolated outside the networks.

Mayo Clinic in Rochester was not immune to these concerns. Major clinics and hospitals on every side of Rochester began assembling their networks through mergers and acquisitions. With just over 50 percent of the patient volume in Rochester coming from the farms, towns, and small cities within 120 miles of Rochester, Mayo needed to protect its "turf" lest important business be funneled off to competitors. Mayo Clinic was an attractive partner for a number of clinics and hospitals whose administrators initiated conversations about joining with Mayo in some way. By the end of 1992, two multispecialty clinics and one community hospital became the beginning of what is arguably one of the most successful networks that dates from this era.[14]

The first clinic from Decorah, Iowa, was branded, Decorah Clinic, a Mayo Regional Practice. Later, Midelfort Clinic of Eau Claire, Wisconsin, joined the network, and the branding followed suit. Then Luther Hospital—the primary hospital used by Midelfort Clinic—became a member of the network and was presented to the community as Luther Hospital, a Mayo Regional Hospital. Mayo's brands contrasted with many other organizations whose acquisitions took on the corporate name followed by a geographic locator.

However, the "Mayo Regional Hospital" and "Mayo Regional Practice" designations did not fit the organizational structure that Mayo Clinic envisioned. Dr. Michael B. O'Sullivan, who, two decades earlier as a young pathologist helped create MML, also led in the development of the regional network clinics and hospitals in the 1990s. He comments, "Still less than a decade into our experience with the merger of Mayo Clinic with its two Rochester hospitals, it was clear that we should strive to achieve integration of the clinics and the hospitals in these regional communities. We wanted to blend the hospitals and the clinics into a single local entity." Dr. William Rupp, who was the president of Midelfort Clinic, helped develop and implement this model and merger in Eau Claire. This was the first of 13 different hospital/physician group mergers within Mayo Health System over the next 12 years.

The final branding strategy was still an open question. Several considerations were at play. First, Mayo Clinic was sensitive to the possibility of its being perceived as the "800-pound gorilla" who marched into communities to take over their local healthcare institutions. It was important not to position the network development as takeovers. Second, observes James G. Anderson, who was the first administrative leader for Mayo Health System and is currently the chief administrative officer in Arizona, "We clearly told the providers that we would not upset the way they were running their practice. We said it was their choice if they referred a patient to Mayo Clinic—we wanted to earn referrals to Mayo. But we did talk about building a larger vision together to help them to do better for their patients." The branding needed to reflect that local control was real. Third, the local hospitals, which were all not-for-profit organizations, belonged to the communities. This was the hospital and clinic that had served local families for as much as three generations. Those families had donated to the local hospital, not Mayo Clinic. The branding strategy needed to honor the affection and loyalty that the communities had for *their* hospitals. Furthermore, these local hospitals and clinics had developed their own brand equity in their local markets. Finally, these new affiliations, which resulted from their merger into Mayo Foundation, were not conceived as Mayo Clinics, for the brand meaning of Mayo Clinic is associated with high-level tertiary and quaternary medicine not available in most local communities. Mayo Clinic is where one goes when no one else can help. The Mayo Health System clinics were the first place to go. Even today, over 70 percent of Mayo Health System doctors are primary care providers, although some of the larger clinics have a number of specialists.

The solution was to preserve to the extent possible the identities of the local hospitals and clinics while also stating clearly their affiliation with Mayo. The merger of the operations of Midelfort Clinic and Luther Hospital in Eau Claire resulted in calling the entity Luther Midelfort/Mayo Health System. In some communities the merged hospital and Clinic used the city name plus "Medical Center" as, for instance, Austin Medical Center/Mayo Health System. The primary identity of these hospital/physician organizations is with the locally familiar names—in Eau Claire the blending of the hospital and clinic names. (See Exhibit 8-3.) In the logo design, "Mayo Health System" is a subhead in a typeface smaller than that of the local hospital to signify a brand endorsement strategy. "Mayo" rather than "Mayo Clinic" is used deliberately to create a degree of separation from "Mayo Clinic;" still, the presence of "Mayo" indicates that the operation is endorsed by Mayo—a stamp of approval. Further, by association there is an implicit promise that Mayo Clinic will be involved in helping to ensure that high-quality community medicine is practiced.

This health system has been successful from the perspective of both Mayo Clinic and the local communities. "Through Mayo Health System, the healthcare service in the local communities was first stabilized and is now enhanced: hospitals and hospital services were often at risk. We've doubled the number of doctors in most of these communities," says Dr. Peter Carryer, medical director of Mayo Health System. "In addition, with efficiencies brought to their

Exhibit 8-3
Mayo Health System Logo

Luther Midelfort

Mayo Health System

operations, the community systems could afford to improve their facilities significantly. The Health System has generated a positive bottom line every year. Most importantly, care for patients has been improved in 67 regional communities. In the end it is about the patient." Rochester has seen steady increases in patients from these communities as well. This has been a successful brand extension from every perspective.

Protecting the Brand

At first, the Clinic's goal was to just protect the family honor and name. Doubters, cynics, enemies, and quacks were the dark side of the celebrity status that the Mayo brothers had earned. The most disturbing of the backlashes came from the medical community, particularly in the upper Midwest. The "third party" in this tension was the press—yellow journalists who sensationalized the Mayo story with details and claims that had no basis in fact. The most inflaming article appeared in the April 1909 issue of *Human Life* in which the journalist made outlandish claims of achievement by the Mayo brothers: "Not a single patient died under their knife," "The Kaiser sought strenuously to persuade them to live in Germany," and "Court of last appeal for the sick of all the world." The publisher, in an unfortunate marketing move, sent free copies to physicians across the country. The doctors, however, concluded that the Mayo brothers had financed this unsolicited circulation as a self-promotion. In fact, the journalist had never even interviewed either of the brothers.

Dr. Will was humiliated when a colleague in Iowa wrote to "uninvite" him to speak at a state AMA meeting because of the furor this publication raised among the physicians of the state. Ultimately, the brothers responded with an article published in the *Journal of the American Medical Association*. They presented their case: "It seems incredible that any fair-minded man in the medical profession could read this article [that had been published by *Human Life*] and believe that we had anything to do with its production.... It is incomprehensible how anyone could suppose that two men over 40 years of age and one at 90 years of age would deliberately take measures to discredit the work of a lifetime."[15] The Mayo brothers had been skittish about publicity even before the *Human Life* story. For instance, in responding to a request for an interview with a newspaper, Dr. Will declined the interview in a 1908 letter where he explains: "The only way in which the public can distinguish a man of reputation from a charlatan is in the question of publicity, as no honorable man will permit the use of his name in this way."[16] The cautious approach to publicity prevailed at the Clinic for decades.

Today's leaders at Mayo Clinic know what the founders sensed: the brand—the reputation of Mayo Clinic—is its most valuable asset. John La Forgia states, "A specific financial value has not been determined for it is enough to know that the brand is invaluable and that if lost, the reputation that is the brand would be gone forever. Any recovery would be partial at best." In 1997, Mayo Clinic established a formal management process to protect the brand over time. The primary players in protecting the brand are the brand team, the in-house legal department, and the board of governors. Loyal patients and employees also play a brand protection role, as these self-appointed brand monitors frequently report possible problems to the brand team.

Protective action against external forces is required to maintain control of the presented brand. For instance, when an organization uses Mayo's name in an advertisement or other marketing materials without Mayo approval, internal legal counsel takes appropriate measures. A Mayo Clinic attorney vacationing in Canada was surprised to read that a new clinic there was considering "The Mayo Clinic of the North" as its name. A single letter from the legal department took care of the matter. Weekly scans of new domain name registrations catch virtually all new applications using the protected versions of the Mayo name. The brand is registered and protected internationally. Yet, in 2006 a Web scan revealed that a "Mayo Clinic" hair removal parlor had recently opened and was operating under that name in England. Mayo Clinic's attorneys contacted the owner and a settlement was reached in which the name of the business was changed. As in this case, external issues are usually remedied by Mayo's internal intellectual property attorneys. Although the legal system works slowly and expensively, these matters typically reach a definitive conclusion.

The greatest risks to the brand come from inside Mayo Clinic itself. The proponents are usually well meaning, but some proposals, if played out in the market, could potentially damage the reputation of the brand. The brand team, which has access to a wealth of market research information about the brand, adjudicates these matters. The *Mayo Clinic Brand Management Guidelines*, developed from a deep understanding of the brand and culture, facilitates these deliberations with four key principles:

1. *A product, service, or relationship using the "Mayo" or "Mayo Clinic" brand name must be owned by Mayo Clinic or be under Mayo Clinic's full (ultimate) control.* This principle was crystallized while Mayo Health System was being developed in the early to mid-1990s. Mayo had extended but ultimately fruitless discussions with several hospitals or physician groups that had expressed interest in an affiliation. Many were large, successful systems that provided excellent medical care. Unlike the hospitals and clinics that joined Mayo Health System, some of these suitors were interested in an "affiliation" short of merging their assets and operations into Mayo Foundation. After serious and extended negotiations, however, Mayo Clinic leadership realized that it was comfortable only in situations in which full, immediate control was in place. Mayo Health System members are all located within 120 miles of Rochester, so it is possible to manage the relationship closely. Nothing that smacked of a "franchise" of Mayo's brand could deliver the valued promise that the brand had developed with its millions of past patients. Nothing that suggested Mayo Clinic was trying to exchange use of its name for cash could ever be reconciled. The principle applies not only to clinic operations but also to all products the brand is applied to today.

2. *Use of the Mayo Clinic name solely to assure success or name recognition of a service, product, or relationship is not appropriate.* On a few occasions, Mayo leadership has been faced with decisions in

which internal proponents of a product concept have argued that its success in the marketplace required use of the Mayo Clinic name. Leadership, however, has held to the principle that the product must first have market viability without the Mayo brand and that only a product or service that will be successful without Mayo Clinic branding will earn the right to the extra boost that the brand offers. The Clinic seeks to use its brand name on internally developed high-quality goods and services that fill a genuine need and will enhance brand equity; the Mayo brand should not be diminished by being used to try to prop up a marginal offering to the market. The pre-1997 brand portfolio did contain a few offerings that probably did not meet this criterion. None exist today. This evolution occurred through the normal course of market forces rather than by formal action of brand governance.

3. *The Mayo Clinic brand is not to be used in a manner that trivializes the name or institution.* This subjective principle comes into play in a wide array of decisions that concern the presented brand. For instance, in a joint advertising program with a major retailer offering Mayo health information, the Clinic's brand leadership could not find a zone of comfort, so the relationship ultimately faded. The partner had developed a successful but light-hearted and humorous advertising style incongruent with Mayo Clinic's being viewed as the "court of last resort" by many people with life-threatening diseases. Because this principle is subjective, rejecting requests from internal colleagues challenges the collegial spirit in which the organization endeavors to work. Many proposals are well-meaning but amateur in nature—names chosen in a contest or promotional posters designed by a staff member. This principle has been used in turning down proposals for a Mayo Clinic hot-air balloon, T-shirt designs, and numerous promotional items.

4. *Agreements must be in place to enable Mayo Clinic Brand Management Guidelines to be in force when any part of Mayo Clinic's organization works with other healthcare providers, industries, or brands.* In recent years academic medical centers have faced increased public scrutiny regarding the relationships between medical researchers

and pharmaceutical and medical equipment companies. This has long been a concern of Mayo Clinic. Since 1910, Mayo Clinic has had an oversight group to monitor relationships with industry. The current group, the medical/industry relations committee, is just the most recent version. At the heart of its responsibilities are concerns about conflicts of interest between Mayo Clinic and corporations serving healthcare providers and patients. The committee's charge emphasizes that the primacy of the interests of the patient will be reflected in all business relationships.

This is a challenging area for Mayo Clinic and most other academic organizations that conduct research and are developing tomorrow's treatments and technology. Relationships with industry are necessary to obtain capital funds to develop products to the point where they are ready for the market. This environment has increased the importance and the tasks of the medical/industry relations committee, for it oversees all relations of all individual physicians, researchers, and administrators in consulting, speaking, and research relationships with for-profit organizations. A dedicated group of attorneys and paralegals negotiates contracts that address use of the Mayo name and explicitly require approval of all communications. The brand team also has developed a complex set of "common law" guidelines for these sometimes challenging brand relationships.

The issues are not confined to conflict of interest; the simple principle of win-win also guides. For example, companies that provide goods and services to Mayo Clinic often want to tout this fact in their marketing materials. To guard against those who might want to leverage Mayo's name as an implied endorsement, Mayo allows its name to be used only in a list in which five or more other organizations are listed and requires that all names be in the same type size and listed alphabetically.

Finally, Mayo Clinic has developed an acid test to be used for making branding decisions (see Exhibit 8-4). The activity must be compatible with the stated values and principles of the organization and reinforce the Clinic's attributes and essence, which have been

Exhibit 8-4
Brand Management Acid Test

The following criteria should be applied to determine if a proposed product, service, or relationship merits the Mayo Clinic name:

1. Is it consistent with the Mayo Clinic vision and core principles?
2. Does it reinforce the brand attributes, essence, and values patients and consumers associate with Mayo Clinic?
3. By user and industry standards, would it be judged among the best in its category?
4. Is the service or product clearly related and committed to health and healing?
5. Does the product or service reinforce in the minds of the consumer that Mayo Clinic exists first and foremost for the benefit of humanity rather than for the accumulation of wealth or other commercial purposes?
6. Does the service, product, or relationship deliver the benefits patients and consumers say they expect from Mayo Clinic?

identified by extensive brand research. Mayo's brand elasticity research indicates that the market expects Mayo to offer only goods and services of the highest quality. Brand elasticity research also shows that Mayo's brand reputation limits its use to goods and services that focus on health and healing. Mayo is expected to operate above the zone of style, fads, and vanity. Sunglass frames, cosmetics, and high-fashion sportswear would trivialize the distinctive clinical brand. In its extensions of the brand, Mayo Clinic must remain true to its focus on advocacy for the needs of patients and humanity and not the accumulation of wealth.

Protecting a brand is much more a human art than a quantitative science. For instance, in the mid-1990s prior to any brand research, Mayo's board of governors turned down a mature business proposal to create Mayo Clinic branded cosmetics that research in Mayo's department of dermatology determined would be superior to other commercial products on the market. The board of governors rejected the plan not out of concerns about its potential profitability, but rather because board members sensed that somehow the product did not feel like the right thing for Mayo. So leaders must artfully manage each type of influence in the service branding model: the presented brand, external brand communications, and customer experience with the organization. Brand research has now supplied data that provide a sound structure for understanding the brand and for processing decisions, but these decisions are not always clear-cut. In the end, leaders must depend on their gut feelings—the intuition based on a genuine understanding of the culture and values. To date, the record at Mayo Clinic is quite positive.

Lessons for Managers

Sustained brand leadership for more than 100 years is rare, but this is what Mayo Clinic has achieved. It is difficult to identify other organizations that have demonstrated such brand strength durability. Managers can draw multiple branding lessons from the Mayo Clinic case study. Here we discuss three especially salient lessons.

Lesson 1: Focus on the performers.   A labor-intensive service brand can be only as good as the people creating the experience that forms brand meaning. As discussed in Chapter 2, the personal values of the service providers directly influence the quality and value of the service they provide. When the Clinic extended its brand to Florida and Arizona, Mayo went a step beyond hiring for values and talent since virtually every unit of these new organizations had a seasoned Rochester employee, usually in a leadership position, to model Mayo Clinic service and culture.

In addition, the "stage" on which the service is performed offers clues to the employee/performers as well as the audience of patients. Mayo's careful design of its newly created space in Jacksonville and

Scottsdale provides clues about Mayo-branded quality to patients, but at the same time it suggests a high service expectation to the employees. The presence of beautiful wood paneling and stone, attractive and interesting art, and quality furnishings in Mayo Clinic might be compared to a fine restaurant with an attractive decor, linen cloths on tables, and waiters in formal wear. Mayo's environment encourages employee service appropriate to the values, culture, and history of the brand.

Furthermore, the generous ethos established by the Mayos—and still prevailing inside Mayo Clinic—encourages the generous volunteerism of employees in their roles as service providers. Mayo's practice of finding the right niches for employees is seen as generous to those who work there. A relatively rich offering of employee benefits also positions Mayo Clinic as a benevolent employer. Because Mayo Clinic, the employer, takes good care of its employees, the employees are more likely to take good care of those they serve.

Lesson 2: Play defense, not just offense.   In 1983, Mayo Clinic was playing offense with the three boldest initiatives in its history: the geographic expansions in Florida and Arizona, an aggressive shift in MML strategy, and publication of consumer health information. These bold offensive plays are the exception rather than the rule when viewed in the context of more than a century of operation. Less dramatic but critically important is Mayo's consistent brand defense. Mayo Clinic remains a cautious institution that prizes quality and consistency over growth. The reputation being defended is no longer that of the founding Mayo family but the reputation of the organization thriving today on the good work of over 42,000 employees. The Mayo brand is a trusted brand. The Clinic's leadership views the trust of patients and referring physicians as a priceless resource to be protected at all costs. The institution's carefulness implemented through an elaborate committee structure, clearly articulated brand management guidelines, a brand team to enforce them, and, of course, the organization's core values have been instrumental in preserving the trust that defines the Mayo Clinic brand. Mayo Clinic plays aggressive brand defense and cautious brand offense.

Lesson 3: Turn customers into marketers.   An astonishing 91 percent of Mayo Clinic patients indicate that they praise the Clinic to others.[17] Mayo Clinic's patients do the advertising. Services that are important, complex, and variable (as healthcare is) are especially prone to word-of-mouth communications. Prospective customers benefit from the unvarnished, credible input of experienced customers. Fully capitalizing on word of mouth, however, requires providing a service that exceeds customers' expectations. Services that meet expectations are common; uncommon services generate word-of-mouth communications. Mayo Clinic's medical experts working as a team offer a healthcare experience that is not readily available to patients in their local markets. The Clinic's emphasis on systems efficiency and excellent interpersonal service further distinguishes what it offers its market. The Clinic evokes the element of pleasant surprise, which is necessary to exceed expectations. Patients want to tell others about the Mayo Clinic. A common assumption in services branding is that the marketing department and its advertising create the brand, but as our model and Mayo Clinic demonstrate, the brand heroes are those industrial engineers and other leaders who design the service processes and the line employees who perform their individualized service one patient at a time.

Summary

We know of no other organization that better illustrates the services branding model presented in this chapter than Mayo Clinic. That Mayo Clinic is a powerhouse brand cannot be disputed. Just as certain is the fact that the brand came about as the by-product of consistent focus on the service experience of patients. In organizations that deliver consequential, complex, variable, and personal service, the performance is critically important. Customers of these services become conveyers of information that can help those they know and love. Great service brands, in the end, are built on excellent customer experiences and this is the metabranding lesson the Mayo Clinic teaches.

NOTES

1. Joe M. Inguanzo, "PRC National Consumer Perception Study," Professional Research Corporation, Omaha, NE, publication pending.
2. The framework for this chapter and some of the content is adapted from Leonard L. Berry and Kent D. Seltman, "Building a Strong Services Brand: Lessons from Mayo Clinic," *Business Horizons*, May–June 2007, pp. 199–209.
3. Leonard L. Berry, "Cultivating Service Brand Equity," *Journal of the Academy of Marketing Science*, Winter 2000, pp. 128–137.
4. Stan Richards, "Building a Brand," a presentation at Texas A&M University's Center for Retailing Studies Symposium, Dallas, TX, October 8, 1998.
5. Berry, 2000, p. 129.
6. Leonard L. Berry and A. Parasuraman, *Marketing Services: Competing through Quality* (New York: The Free Press, 1991).
7. Kevin Keller, "Conceptualization, Measuring, and Managing Customer-Based Brand Equity," *Journal of Marketing*, January 1993, pp. 1–22.
8. As quoted in Leonard L. Berry and Sandra S. Lampo, "Branding Labor-Intensive Services," *Business Strategy Review*, Spring 2004, p. 20.
9. Helen Clapesattle, *The Doctors Mayo* [abridged] (Rochester, MN: Mayo Foundation for Medical Education and Research, 1969), p. 242.
10. Clapesattle, pp. 243–244.
11. Mayo Clinic proprietary market study, 2007.
12. John T. Shepherd, *Inside the Mayo Clinic: A Memoir* (Afton, MN: Afton Historical Press, 2003), p. 135.
13. Robert Waller, "Diversification Update to the Board of Governors," September, 1894. Private papers of Robert Waller, p. 6.
14. Peter W. Carryer and Sylvester Steriotf, "Mayo Health System: A Decade of Achievement," *Mayo Clinic Proceedings*, vol. 78, 2003, pp. 1047–1053.
15. William J. Mayo and Charles H. Mayo, "A Disclaimer from the Mayo Brothers," *JAMA*, May 15, 1909, p. 2.
16. Letter from William J. Mayo to J. F. Percy and Fred Ewing, November 4, 1908.
17. Mayo Clinic proprietary market study, 2007.

CHAPTER 9

INVESTING IN TOMORROW'S ORGANIZATION

*I*n 1994, we found out that our large practice of complex knee- and hip-joint replacements lost money—actually about $2 million per year. When you are an orthopedic surgeon and working very hard and dealing with patients referred by other orthopedic surgeons, this is very difficult to accept. Partly this reflected the nature of our practice, as we do a fair number of surgeries to replace failed implants, but it also resulted from things we were doing—keeping people in the hospital too long, for instance. Most significantly, however, the loss stemmed from the implants we were using, for we were implanting 10 to 12 versions of half a dozen major designs for any one clinical indication. Clearly, things needed to change.

It is important to remember that the Mayo Clinic culture is very strong. My colleagues and I have all given up our ability to earn as much money as we could in private practice. We have bought into a culture where we labor for the common good and are focused on doing what is in the patient's best interest. When you say to these MDs, "We have to reduce cost in caring for patients," that flies in the face of what we are doing here.

Physicians revert to primal instincts when confronted with information strongly suggesting that they change the care of patients. They begin hiding behind rocks—the first is the data quality rock. They will argue, "Your data are flawed. Go back and look at this again." It is a cultural expression saying,

"We are unwilling to change." So we made sure the data presented to physicians were accurate. And, since this was physician-led, it was physician-to-physician communication rather than financial analyst-to-physician. So, I was able to say, "The data are accurate, and you can't question them. But if you can demonstrate to me that they are inaccurate, then I'll rework the data. Lacking the demonstration, however, the data are accurate." So, we blew up the first rock.

Then most physicians will hide behind the clinical quality rock. It is usually expressed in some variation of this message, "I'm not going to do that because I have the best interest of my patient in mind." We needed a logical argument that enabled the physicians to see the needed change as an expression of our culture. For years we had held such a strong commitment to the best interests of the patient that there was hesitancy to question physicians' clinical preferences when they hid behind this rock. Consequently, we'd come to this wide variation in our practice based on the surgeons' personal perceptions of what was best.

The first step in change was to get my colleagues to accept the premise that each of 12 different prosthetic knee implants was probably not "in the best interests of the patient," particularly when surgeons had their favorite implants and their cost varied widely. And, when we faced the losses from our practice, it seemed that cost did matter. So, as medical scientists we came to understand that variation is expensive and standardization is a way both to control cost and to improve quality. We blew up the clinical quality rock with this ground rule: We will adopt evidence-based criteria to identify what is best for patients and then choose the lowest-cost prosthetic joints that do not compromise the quality of patient outcomes. Our goal was to reduce the choice to two implants for any one clinical indication.

So, we partnered with our colleagues in supply-chain management who negotiated with the manufacturers of the implants. It turns out that we moved the net operating income of the knee and hip practice from a negative number to a positive number in two years—an $8 million swing in the Rochester practice alone. Even more important, there was no compromise in the patient outcomes; the complication rate in our patients did not change. The savings have held for a decade and been multiplied as the Florida and Arizona practices as well as Mayo Health System have adopted this approach.

This account by Dr. Bernard Morrey, past chair of orthopedic surgery and past member of the board of governors, illustrates the primary principle guiding Mayo Clinic as it invests in its future: Mayo Clinic will succeed best by being Mayo Clinic.

As Dr. Morrey negotiated this change in the clinical practice among his colleagues, there was no compromise of the core value: the needs of the patient come first. In fact, by working together on the problem, they also lived the teamwork value while better meeting the needs of their individual patients because they lowered expense without compromising clinical care. This case study became the model for other Mayo initiatives. According to James R. Francis, chair of supply chain management for Mayo Clinic, a similar project in the pharmacies has saved more than $40 million during the past five years. Other projects—all physician-led—have produced efficiencies in cardiovascular medicine, gastroenterology, radiology, and capital equipment.

The discipline that Mayo exhibits in these supply-chain examples reveals an organization fueled by the internal power of teamwork and focused simultaneously on the customer's needs and on the financial outcomes required to sustain Mayo Clinic for future generations of patients. As discussed later in the chapter, this organizational discipline and power is now implementing *evidence-based* quality measures across the organization. In service organizations, "Control of destiny is a success sustainer.... The senior leaders of the business determine its course—not competitors, not lenders, not institutional shareholders, not unions, not suppliers, not community activists, not the media, not politicians. The senior leaders keep the organization focused on creating superior value for customers, and this focus helps secure the organization's future."[1]

In this chapter, we explore Mayo Clinic's commitment to tomorrow as seen through the strategic priorities it pursues today: *integration* of the three campuses into a single, smoothly functioning organization is our first topic. Following are *improved quality* and *safety* in the clinical practice, *high-value care* based on clinical outcomes over time, *innovation* in healthcare delivery, *advocacy* on behalf of patient-first interests in healthcare practice and policy reform, and *leadership development*.

Realizing the Power of One

Dr. Denis Cortese, CEO of Mayo Clinic, is clear: "Mayo Clinic's purpose in life is caring for patients. We have a hundred years of practice at building a delivery system centered on the individual patient." Mayo knows where it comes from and where it wants to go, but Mayo Clinic's destiny is being forged in perhaps the most complex scientific, social, and political environment in its history. The United States is engaged in a national conversation about a healthcare delivery system that most analysts agree is broken; cynics even ask, "What system?" Also looming are questions about how to finance the healthcare that Americans have come to expect. As the entire industry deals with the social and political demand for change, Dr. Cortese sees a national movement toward the vision Mayo has developed: "A healthcare system delivering care focused on the individual patient while providing high value, better outcomes, better safety, better service, and lower cost by integrating and coordinating care among different providers and organizations." He asserts, "Mayo Clinic is better prepared to live through this than any other large institution." But Mayo Clinic is not perfect. Its leadership is working to ensure that the organization lives up to its reputation— that it consistently delivers the implicit promise of the brand that brings comfort and peace of mind to those who think of Mayo Clinic when grave illness strikes.

The first order of business under Dr. Cortese's leadership as president and CEO has been the integration of the three campuses into a single organization. As discussed in Chapter 8, when the Florida and Arizona campuses were opened, it was unclear whether they needed to function as part of a single organization. Some of Mayo's leaders thought that the parent organization, known as Mayo Foundation at the time, should serve as a holding company with various business units operating with some significant autonomy. When the decisions to expand were made in 1983, Mayo's leadership was responsible only for Mayo Clinic in Rochester—an outpatient clinic with fewer than 8,000 employees. Many of the organization's leaders believed that Mayo Clinic was about to reach the maximum size that could be managed effectively. Furthermore, in 1983 the Mayo Clinic operation in Rochester was poised to assume responsibility in 1986 for two local hospitals—Saint Marys and Methodist—which would more than double the number of employees and add untold complexity to the Rochester operation. Given this challenge, Mayo's leaders were reluctant to become deeply involved in two fledging campuses. It also seemed reasonable to allow the new campuses to have some distance from Rochester's culture and practices because they were operating in new, unfamiliar regional markets.

However, by 2003 when Dr. Cortese became CEO, it was clear that integration into a single Mayo Clinic organization was necessary. Dr. Dawn Milliner is chair of the clinical practice advisory group. This group consists of leaders from the clinical practice committees on each of the three campuses and is charged with increasing coordination of Mayo's entire clinical practice. As chair of the clinical practice advisory group, Dr. Milliner has been at the center of the campus integration project. "When we started, people didn't know each other or where expertise even resided, because we had grown so rapidly and were so separated by geography." Since the late 1960s Mayo has had a powerful priority paging system that connects two consultants by phone in seconds. It was extended to Jacksonville and Scottsdale in the 1980s. It is a vital communications tool, particularly within the staff on each campus. This technology, however, could not solve the underlying problem: consultants who did not know one another. Videoconferencing also has been available since the practices started in Florida and Arizona. Videoconferencing is helpful, but it also works best after some face-to-face familiarity is established. Shirley Weis, chief administrative officer, indicates that Mayo now realizes the importance of establishing more personal familiarity across the campuses to facilitate integration. This means more travel than in the past.

Dr. Milliner sees the integration initiative as a chance to recapture what the Mayo brothers accomplished in their day—bringing every resource they could to each individual patient. "However, today," she says, "we have a wonderful opportunity to bring the best of Mayo Clinic care to each patient, no matter where in our system the expertise resides or where the patient is receiving care. We are in a digital age where communication tools permit integration within a much larger organization." The use of the electronic medical record or a digital CT scan combined with a phone call or an e-mail, for instance, permits real-time consultation with the most qualified expert among all 2,500 Mayo Clinic physicians without regard to geographic location. As we will see later in the chapter, the enterprise learning system has powerful potential to provide automated just-in-time patient management information to any Mayo physician whose patient has a rare clinical finding. Dr. Milliner concludes, "It is a daunting task and won't be easily accomplished. But for me the exciting part is that we are going back to what we inadvertently lost—the ability to leverage our entire system to address each patient's needs."

Because integration is a work in progress, its full implications are, as yet, undetermined. But even now, the organization can understand some of what integration means to the Mayo organization. Most importantly, it means that patients will receive the same high-quality service, diagnosis, and treatment regardless of which campuses they use. It means that any physician hired to work on a Mayo Clinic campus is qualified to work on the other two, and today, in contrast to the past, hires are frequently vetted by clinical peers across more than one campus. It means that ultimately there may be one appointment office where now there are three. Integration is leading to common information management systems instead of each campus selecting its own software infrastructure. And very importantly, capital investments and growth decisions will reflect judgments about what is best for Mayo Clinic overall rather than the interests of a single campus. Dr. Cortese speaks of today's Mayo Clinic as "an organism—a single entity—so if any part of it is not doing well, the whole organism is affected."

Quality—"We Can Do Better"

Mayo Clinic seeks to control its destiny by accelerating its efforts and investments to improve quality. Dr. Cortese explains that quality—defined by clinical outcomes, safety, and service—at Mayo is excellent, but he believes that the organization can do better. Dr. Stephen Swensen, professor of radiology and Mayo Clinic director for quality, notes, "Mayo Clinic leads all other U.S. providers when you look at objective measures of outcomes, safety, service, preventable death, mortality rates adjusted to account for preexisting medical problems and health status, and adverse events with harm to the patient. For instance, when the hospital standardized mortality rates were first released a couple years ago, Saint Marys Hospital had the lowest mortality rate of any general hospital in the United States and the United Kingdom. When you look at all these measures as a composite, Mayo is at the top." But, he warns, "We are *just* at the top of the group of elite providers; we are not as far ahead as we aspire to be." The caution that Dr. Swensen articulates has become a rallying call from leadership throughout the organization. Dr. Swensen is confident that Mayo will rise to the challenge, "No one is better positioned to break away from the rest of the leaders in clinical reliability than an integrated group practice that values teamwork, understands the dividends of a more horizontal, cross-functional team of nurses, technicians, doctors, pharmacists, and administrators, and has a century-long history of patient-centered care facilitated by a large contingent of systems engineers." It is clear from interviews with Mayo leaders that they expect improvement.

Mayo Clinic is not isolated from the rest of U.S. healthcare. Although more than 60 percent of Mayo's physicians have had some training at Mayo Clinic, few have trained there exclusively. Dr. Milliner explains, "Those of us in American medicine accepted error and poor outcomes as inevitable. We told ourselves, 'That's just the way it is when you treat complex conditions—there will be some number of adverse effects—we can't help it.' Still everyone working from this mindset was trying to get better, while they tolerated some bad outcomes." Dr. Milliner also suggests that between the 1960s and the end of the 1980s, U.S. medicine experienced tremendous technological advances. "Everyone was focused on new treatments and procedural interventions—using those to improve outcomes. They were not paying much attention to errors in judgment, handoff problems, and safety issues." In 2000, the Institute of Medicine startled Americans by asserting that as many as 98,000 patients died needlessly each year in U.S. hospitals.[2] Mayo Clinic, with the rest of U.S. healthcare, took notice. "We need to take a critical look at ourselves," Dr. Milliner suggests. "Mayo has been at the front of the curve from the start, but the whole curve is shifting. Even though we do well today, it is not good enough. We know now that it is not the best we can do."

The rallying call for improving quality is seen, in a sense, as a corrective action. In the early days of Mayo Clinic, the physicians practiced with clear standard procedures. Dr. Swensen notes, "The archives in radiology show, for instance, that a barium exam had an absolute template procedure down to how the tech handed the cup to the patient. We drifted away from that standard work to a more autonomous model where we let physicians come here and practice the way they wanted. So we developed a more heterogeneous practice, which is not a hallmark of high reliability and the ultimate safety environment." Because Mayo Clinic has hired superb physicians and support staff, its outcomes are still excellent. However, the increased availability of publicly reported data revealed that Mayo has only a narrow lead in positive outcomes generally and that it lags behind other elite providers in some specific cases. "We have a tinge of complacency where we assumed that we were always giving the best care and that our outcomes were always world class—without an opportunity to get much better," Dr. Swensen adds.

The catalyst to change in this broad initiative is transparency—open sharing of the performance measures of the clinical groups both inside and outside of Mayo Clinic. According to Dr. Cortese, "Transparency means measuring our performance, sharing what we learn broadly, working together to find ways to improve, and reporting our outcomes so that we're honest with ourselves and others about whether we're meeting our goals. Mistakes can be a great catalyst for change. Learning from our mistakes is the only way to prevent them from happening again." Dr. Swensen concurs, "The more we share with one another about our performance—how often diabetics get the best care or when the wrong dose of a medicine is given to a patient or when the right dose goes to the wrong patient—the more we have a catalyst for change, for being the best we can be," Dr. Swensen says. Mayo Clinic started posting performance outcomes by each practice site on its intranet in October 2007. These outcomes were placed on Mayo Clinic's Internet site www.MayoClinic.org in December 2007 for public viewing.

Complementing the quality improvement journey are two additional strategic priorities: individualized medicine and the science of healthcare delivery. Individualized medicine stems from recent developments in genomics, "the study of all the genes in a person, as well as interactions of those genes with each other and with that person's environment."[3] This science opens a new era in which the tools of genomics will likely predict disease and in many cases point to the optimal preventive strategies or treatments. For instance, a patient with genes associated with early onset of colon cancer might be screened with a colonoscopy beginning at age 30 rather than age 50 as recommended for the general population. With early identification and removal of precancerous polyps, colon cancer can be prevented. Individualized medicine may also be applied in cancer treatment where the chemotherapy agent selected for a patient could be determined in some cases by his or her genes.

With a tragic story, Dr. Swensen illustrates the power and vital importance of harnessing the power of genomics and the science of healthcare delivery so as to increase the quality of outcomes, safety, and service. In the recent past, a young Mayo Clinic patient died unnecessarily. "It was a preventable death," Dr. Swensen says, "The death happened because 'Mayo didn't know what Mayo knows.'" The patient was experiencing cardiac symptoms, and the electrocardiogram (ECG) showed a rare "long QT interval," which is a disorder of the heart's electrical system. The patient was scheduled for a follow-up appointment in cardiology but died a week before the appointment date.

Dr. Michael Ackerman, a pediatric cardiologist at Mayo Clinic, is the world's leading authority on long QT interval. He sequenced the gene for an ion channel (a potassium channel in the heart). Out of the three billion nucleotides in the human genome, he determined that when a particular nucleotide is wrong, the patient can suffer a fatal cardiac arrhythmia. The long QT interval on an ECG is clinical evidence often associated with the rare genetic syndrome that leads to the sudden death of a number of children and young adults each year. The lifesaving treatment is the implantation of a defibrillator that is activated when it detects the fatal arrhythmia. Dr. Ackerman's treatment standards also identify medications that should and should not be used in the presence of this syndrome. But not all caregivers at Mayo Clinic know what Dr. Ackerman knows. Disseminating his knowledge throughout the institution called for a new capability in the science of healthcare delivery.

The parents of a deceased patient made a large donation to Mayo Clinic for the express purpose of improving the reliability of care at Mayo. The initial project creates an electronic means of moving Dr. Ackerman's knowledge to any Mayo Clinic physician at the moment he or she needs it, whether or not the doctor knows the information is needed. Specifically, Mayo Clinic's systems engineers built a link between the computer that analyzes the ECG and the mind of the patient's ordering physician. Today, when the ECG computer identifies the long QT interval and it is verified by a cardiologist, the ECG computer routes the information into the outpatient's electronic medical record and also routes an automated message to the physician who ordered the ECG. The system has a feedback loop to confirm that the physician received the message. The automated message has a link to Mayo's enterprise learning system (ELS) which first provides a directory of Mayo Clinic experts on the disease or condition, and then offers answers to frequently asked questions, key facts, and clinical guidelines. The electronic systems provide specialized knowledge to the managing physicians so that they can know what they don't know about safe care for their patient. This innovation in the science of healthcare delivery helps ensure that patients always get the best care regardless of whom they see or where they are seen in the system.

The ELS represents a large and essential investment in the science of healthcare delivery. Dr. Farrell Lloyd, director of the Education Technology Center, emphasizes that it is impossible for doctors to stay current on all the medical literature produced today as more than 500,000 new reports are added each year to Medline, an online database of published medical research, a service of the U.S. National Library of Medicine. In testimony before Congress, the director of the Library of Medicine described a conscientious physician who faithfully reads two articles each day for a year, and, "By the end of such a year, this good doctor will have fallen 648 years behind on reading the new publications."[4] Moving knowledge from research to patient care is slow and difficult; one study determined that it takes 17 years to translate 14 percent of original research to the benefit of patient care.[5] Today, medical education is moving from an emphasis on memorization to the skills of locating and using critical information at the point-of-need in the day-by-day practice of medicine. "The enterprise learning system," says Dr. Lloyd, "is Mayo Clinic's way of making the needed information accessible to the physicians as quickly and simply as possible."

Dr. Swensen admits, "A standard treatment protocol is an incendiary concept for many doctors—they call it 'cookbook medicine'—because it means they have to perform like the physician next to them and their colleagues on other campuses. But the Mayo Clinic model of care is patient-centered—what would the patient want? Patients come to get Mayo Clinic world-class care. They should get it no matter what door they open. Our quality initiative takes the model of care off the wall and makes it part of how we perform reliable care."

Others echo Dr. Swensen's message. James G. Anderson, chief administrative officer in Arizona whose career spans nearly 40 years in healthcare administration inside and outside Mayo, is adamant, "The model that we know as the Mayo Clinic—the integrated practice, shared physician/administrator management, salaried physicians, practice emphasis complemented by research and education—is a powerful and differentiated model in the marketplace. If we are not satisfied with our results, the problem is in our execution, not who we are or our strategic approach to the market." Mayo Clinic at its best—a team focused on a challenge, responsible for change with resources at hand—is a powerful force. Dr. Swensen describes how Mayo Clinic becomes Mayo Clinic at its best through its approach to quality improvement:

> *We identify a physician leader who owns the responsibility and assign key team members including a systems engineer who has no other responsibility for the 100-day duration of the project, an administrative project manager, and a data specialist. In addition, a cross-functional team is assembled—physician experts in the disease, nurses, technologists, pharmacists, technicians—with members from across the campuses of the Mayo system. The team is keyed up with a charter so we will know what we are going to measure. And then there is a control phase afterwards. Basically there are 100 days of intense focus on an opportunity for improvement. So with pneumonia in the hospital our team was to identify the best practice. Then they deployed that and measured it. Did it make a difference? We decreased the length of stay, lowered the readmission rate, and demonstrated a lower disease-specific mortality rate for patients with pneumonia who got optimal treatment. We started from a baseline where we had excellent performance, but we thought there was opportunity to get even better. We did that.*

Mayo Clinic today holds this belief: the highest quality outcomes, a reliably safe environment, and stellar service come when colleagues work together to determine what is the best care for the individual patient and then execute this care model and patient experience consistently in every clinic and hospital at Mayo Clinic. In other words, every door—including virtual doors—provides the same experience. "Then from that standard of excellence we can innovate because we have something to compare it to," Dr. Swensen concludes. "Our approach to quality has to be scientific, evidence-based. We need control charts and biostatisticians. This is the science of healthcare delivery."

Prudent, High-Value Care

As one Mayo leader shared, "We are doing quality for the right reason—to improve the outcomes and safety and reliability of our care. No question that this is the right reason." There is, of course, a business case as well for driving out needless variation, waste, and defects from the care of patients. Most organizations outside of healthcare do this to improve the bottom line. But for Mayo Clinic, the primary business case is not the net revenue published in the annual report. Rather it is in the affirmation of the fiscal efficiency of Mayo Clinic's integrated care model. Mayo Clinic must be able to tell its patients and their insurance companies or employers that this high-quality care is not a luxury but a prudent, high-value purchase.

Healthcare is the largest business sector in the United States, and it underperforms all others in terms of efficiency and defect rates. It is frequently not a high-value purchase. A recent study in the *New England Journal of Medicine* shows that about one-half of the care delivered by physicians in the United States is not based on current best practices.[6] As we discuss in Chapter 4, Mayo gets high marks from patients for its efficient use of their time, but some insurers and patients are not quite as sure that Mayo's care is an efficient use of their money. Mayo Clinic bills can be large in part because all services from physicians, all laboratory tests, and all hospital charges are bundled into a single bill. Integrated bills for care are not the norm in healthcare because services are frequently obtained from several different organizations.

Robert Smoldt, recently retired chief administrative officer of Mayo Clinic, and Dr. Denis Cortese, president and CEO, have led internal efforts to ensure that Mayo's care is high-value care. They advocate that *value* is the best metric to identify high-quality, cost-effective medical care among all providers across the nation. In a recent article, they offer a value equation dividing quality (outcomes of care, safety, service) by the cost per patient over time.[7] Dr. Cortese observes, "While our charges may be near the top for individual line items on a bill, we don't do things as often as most others, so the cost over time is favorable." He also notes that every Mayo Clinic doctor has access to all the laboratory studies, radiology reports, and notes from the other doctors, and this provides fiscal efficiency as well— no need for duplication. Furthermore, if Mayo can prevent a patient from developing a disease such as type-2 diabetes, then the value over time is very high. Diabetes is expensive to manage as a chronic disease for the balance of a lifetime and, if poorly managed, multiple complications create even greater expenses and a compromised quality of life for the patients. Dr. Cortese adds, "By predicting the potential for disease, preventing it when possible, accurately diagnosing disease when it occurs, and then specifically treating, for instance, the type of breast cancer or diabetes, we will over time provide high-quality, high-value care."

Dr. Dawn Milliner, who led a task force that studied the value equation, takes a big-picture view on the cost issue: "All of us delivering healthcare in the United States need to step back and ask ourselves, 'What is it about our national system that creates these high costs and poor outcomes.' Mayo cannot be a responsible provider of healthcare if we don't look critically at this issue. Mayo Clinic *needs* to do its part in helping lead the effort to provide better value in healthcare. It is a responsibility to our patients as it is in their best interests—it absolutely squares with our primary value." Many purchasers of healthcare services—the federal government, major employers, and health plans—have themselves stepped forward with incentives for providers to improve. Under the general rubric of "pay for performance," these payers have been using money—slightly higher reimbursement levels—in an effort to ensure that their beneficiaries get quality care. However, Smoldt and Dr. Cortese argue that these programs pay for processes, not specifically for outcomes. Further, several of the programs increase payment on a percentage basis, so the inefficient providers whose cost of care is high earn higher dollar rewards than do the efficient providers.

"We have quite a bit of evidence to show that Mayo Clinic's care model does produce high-value care," says Smoldt. He points to *The Dartmouth Atlas of Health Care* as the best source of data.[8] The Dartmouth researchers contend that the data on healthcare costs in the last six months and the last two years of life are a good measure of efficiency. These costs are high since about a third of all Medicare expenditures for individual patients is made in the last two years of a person's life. Using the massive data sets for all U.S. Medicare patients, the Dartmouth researchers argue that more care is not necessarily better care: "The extra spending, resources, physician visits, hospitalizations, and diagnostic tests provided in high spending states, regions and hospitals doesn't [sic] buy longer life or better quality of life.... The problem is waste, and overuse ... not underuse and healthcare rationing."[9] In discussing academic medical centers, the Dartmouth researchers note that, in their last six months of life, patients using one university hospital in New York City "had 76 physician visits per person; Mayo Clinic patients had only 24 visits." In the last two years of life, patients at one California university hospital used "twice as much physician labor—measured as full-time equivalent physicians—as does the Mayo Clinic."[10] Although the report does not rank Mayo Clinic as the most efficient provider on every measure in the academic medical center peer group, Mayo is consistently among the most efficient. The authors conclude that most patients near the end of life have no one in charge of their care. However, "Large group practices like Mayo Clinic and integrated delivery systems like Intermountain Healthcare provide examples of how it can be done."[11]

In the end, by making the case for recognizing and rewarding high-value providers, Mayo Clinic is advocating for patients. They get higher-quality clinical outcomes, safer treatment, and better service. Making the case for an evidence-based value score will, in the view of Mayo's leaders, provide two paybacks. First, it will encourage the U.S. healthcare establishment, including doctors, hospitals, payers, and health policy makers, to consider both quality and cost *over time* in the payment systems of the future. Second, it will position Mayo Clinic as a prudent, high-value purchase.

Delivering Health

Dr. Nicholas LaRusso wants Mayo Clinic to become a leader in the coming transformation of healthcare delivery. An imperative for change seems to be forming around forces that promise to disrupt healthcare business as usual—genomics, communications technologies, a broken and expensive healthcare system, and a maturing Facebook generation that is already breaking many conventional rules. As the founding director of Mayo Clinic's Center of Innovation and Healthcare Transformation, Dr. LaRusso is focused on things new. He is particularly interested in healthcare delivery that emphasizes maintaining health rather than treating illness. This may well be the dividing line between the medicine of today and the medicine of tomorrow.

In the early 1980s, the Clinic's leaders were deeply concerned that patients could not or would not continue traveling to Rochester, Minnesota, for care. Today's leaders have a similar, nagging fear that centers on a potentially more radical revolution of healthcare delivery that would render some types of on-site care obsolete. Communication technologies could—and likely will—replace some, if not much, of the current face-to-face consultation between patients and their physicians. Dr. LaRusso, who is also a past chair of the department of internal medicine in Rochester, sees a distinct possibility that the "annual exam" as now traditionally performed with a standard medical history and a head-to-toes physical exam may become obsolete. A health risk assessment coupled with genetic analysis of the patient may eventually predict disease much more efficiently than a traditional general exam could ever detect it. "Personalized genomic medicine, coupled with evolving imaging techniques, may very well become a disruptive force that will revolutionize the practice of medicine," states Dr. LaRusso. "While Mayo Clinic will participate in the *discovery* revolution, it should lead the *delivery* revolution—we need to create a system of delivery that can rapidly introduce these and other innovations as they become available."

Dr. Glenn Forbes, CEO of Mayo Clinic Rochester, suggests, "With knowledge of the individual's genetic makeup, people and the medical community will, in the future, shift more focus on the predictive and preventive part of the healthcare curve." He sees the role of the Center of Innovation and Healthcare Transformation as developing innovations required for bidirectional, interactive wellness relationships. Dr. Forbes illustrates:

> *Sometime in the future, I could be living anywhere on the planet, or I could be traveling. I have some type of communication with Mayo because I'm partnering with Mayo in my wellness. It may be a*

computer chip embedded in a card, or it may be a computer chip embedded in me. Mayo knows my genetic makeup and has cross-referenced my genetic profile with millions of aberrations and cohorts that are similar to my situation to identify several predictive and preventive issues to address. Mayo knows my vulnerabilities, risks, my strengths—that is part of the database.

I feel fine, but I check in every once in a while. If I have a chip embedded, I might even be unknowingly "checking in." Every seven days, Mayo checks my blood sugar and could send me a message about needing to cut back on the cookies because my sugar level went up from 116 to 124. This information and advice is part of my partnership— part of what I have decided to purchase for my personal benefit.

But now, I'm traveling in France and I feel ill and need some interaction with Mayo. To stimulate my chip—if on a plastic card— I stick it into the Health Maintenance "ATM" in the hotel, and the ATM recognizes me—just like a bank today recognizes me when I use my bank card on the streets of Paris. I tell Mayo what is going on—I've been having headaches. Mayo responds, "Your genetics suggest that you are prone to headaches if you've been eating too much pasta. But, if you want to see a doctor, we have a Mayo Clinic alumnus or affiliated provider located, according to your GPS information, just two miles away. Here are the coordinates for the office, and we've already alerted the office that you will probably be coming."

Here, I have a partnership with Mayo, and I'm using whatever communications technology is available at the time to give intelligent consultations and interactions as I live my life in wellness.

Physicians in this new era will still analyze clinical data and convey its meaning to patients; the conversations will still require listening skills and sensitivity to the uniqueness of individuals. New, however, will be the conversation about the meaning of the risks identified in a patient's genetic profile. Dr. LaRusso illustrates, "We already have two genetic patterns that predict one's chances of getting breast cancer—breast cancer gene mutation 1 (BRCA1) and BRCA2. But these together account for only a small percentage of all breast cancer. When we get BRCA3, 4, 5, 6, 7, ... 10, tests which are on the horizon, we may identify genetic patterns for early disease onset where the individual should start getting mammograms or another special diagnostic test at age 20. Other patterns might suggest an optimal window in which the woman should have children." Likewise, some patients may have genetic patterns associated with cancer onset after menopause, so mammograms could safely wait years beyond today's recommendations.

Much of this testing and information exchange does not require that the patient be present in front of a Mayo Clinic doctor. Increasingly, such care could be delivered to patients anywhere in the world through new communications technology. "This could lead to a new concept of Mayo Clinic as a destination medical center—a URL," observes Dr. LaRusso. "An appointment with Mayo would not always require you to leave your home." In fact, Mayo, in partnership with Blue Cross Blue Shield of Minnesota, is already conducting a feasibility project between clinics in the Duluth, Minnesota, area and Mayo Clinic Rochester. If the patient and the primary care doctor in Duluth feel a referral to Rochester is in order, they can opt for a "virtual consultation" where a doctor in Rochester reviews the provided information from a secure Web portal and shares an opinion electronically within 48 hours. Business models for this type of service are already being tested. "We've learned from our proof of concept testing so far that most patients and their primary care doctors can be served in this virtual model and that the patient will not need to travel to Rochester," says Barbara Spurrier, senior administrator for Mayo's Center of Innovation and Healthcare Transformation. "When it is determined that the patient needs to come to a place like Mayo Clinic for a major surgical or procedural intervention, their care management is expedited because of the virtual consult."

Mayo Clinic's reputation for reliability and patient advocacy should position the Clinic favorably in the business of this healthcare information exchange. But before a new idea can become a reality in the marketplace, it must be transformed into a viable customer experience and a solid business proposition. This is where the new Center enters the picture. Barbara Spurrier emphasizes that transforming ideas and innovations requires expertise that does not fully exist inside Mayo Clinic today: "Innovation will be approached as a discipline."

The innovation center grows from the SPARC (see, plan, act, refine, communicate) project that was based in the department of internal medicine under the leadership of Dr. LaRusso and Spurrier, who was the lead administrator for the department at the time. SPARC has focused on redefining how in-person healthcare is delivered. A large suite of office and examination space in Mayo's outpatient facility in Rochester was converted into a care delivery laboratory. The facility features movable walls, for instance, that can be reconfigured to test the functionality of space. After a care delivery prototype is created, it is studied in real time as it serves as an outpatient clinic used by doctors and patients for actual appointments. More than 25 major explorations in care delivery have been conducted in SPARC.

Both Dr. LaRusso and Dr. Forbes emphasize that the transformation envisioned will not make bricks and mortar institutions obsolete. The relationships formed in wellness healthcare would convert to illness healthcare if necessary and, perhaps, even on a Mayo Clinic campus. "Patients will still need hands-on, in-person medical care for procedures and surgeries. Patients will also require access to sophisticated diagnostic and treatment equipment," says Dr. Forbes. "We intend to maintain Mayo Clinic as an attractive destination—both in the virtual sense and in the sense of a physical location."

Speaking Out

In 2006, the Mayo Clinic Health Policy Center officially entered the high-level public conversation on healthcare reform. "Our public trustees asked Mayo Clinic's leadership to invest some of Mayo's reputation for patient advocacy in the dialogue and debate on reform of the U.S. healthcare system," says Robert Smoldt who became the founding director of the Health Policy Center in 2005 while still serving as Mayo Clinic's chief administrative officer. Looking back at the proposals of the 1980s and even the efforts of President Bill

Clinton's administration beginning in 1993, it is clear that the voice of the patient doomed what policymakers thought were good ideas. Patients wanted choice, and they wanted care from doctors and hospitals that were motivated by the patient's clinical best interests. "The long success of Mayo Clinic, our high patient satisfaction, and the early evidence of Mayo Clinic as a high-value provider create much of the credibility for our voice in the discussions," says Smoldt.

Three tenets underscore Mayo Clinic's position on health reform: First, everyone in the United States needs *health insurance*. Second, everyone needs access to *integrated care*. This idea suggests that community medicine everywhere should reflect key elements, such as common medical records, doctors working collaboratively and seamlessly between clinical specialties, and doctors and hospitals functioning smoothly together in the best interests of patients. Third, all healthcare provided should be evaluated by a *value metric* that considers medical outcomes as well as cost over time. These positions have been formulated from patients, patient advocacy groups, and leading healthcare thinkers who have attended Mayo-sponsored symposia and working sessions around the country since 2006.

In an interview conducted for this book, Smoldt paused, and then told this story:

> *In the 1970s, early in my career at Mayo Clinic, I had a chance to work for Dr. Jack Hodgson, who was the chair of radiology and on the board of governors. He just loved Mayo Clinic like a lot of us do. Outside of his work at Mayo, he was a visible and outspoken pacifist. After I'd gotten to know him for a year or so, he asked, "What do you think of Mayo Clinic?" I didn't have a quick response, so he continued, "You know, I'm a pacifist, but I think that I'd kill for Mayo Clinic."*

Smoldt then acknowledges that, like Dr. Hodgson, he is of two minds. The first is an altruistic emphasis on a healthcare policy that focuses on the needs of patients. The second is his personal desire that organizations like Mayo Clinic be protected and preserved for future generations of patients. Smoldt's second concern is not just his own; it is shared by Mayo's trustees and leaders as well as by patients. Healthcare is not fully controlled by market forces. Medicare and Medicaid patients make up 30 to 60 percent of the patients treated on the individual campuses of Mayo Clinic. Those patients do not pay "market rates" for their services because price caps have been imposed by public policy. Healthcare providers work in a market where public policy, political philosophies, and political "horse trading" can have rich or devastating impacts. Smoldt continues:

> *We in the Health Policy Center believe that sometime in the next decade the United States will either undertake major healthcare reform or will have to reform the Medicare program. The huge inflow of baby boomers into an environment where medicine can do more and more for patients makes Medicare as it exists today unsustainable. Something has to happen. Some ask, "Do you think how Medicare gets reformed will have much of an impact on Mayo Clinic?" I think it will be huge. It is in Mayo Clinic's own self-interest to be very involved in the discussion and seek a result that will enable us to continue our long tradition of patient-centric medical care.*

Cultivating Tomorrow's Leaders

Mayo Clinic's senior leaders have few worries about the next generation of Clinic leaders, including the physician leaders. In fact, two generations of future leaders are mostly on campus today, and they are being deliberately readied for senior leadership positions. The talent pool includes many from which a smaller number will become candidates for major positions as they open over time. This speaks to two important commitments: First, Mayo's commitment to find internal talent to sustain the values, culture, and clinical model that have proven to be effective for so long. Never has the chief executive officer come from outside of Mayo, and in only a few cases has an individual been hired from outside Mayo to fill a senior administrative leadership position. Second, Mayo has a commitment to deliberately cultivate physician and high-level administrative leaders.

The talent pool seems deeper than in the past, thanks in part to the Mayo Clinic career and leadership development program.

The current program is a successor to training courses conducted on campus beginning in the mid-1990s. In 2005, the new program began to take shape with the realization that Mayo's general introduction to management skills and fundamental content from short courses in finance, marketing, and management were not sufficient for the physician/scientist leaders needed in the twenty-first century. "Also most external programs were not specific enough to address Mayo's needs," states Dr. Teresa Rummans, chair of the career and leadership development program at Mayo Clinic and a member of the executive board in Rochester. "This program does address the unique needs of Mayo and its future leaders in an economically feasible way." The facilitators and presenters are predominantly internal, but external experts from academia lead topics such as individual development and change management.

"This program strives to create leaders who can lead comprehensive changes in care management," wrote its designers.[12] Change in healthcare is difficult because leaders lead peers, not underlings. Physician leaders must persuade and inspire physicians to change. "We try to explain to those in the course how one can drive change in Mayo Clinic with its various committees and its commitment to consensus management," says Dr. Robert Nesse, currently the CEO of Franciscan Skemp, a Mayo Health System organization in La Crosse, Wisconsin, and a member of the board of governors. Dr. Nesse was selected as a presenter in the course based on his deep leadership experience in Rochester before going to La Crosse; he speaks with an authority about Mayo Clinic's management culture as no one from outside Mayo could.

The program (outlined in Table 9-1) begins with three modules (identified in the left column) that all new physicians go through. These three modules are spread over a week. The level II program, taught over three and one-half days, is required of all new chairs and their leadership team members. Both physicians and administrators participate in this program. In level III, selected department chairs and other leaders—sometimes as many as 250 individuals—participate

Table 9-1
Mayo Clinic's Career and Leadership Program

Career and Leadership Development I	Career and Leadership Development II	Career and Leadership Development III	Career and Leadership Development IV
Newly appointed staff	*Newly appointed leaders and members of their leadership teams*	*Experienced leaders*	*Senior leadership*
Module I-A Mayo Clinic Heritage: Institutional Orientation	**Module II-A** Understanding Your Role as Leader	**Module III-A** Providing Value: Building a Culture of Quality, Safety, and Service to Produce the Best Outcomes	**Module IV-A** Strategic Planning: Developing the Direction and Implementing Change
Module I-B The Individual: Personal Development	**Module II-B** Maximizing Our Financial Performance to Achieve Our Mission	**Module III-B** Providing Value: Driving Down Expense to Arrive at the Most Reasonable Cost	**Module IV-B** Execution Assessment: Assessing the Progress and Modifying the Course if Needed
Module I-C The Team: Team Development	**Module II-C** Leading Organizational Change **Module II-D** Developing Our People		

in the one and one-half day program. Finally, level IV serves the combined executive boards of the three campuses as well as the board of governors. "One special feature of this program is that it is just-in-time education. The courses are offered just before or after the participants first need the information," explains Dr. Rummans.

Dr. Nesse observes that another objective of the program is to create "a community of leaders" among the newly appointed young leaders who may interact with one another over the next decade or two.

By thinking of themselves as leaders rather than as just ophthalmologists, or pathologists, or rheumatologists, they can identify with a new role in their career of Mayo Clinic leadership.

Lessons for Managers

Great leaders create the future of their organizations. That is a tall order for any company in the twenty-first century and quite challenging in healthcare. Healthcare delivery of tomorrow is being shaped today by forces that a healthcare provider, even a very large provider like Mayo Clinic, can influence but not control. Around the world, laboratories in universities and corporations are developing new science and technology. In executive conference rooms and legislative halls, committed minds are grappling with healthcare policy, costs, and controls. Society wrestles with issues of equity and rights that determine who has access to the best that healthcare can offer. Physicians try to make the delivery system work for patients even as they often struggle with conflicting interests within this system that includes hospitals, insurers, employers, and pharmaceutical companies in addition to themselves. Yet, as one participant in this complex web of interests and players, Mayo Clinic strives to control its own destiny by being true to its core values and strategies while investing to ensure its strategic relevance and quality leadership tomorrow. Managers can learn from this organization where power is distributed widely and leaders can lead but not control.

Lesson 1: Excellence is a journey.   Excellence is a journey and perfection—zero defects—is the elusive destination. The first great leap in excellence at Mayo Clinic came when the Mayo brothers decided to wash their hands between surgical cases—an idea they got from others. Though their father first scoffed at the idea, the low mortality in their subsequent work convinced him and also earned their clinic its initial reputation for excellence. The battle against hospital-acquired infections, a century later, still has not been won, and the hand-washing journey at Mayo and other healthcare institutions continues.

Every organization that strives for excellence must define the goal and map the journey. Mayo Clinic is not content to be a leader in a cluster of excellence, so it has embarked on an aggressive effort to widen the distance between its measured quality and the rest of the best. The map reflects the "Mayo way"—a collaborative effort using the best resources available to produce a higher level of quality to serve the best interests of the patient. This is difficult work, and, in part, the employees are powered on this journey by leaders who challenge and inspire—extrinsic fuel.

Mayo Clinic is fortunate because its work force is intrinsically driven. There is no bonus for extra effort, no extra vacation days at Mayo. Mayo endeavors to hire the best—those achievers who earlier were satisfied only when their name was at the top of the grade curve posted after exams. Transparency of the gap between what is and what could be will further energize an organization whose workforce is committed to learning, high achievement, and the best for its customers.

Mayo Clinic, the strongest healthcare brand in the United States, has a sense of urgency about improving the quality of service it delivers and the range of services it offers. That Mayo is an industry leader in various quality metrics takes a back seat to its desire to get better. Having built its stellar reputation by delivering care to the sickest of patients, Mayo is now embarking on extending its care model to help prevent sickness. Excellent organizations such as Mayo Clinic always focus their energies on getting better—the journey—and this is a valuable lesson for all managers.

Lesson 2: Align structure with the brand.   The brand must be the same in every venue and offering. Mayo Clinic's patients expect to find Mayo Clinic behind every door and every portal that bears the name. Although the patient satisfaction studies showed that the patient experience was successfully replicated and the culture of service had been transplanted in the new clinics in Florida and Arizona, something was still not right after 15 years of operation. The collegial teamwork value suffered when sister organizations competed with one another, when physician colleagues over a thousand miles away were strangers, and when leaders grumbled as central resources were allocated. The clinical services Mayo provides are not always completed at the site where they begin; complex patient care is sometimes handed off from one campus to another. So it is not sufficient for each campus to execute the Mayo model of care independently. Patients appropriately expect that the teamwork between campuses be equivalent to the teamwork on one campus.

Controlling the destiny of an organization requires an alignment of forces in services and in management. Though rare, service lapses clarified that the holding company model did not work for the geographic extensions of the Mayo Clinic brand. "One Mayo" became the mantra, and its definition is maturing through personal relationships, clinical collaborations, investment in common systems, more staff movement between campuses, and numerous multicampus experiments. For instance, Dr. Wyatt Decker serves as the chair of the department of emergency medicine in both Rochester and Jacksonville. The department of neurology has a "division" structure in neurology subspecialties such as clinical neurophysiology and behavioral neurology with membership that spans the three campuses to coordinate research and education. Determined senior leaders are investing significant resources toward the journey to "one Mayo." For an organization that invented the concept of an integrated, multispecialty medical practice, a concerted effort to strengthen geographic teamwork became inevitable once the decision was made to expand geographically. It was a matter of "when" and "how," not "if." Culture could take the organization only so far; structure had to do its part, too.

One of the most vexing issues that leaders of all multiunit organizations face is determining and implementing the proper balance between centralization and decentralization. The issue is not, "What is the best structure?" but, rather, "What is the best structure to execute the strategy?" As discussed in Chapter 8, a brand is a promise of performance. It is instructive that Mayo's leadership is using an internal brand—one Mayo—to help strengthen its external brand.

Lesson 3: Challenge the performers to improve the performance.
Few employees, regardless of profession or vocation, who have

become proficient in their work take kindly to advice from "management" or outsiders who have never sat in their chair. The teamwork value takes some of the edge away from Mayo doctors as the clinical decision is often a shared rather than a solo performance, and in general, physicians surrender some autonomy to serve at Mayo Clinic. Examples earlier in this chapter show physicians leading successful changes in the clinical practice of their peers; for instance, establishing a higher standard of care in the management of pneumonia and instigating a cost reduction resulting in a positive $8 million savings on the bottom line for the orthopedic practice in Rochester. Here surgeons using evidence-based research both honored Mayo's underlying values and determined scientifically the changes needed in their own practice. They, not the CEO or the chief financial officer or even the department chair, brought the changes into being.

In preparing for tomorrow today, Mayo is redoubling efforts to improve in every part of the organization (Lesson 1). It is doing so by delegating improvement to the people who know the work best; the performers are being challenged to improve the performance. Teams of employees are being charged with achieving higher standards of quality for the practice. Doctors lead, but representatives from the whole care team—nurses, therapists, technicians, computer programmers, systems engineers—gather to solve the problems. The team members are drawn from the various campuses in the spirit of "one Mayo." Together these experts design the care protocols and implementation plan and then measure the results. The authority to take an organization to a higher level of performance is in the minds and hands of the subject experts who do the work. Although leaders must articulate the vision, communicate its importance, and provide the resources of time and tools, they become active spectators as the teams transform service delivery.

Summary

A pivotal question for any service provider is, "What is the impact of the Facebook generation on my organization?" Investing in the future requires an answer to this and other questions. Sustaining yet extending an excellent organization to serve a new generation of customers means transformation, but it begins with a clear sense of identity based on commitment to core values. It requires innovation and leaders who can lead change. It depends on performers who are committed to improving the performance. It is a daily challenge, a quest without end centered on serving the needs of tomorrow's customers.

NOTES

1. Leonard L. Berry, *Discovering the Soul of Service: The Nine Drivers of Sustainable Business Success* (New York: The Free Press, 1999), p. 111.
2. Committee on Quality Health Care in America, Institute of Medicine, *To Err Is Human: Building a Safer Health System* (Washington, DC: National Academies Press, 2000).
3. Centers for Disease Control and Prevention, available at: www.cdc.gov.
4. Donald A. B. Lindberg, "NIH: Moving Research from the Bench to the Bedside," statement to U.S. House of Representatives Committee on Energy and Commerce; subcommittee on Health, 108th Congress, 1st Session, July 10, 2003.
5. E. Andrew Balas and Suzanne A. Boren, "Managing Clinical Knowledge for Health Care Improvement," *2000 Yearbook of Medical Informatics* (Bethesda, MD: National Library of Medicine) pp. 65–70.
6. E. A. McGlynn, S. M. Asch, J. Adams, et al., "The Quality of Healthcare Delivered to Adults in the United States," *New England Journal of Medicine*, 2003, pp. 2635–2645.
7. Robert K. Smoldt and Denis A. Cortese, "Pay-for-Performance or Pay for Value?" *Mayo Clinic Proceedings*, February 2007, pp. 210–213.
8. Dartmouth Medical School Center for the Evaluative Clinical Sciences, *Dartmouth Atlas of Health Care*, available at: www.dartmouthatlas.org.
9. John Wennberg, Elliott Fisher, and Sandra Sharp, "Executive Summary" from *The Care of Patients with Severe Chronic Illness: An Online Report on the Medicare Program*, (Trustees of Dartmouth College, 2006), p. 1. Available at: http://www.dartmouthatlas.org/atlases/2006_Atlas_Exec_Summary.pdf.
10. Wennberg, Fisher, and Sharp, p. 2.
11. John Wennberg, Elliott Fisher, and Sandra Sharp, *The Care of Patients with Severe Chronic Illness: An Online Report on the Medicare Program*, (Trustees of Dartmouth College, 2006), p. 71. Available at: http://www.dartmouthatlas.org/atlases/2006_Chronic_Care_Atlas.pdf.
12. Robert Nesse, Teresa Rummans, and Scott Gorman, "The New Physician/Scientist Leaders: Mayo Clinic Responds to Changing Trends in Healthcare Executive Education," *Group Practice Journal*, April 2007, pp. 13–17.

CHAPTER **10**

REALIZING HUMAN POTENTIAL

I *have been a registered nurse for many years, practicing mostly in*
critical-care and postanesthesia care. I've worked at the bedside and also
in leadership roles. I was at Mayo Clinic in Arizona from 2000 to 2004
before moving to New Jersey because of my husband's job. I currently work
as a legal nurse consultant.

I miss Mayo every day, and after moving I tried to work in a local hos-
pital part-time. But once a Mayo nurse, it is very hard to go anywhere else.
Mayo is an amazing place to be a nurse. I called it "Disneyland for Nurses"
because finally, after 17 years of nursing, I could be the nurse I always
wanted to be. The patient really did come first. There was a team approach
to patient care. I can remember when first starting at Mayo that I was
amazed at the level of proactive medical care and how the team approach
prevented major disasters. Patients who would never have survived where
I had worked before went home to live normal lives. It was common for a
group of healthcare workers to put their heads together to come up with a
solution rather than give up. Every team member was asked to contribute,
and their input was valued; this included doctors, nurses, physical and
respiratory therapists, social workers, and family members.

There is a mutual respect for all healthcare providers at Mayo. I recall a
day when a physical therapist went into the room to help my post-op patient
out of bed, and the patient needed to use the bathroom. I immediately ran
into the room to help the patient, but the therapist said, "I got it, go back to
what you were doing." Where I worked before, anything to do with bodily
functions was the "nurse's job." I never heard, "It's not my job," at Mayo.

Mayo is selective about whom they hire, and they hire people who fit the vision rather than trying to mold people into the Mayo way. So many times in my career, the mission and vision of the hospital were spoon-fed to me, and I was asked to memorize them for accreditation visits. No one ever thought I held those values already. Mayo did.

At Mayo I had the time and resources to care for my patients the way I wanted to care for them. I could take an hour to do a dressing change carefully after premedicating the patient for pain and know that I would be able to complete the painful procedure without being interrupted because of another patient. My coworker would have time to watch my other patient(s) and would willingly do so because that was our culture. I could spend an hour in a family conference or comfort a dying patient's family because that was not considered frivolous; it was part of my job. Hospitals typically allocate more nursing time to critically ill patients. The difference at Mayo is that all patients who are hospitalized are considered to need special care, and staffing is done accordingly. Of course not every day was perfect, and there certainly were days when I did not have enough hours in the day, but 90 percent of the time it was as I have described.

The opening words of our final chapter come from Lori Plate, an experienced, award-winning hospital nurse who has worked at Mayo Clinic and elsewhere. She has been recognized by her Mayo peers for her service excellence, and her comments highlight the primary attribute that distinguishes and sustains Mayo Clinic as an exemplary healthcare provider and service organization—the people. A labor-intensive service organization cannot be excellent unless its people deliver excellent service. The reality of pure service organizations is that the "product" is actually a series of performances. Thus product quality depends on the quality of the performers. Mayo Clinic's people consistently perform services at a high level—services that people need performed at a high level. Patients' quality of life—and sometimes life itself—depends on performer quality.

Although most service companies do not serve customers in as vulnerable a state as healthcare providers do, the lessons Mayo Clinic's story teaches are just as important outside of healthcare as inside. All service organization managers should benefit from learning how an organization in existence for more than 100 years that has grown robustly in size and complexity has been able to consistently deliver a skill- and labor-intensive service so well that more than 90 percent of its patients praise it to others (see Chapter 8).

Global brands are rare for healthcare services, which are usually delivered to people who live within driving distance of the provider. We researched and wrote this book to understand how a family medical practice started in the late nineteenth century in a small Midwestern community became a world-class brand. How did this happen? What could we learn and share with readers if we explored deeply, did our homework, and then reflected on what we were learning in conjunction with our respective experiences: Berry as a career-long academic services researcher who did an in-depth sabbatical service research study at Mayo; Seltman as a healthcare marketing executive who served as Mayo Clinic's marketing director from 1992 to 2006. Although we knew many things about Mayo before we decided to write a book, we did not know enough to write the book we wanted to write, a book that would answer the question, how did this happen? To answer the question for our readers, we first had to answer it for ourselves.

The chapters that precede this one transfer our discoveries to the printed page. In this last chapter, we reflect on what we have learned from researching and writing the previous chapters. Mayo Clinic is a remarkable institution. Perhaps any organization that lives for more than a century deserves the label "remarkable." But surely one that has lived so long and remains much admired and much in demand deserves it.

Yes, the Mayo Clinic story is about realizing human potential; it is about exceptional people doing exceptional work one patient or one lab specimen or one room cleanup at a time. In this chapter, we distill the lessons behind the lessons of Mayo's durable success. We could not have written this chapter without researching and writing the previous chapters. We needed to climb the stairs to this final chapter, and this rule holds for our readers, too. This is not a book that allows reading the last chapter first. Readers also need to climb the stairs.

Three Big Ideas

Mayo Clinic was built from three big ideas. The first was to place the interests of the patient above all other interests. The second was to pool talent—to create a "union of forces" as Dr. William J. Mayo referred to it. The third was to deliver clinical care with time-condensed efficiency—what we refer to as "destination medicine" in Chapter 4. Putting the patients' interests first is "aspirational"; it is what the Clinic aspires to be. Mayo Clinic staff members commonly refer to this as "the primary value." Team and destination medicine are the ways the Clinic serves the interests of its patients. It offers patients the benefit of specially configured medical teams whose members' skills and knowledge are integrated just for them, and it offers these services in an efficient manner that condenses the time between the decision to provide clinical services and the actual delivery of those services. These latter two ideas are "implementive."

Business texts (and professors) distinguish between organizational values and strategies. In considering the soul of Mayo Clinic and the legacy of its founders, such a distinction is difficult to make. In classic terms, putting patients first is an objective, and practicing team and destination medicine are strategies to achieve the objective. The Clinic cherishes these three ideas, which represent its core values. At Mayo core values and core strategies converge. The core strategies are so embedded, so fundamental to Mayo that they also are values. As we state in Chapter 3, "The conventional wisdom in business is that a company's core values remain stable while its strategies and tactics change with the times. However, Mayo Clinic teaches that excellent organizations can have one or more strategies that are so central to their belief system, so integral to who they are, that they rise to the level of a core value."

Big Ideas Are Not Enough

Mayo Clinic's big ideas from its early years remain its big ideas today. And why not? Most patients with a serious or undiagnosed illness would want to have their interests put first, benefit from the pooling of specialized medical knowledge and skills, and receive efficient, time-condensed care. And, as discussed in Chapter 9, another big idea—preventing illness—is in Mayo's future. But big ideas are not enough. They need to be transformed from the orientation classes and care model booklets to the patients' actual experience; the ideas need to be executed; they need to be put into practice.

Great service organizations focus on execution. They focus on delivering the performance that is promised and expected. Strategy cannot be hidden, and success encourages imitation. The only viable option is to outperform the competitors that are sure to follow a successful innovation such as an integrated, multispecialty group medical practice. Other healthcare organizations have followed Mayo's model—at least in some respects—but Mayo remains the leading healthcare brand as data presented in Chapter 8 demonstrate. The key is execution. In reflecting on what we have learned in researching and writing this book, we conclude that what is *most* impressive about Mayo Clinic is how well it has executed its core values and strategies for more than a century. And this is the basis for our conclusion that the people of Mayo Clinic—the performers of the services—represent the crucial explanatory variable in the Clinic's sustained excellence. As Leonard Berry states in an earlier work: "Attracting great people is the first rule of execution. Great service companies attract great people to perform the service. It is a simple idea. It is a powerful idea. And it is—for most companies—an elusive idea."[1]

Staff quality at Mayo has three components which, in turn, are a function of organizational attributes described in this book. First, Mayo attracts—and retains—top-notch people. Chapter 6 discusses the Clinic's investment and effort in attracting employees possessing not only the ability and background to be successful in executing the strategy but also the personal values to be successful. The investment Mayo makes in finding people whose values align with the organization's values produces profound benefits. Because the Clinic's values are so patient-centered and collaborative, Mayo attracts people who are patient-centered and collaborative. The best way to implement a values-based strategy is to hire people who already have the desired values. Mayo does this exceptionally well. The compatibility of values creates a quality of work life that many talented employees seek, and it keeps them from leaving. Mayo is not a good fit for everyone as Chapter 6 points out, but it is a good fit for some. The Clinic's employee turnover rates are well below healthcare industry averages, and Mayo has many "career" employees. By attracting excellent people with the requisite values, Mayo rarely needs to go outside the organization to fill leadership positions. Clinic leaders know the values of people they promote to leadership positions because they promote from within, helping preserve core values in so doing.[2]

In labor-intensive, interactive service organizations, the personal values of the performer directly influence the value of the performance. This is a crucial point in understanding Mayo's success. The Clinic's values are its strategies; its strategies are its values. Mayo Clinic needs talented people with humane values to be Mayo Clinic; it attracts and keeps talented people with humane values because it is Mayo Clinic. Dr. Victor Trastek, a thoracic surgeon and CEO of Mayo Clinic Arizona, states: "My colleagues, the people I work with, are outstanding. There is nothing they wouldn't do for you, or you for them, to help a patient. You don't have to ask them twice."

Second, the combination of the Mayo culture and mystique encourages people's best efforts. Thus, the institution not only benefits from a superb talent pool but also from a staff working up to its potential. A key question for any manager is: "Do our employees work up to their potential, or do they work below it?" At Mayo, most employees rise to the level of effort called for by the Clinic's stature, by its core values, and by the high peer expectations that are embedded in a collaborative culture. Making a modest effort is not usually a comfortable performance level for a staff member at Mayo. Some staff members do perform at that level, of course, but most exhibit strong discretionary effort; they exert the maximum amount of effort one can bring to the job rather than the minimum effort required to avoid adverse consequences.[3] As nurse Lori Plate mentions in the chapter opening, she has never heard a fellow employee state, "It's not my job."

Third, Mayo's collaborative culture fosters personal growth. Mayo people not only typically work hard, but they also continually improve their skills and knowledge. While peer pressure encourages extra effort, peer teaching cultivates personal growth. Mayo staff members learn from their teammates; they not only have reason to improve, but they have the teachers willing to help them. As noted in Chapter 1, one of Dr. William J. Mayo's three conditions that he considered essential to the future success of the Clinic was the continuing interest by each staff member in the professional progress of every other member. The team medicine model, consultative culture, and investment in communications technology that facilitates remote teaching, such as Mayo's sophisticated paging system and its integrated electronic medical record, all contribute to the continuing viability of the spirit of this condition even though the time has long passed when a Clinic staff member personally knew most of the other staff members.

Mayo's system of rotational administrative assignments as described in Chapter 5 also fosters personal growth as does the pairing of physician and administrative leaders. The career and leadership development program described in Chapter 9 is an investment that will further enhance personal leadership development.

Attracting excellent employees and eliciting excellent performances from them is a worthy goal for all managers regardless of the industry in which they work. It is critically important when the product is, in essence, the performances of the employees. How does Mayo attract and keep such good people while getting their best efforts and fostering their personal development? Each chapter in the book offers important insights. In the concluding sections, we revisit some of these insights and reframe them in broader terms to help explain why Mayo earns an "A" in human performance.

The Power of High Purpose

Mayo Clinic's reason for being—to help the sickest patients—resonates with people who have humane values and want to make a difference in their work; in other words, people who are likely to be well suited for intensive, high-stakes service work. Not everybody wants to be part of a team, but for those who do, Mayo provides the opportunity to be on a really good one. Not everybody wants to work where the expectations and stakes are sky-high, but for those who do, Mayo offers a perfect opportunity. Not everybody wants to contribute to the quality of life through their work, but for those who do, Mayo makes it possible.

Healthcare needs the Mayo Clinic. In addition to its educational, research, and other health-related contributions, Mayo offers an alternative model for healthcare delivery unlike any other available in most parts of the United States or the world. It is the court of last resort for many patients, a place, perhaps, where an elusive diagnosis can be made, where a specialized surgery unavailable in a patient's hometown can be performed. A key question for any manager is: "If our organization were to disappear overnight, to vanish, would customers really miss us?" Clearly, for Mayo Clinic the answer would be yes. The Clinic's work is important, and this attracts and retains talented people and inspires their efforts.

A high percentage of Mayo staff members embraces the Clinic's core values. They entered a healthcare career to serve patients, and the Clinic's bedrock patients-first value attracts them in the first place and inspires their high discretionary effort once they are on the job. A Mayo Clinic career means a daily opportunity to progressively apply core values of effectively and efficiently serving patients, which is what we mean in Chapter 1 in referring to Mayo as a "modern-traditional organization." Reinforced every day in multiple ways, these values are a decision-making, resource-allocating compass; they guide, they remind, and they energize the people who do the work. As emergency physician Annie Sadosty states: "The value system hits you consciously or subconsciously every day. I didn't train at Mayo, yet it doesn't take long before you are citing 'the needs of the patient come first' as fluently as anyone who has been here for 25 years. I think that's probably the thing that holds it all together, that one phrase. Everyone knows what that means."

The Resources to Be Excellent

Mayo Clinic attracts, retains, and energizes its staff in part by its commitment to pursue success on its own terms. The Clinic has been steadfast in defining success in terms of creating social profit rather than financial profit. Social profit contributes to the betterment of society, which Mayo has pursued through patient care, medical research, and medical education. Mayo Clinic exists to create a better quality of life rather than a better bottom line. The seeds were planted early. As Dr. William Mayo wrote in 1921: "The medical profession can be the greatest factor for good in America. The greatest asset of a nation is the health of its people."[4]

It is not that the Clinic is unconcerned with finances. Faced with declining healthcare reimbursement margins, significant capital needs associated with expanding the practice, and the necessity to properly fund its research and education activities, Clinic leaders for at least a quarter of a century have adhered to the principle that the medical practice must sustain itself financially. The Clinic must exercise the financial discipline to control its own destiny. The only way to control its destiny, to be true to its mission and legacy, is to be fiscally smart. Thus money does matter at Mayo. The difference between Mayo and many organizations (both profit and not-for-profit) is that money doesn't drive the bus. Mission does, and this is a key reason the Clinic can attract such good staff members who do such good work. States Dr. Robert Waller, who retired as Mayo Clinic CEO in 1999: "Rochester, Minnesota, is a wonderful community, but people don't stay in Rochester for the weather or for the money."

The business side of Mayo Clinic doesn't trample the mission of Mayo Clinic. Striving to be fiscally responsible rarely leads to skimping on resources needed to be excellent. Mayo staff members have the time, equipment, and facilities to do their work in the right way. Lori Plate's comment that, "I could be the nurse I always wanted to be" accurately represents how many Clinic staff members feel about their work. They have at their disposal the resources needed that enable them to be excellent.

That Mayo is physician-led is instrumental in its mission-over-profits culture. Teaming physician leaders with administrative leaders, as discussed in Chapter 5, brings business and management acumen to the leadership table. However, the physician perspective wins out when there is a tie vote. Administrators are partners, but they are not equal partners, and this is purposeful. James Anderson, the chief administrative officer at Mayo Clinic Arizona, explains the rationale:

> *We have to service the leadership requirements of the clinical side and the business side. That is why we have these partnerships. So why do we say "physician-led" rather than "administrator-led?" The reason is that physician-led biases our decision making to the primary value upon which Mayo Clinic is founded—the interests of the patient rise above all other interests. When we have tough choices, when we hit an impasse, the physician's judgment, training, and instincts tilt us toward the clinical side of the equation. That is what we want. We want that bias working through the myriad decisions that we are making daily. We want the institutional bias to be aimed toward the patient and the physician in our model.*

Also instrumental in the primacy of mission is the one-bucket philosophy of resource allocation. Mayo follows a governance model in which all revenues are funneled through the central organization and then allocated to fund mission priorities. The fact that certain medical services generate high revenue because of the healthcare reimbursement system (surgeries and diagnostic imaging, for example), and other services do not (pediatric and psychiatric care, for example), does not determine the amount of resources allocated to the various units within Mayo. Rather, resources are distributed based not only on financial considerations but also on how well units are serving patients and their research and education needs. What a particular unit is doing on behalf of the Clinic as a whole is what really counts. Can this system cause some tension with groups that feel they should be getting more? Yes. Internal debates do occur concerning who owns the revenue. Yet, this system is unlikely to change dramatically because it enables Mayo to deliver on its promise of integrated multispecialty excellence. Dr. Waller explains:

> *Society chooses to pay well for some services and not for others. What we do is take in the revenues that society chooses to pay and put them all in one bucket. Our governing bodies and trustees decide how the dollars are allocated. Because of our one-bucket philosophy, we have been able to build, for example, modern facilities for psychiatric and pediatric care as well as invest in other ways to offer needed care that is not highly reimbursable. Our approach allows us to provide the care that patients need.*

A Culture of Respect

Mayo Clinic's core values nurture a culture of respect that contributes to the quality of work life. What is cherished (values) shapes behavior (culture). The profound respect Mayo employees typically have for patients, for each other, and for the institution is palpable. To not respect patients' presence, voice, dignity, and vulnerability in an institution that prides itself on putting patients' interests first is uncomfortable. To not respect coworkers' contributions in an institution that attracts patients with severe and complicated illnesses is foolish. Collaborative medicine is not only a core value at Mayo, it is a necessity. To not respect an institution that exists to serve humanity and has done so successfully for such a long time is arrogant. Mayo is many things, but it is not arrogant. Proud, yes. Protective of its reputation, yes. Slow to make strategic decisions, yes. Arrogant, no. As Dr. Stephen Swenson states, "Mayo is intolerant of prima donnas regardless of whether they are administrators, nurses, doctors, or anyone else. You may find a few here and there, but we rarely hire these kinds of people, and if we do, they usually don't last long."

First-time patients are often surprised at how much time physicians give them. The Clinic practices unhurried medicine, a tenet of its model of care presented in Chapter 2. This tenet, which dates back to the founders, stems not only from the necessity for careful exams to make a proper diagnosis (see the excerpt from Dr. Will's 1895 speech to graduating medical students in Chapter 1), but also from a fundamental respect for the patient's presence, voice, and trust. Mayo patients may have to wait three months for an appointment, but once they get into the system they are typically treated with uncommon respect.

Mayo's consensus culture can be frustratingly slow in terms of decision making, but it is the product of respecting colleagues' voices in addition to the institution's basic cautiousness. In a 1986 speech to Clinic supervisors describing the Mayo culture, former department of administration chair Robert Fleming quoted medical scientist Lewis Thomas's description of consensus and asserted that the words applied to Mayo:

> *We pass the word around; we ponder how the case is put by different people; we read the poetry; we meditate over the literature; we play the music; we change our minds; we reach an understanding. Society evolves this way, not by shouting each other down but by the unique capacity of unique individual human beings to comprehend each other.*[5]

Respect for the institution is revealed in myriad ways, not the least of which is what recently retired senior administrator Carleton Rider calls "an institutional personality trait of self-criticism." Rider explains that Mayo leaders have usually been in the organization for many years and when they assume a leadership position, they are especially respectful of the legacy they inherited. It is now their time to contribute as an institutional leader, and they want to advance the institution, to strengthen it and not weaken it. This leads to an inclination, in Rider's words, "to be hard on ourselves."

It is not just the leaders who are self-critical. Institutional pride encourages considerable worrying throughout the staff. It is not unusual to talk to Mayo employees who are worried that the organization is losing focus on its core values, that people aren't working hard enough, that physicians are less eager to assist on a case than they might have been before. This is partly because there will always be some truth to these concerns. An organization's core values can never be taken for granted and, in a sense, are inherently at risk. And all staff members do not work equally hard or make good teammates. But the institution's self-critical personality also is a function of the enormous pride most staff members take in the Clinic and its legacy. They care deeply. Mayo's brand power leverages internally with the staff, not just with external stakeholders. Staff members don't want to see the brand diminished.

Mayo Clinic's Story

Mayo Clinic's story is a story about people—people with skills, values, and vision—who committed and continue to commit themselves to creating and sustaining an organization in order to deliver an excellent service for the benefit of other people. It is a story about humane values, a spirit of institutional generosity, and the progressive application of traditional ideas. It is a story of brilliant structural arrangements that have stood the test of time. It is a story of a powerful, world-renowned brand that was created not from marketing communications but rather from service performance. It is a story of old-fashioned teamwork and modern efficiency, respecting the past and investing in the future. It is a story of a unique organization marching to its own drumbeat, being true to itself, taking comfort—and pride—in its uniqueness.

But it is also a universal story because the underlying principles can inform other service enterprises. It is a story about consistently executing a vision. It is a story of excellent people performing excellently, of people rising to their best to help keep strong the great institution they inherited so that it can continue to contribute to humanity.

It can be your story.

We close with one more episode in the Mayo Clinic story, turning again to nurse Lori Plate. Her narrative reveals the heroes and heroines common to every great story: the people.[6]

Working in critical care, we often deal with death and dying. It is how our team approached this particular death that represents the ultimate team effort.

Mr. M had recently received a terminal diagnosis, and he and his wife of more than 50 years were struggling with the decision of further aggressive treatment versus palliative care. At Mayo, we function as a team with ease even in the most difficult situations. All the appropriate team members did their part to assist this couple during a very difficult time. Nursing continued to give excellent bedside care. The case manager and social worker spent time with Mr. and Mrs. M detailing options for both hospice and acute care while helping them attend to any personal matters and possible impending arrangements. A family conference was provided at the bedside to allow for Mr. M to participate in the decision making. Physicians, a social worker, a case manager, the chaplain, and nursing were present. Although Mr. M was ready to make the decision to end aggressive treatment, Mrs. M could not accept the end was near. Treatment continued and everything was done to prolong Mr. M's life. The chaplain prayed with the family and told Mr. and Mrs. M to call at any time if they needed him.

This is where the real teamwork begins. W, the young nurse caring for Mr. M, had never cared for a patient who was so close to death. I, being an experienced 20-year veteran, let her know I was there for her during this difficult time if she needed me. W was both thankful and relieved. Mr. M was becoming more critical as the day went by and Mrs. M was realizing how much he was suffering. At approximately 4:00 p.m. that afternoon, Mrs. M called W into the room and asked that her husband be made comfortable and be allowed to pass on in peace. W notified the physician and asked me if I could come into the room when Mr. M's passing was imminent.

An hour later, all the appropriate paperwork (do not resuscitate order) was signed allowing for comfort measures and for Mr. M to die peacefully when his time came. Mrs. M was at his side with both W and me nearby to offer support. The other nurses on our pod continued to care for my patients, so I could help W help this couple say goodbye. I consider myself quite skilled and compassionate when it comes to death, but on this day I became the student and watched and learned.

At 6:00 p.m., Mrs. M requested the chaplain be called to pray with her as her husband became less responsive and closer to his death. I instructed W on how to page the chaplain only to find out he was on another pod with another family who was in a similar situation. He said he would be with us in about 20 minutes. Mr. M did not have 20 minutes. Mrs. M was crying and requesting the chaplain so a prayer could be said while her husband passed on. It was very clear Mr. M would not live another 20 minutes. I grabbed the tissues and prepared to comfort Mrs. M and show W the best compassion I had. When I entered the room, I saw W, who was of a different faith, take Mrs. M's hand in one hand and Mr. M's hand in the other and begin to pray. She asked the Lord to bless their 50-year marriage using their first names (I am not sure I would have been able to recall their first names that quickly). Her voice was strong, clear, and sweet and did not waver as she recited the Lord's Prayer while Mr. M took his last breath.

I stood by the entrance to the room and sobbed. My emotions were mixed. Both sadness for Mrs. M's loss and joy that we, the team, provided what the patient needed. W was the ultimate team player. She assumed another's role, making our system flawless when it mattered most.

NOTES

1. Leonard L. Berry, *Discovering the Soul of Service: The Nine Drivers of Sustainable Business Success* (New York: The Free Press, 1999), p. 239.
2. Berry, *Discovering the Soul of Service*, p. 240.
3. Daniel Yankelovich and John Immerwahr, *Putting the Work Ethic to Work* (New York: Public Agenda Foundation, 1983), p. 1.
4. William J. Mayo, "The Medical Profession and the Public," *Journal of American Medical Association*, vol. 76, 1921, pp. 921–925.
5. As quoted in a speech by Robert W. Fleming at Mayo Clinic on March 4, 1986.
6. This story first appeared in print in Leonard L. Berry, "The Collaborative Organization: Leadership Lessons from Mayo Clinic," *Organizational Dynamics*, no. 3, Fall 2004, pp. 239–240.

INDEX

ABOUT THE AUTHORS

Leonard L. Berry is distinguished professor of marketing and holds the M. B. Zale chair in retailing and marketing leadership in the Mays Business School at Texas A&M University. He also is professor of humanities in medicine in the College of Medicine. He served as a visiting scientist at Mayo Clinic studying healthcare service in 2001–2002. A former national president of the American Marketing Association, Dr. Berry is author of *Discovering the Soul of Service* and *On Great Service*, among other books. He is a recipient of the AMA/Irwin/McGraw-Hill Distinguished Marketing Educator Award and the Outstanding Marketing Educator Award from the Academy of Marketing Science, and the Paul D. Converse Award.

Kent D. Seltman is the past chair of marketing for Mayo Clinic. Prior to his 16-year career at Mayo, he served as a professor of English and department chair in a 19-year career in academia. Dr. Seltman's career in healthcare marketing began in 1984 as director of public relations and marketing communications at Florida Hospital in Orlando, Florida. Upon completion of an MBA in 1987, he served as founding director of the Loma Linda International Heart Institute at Loma Linda University Medical Center prior to coming to Mayo Clinic in 1992. He speaks and publishes widely on healthcare marketing and branding, and served as the editor of the American Marketing Association's *Marketing Health Services* quarterly.